W9-BNT-826

MICHELIN GUIDE

HONG KONG MACAU 2009

RESTAURANTS

& HOTELS

米芝蓮指南
香港 / 澳門 2009
餐廳及酒店

A LETTER FROM OUR C.E.O. TO OUR READERS

Why should a world tire industry leader want to publish a Hong Kong and Macau restaurant and hotel guide? That is a long story...

In 1900, our Company's founders, Édouard and André Michelin, published, in France, the first Michelin Guide to provide motorists with practical information about where they could service and repair their tires and cars and tips about facilitating their travel. In 1921, the Michelin Guide innovated with restaurants acquiring a specific rating system and introduction of a list of hotels.

The famous Michelin star rating system for outstanding restaurants was introduced in 1926. These awards have become, over the years, the benchmark of reliability and excellence in over twenty European countries, more recently in the United States and, since last year, in Tokyo, Japan. Today, the Michelin Guide is the world's top Fine Cuisine guide. It targets a broad audience as it lists Michelin three-star restaurants as well as many other restaurants that deliver good value for money, palaces and charming hotels, thus making it a guide suited for every occasion: dinner for two, family luncheon, etc.
For this second historical step in Asia, our teams immersed themselves in the culinary tradition of Hong Kong to produce a selection that does full justice to the richness and diversity of the Hong Kong and Macau restaurant and hotel scene.

As part of our meticulous and highly confidential evaluation process, Michelin inspectors conducted anonymous visits to restaurants and hotels. Preserving their anonymity is essential to ensure that they are treated as any other customer.

Our Michelin Guide collection for hotels and restaurants is yet another expression of our dedication to excellence and Better Mobility: Michelin always provides a better way forward to make traveling safer, easier, more enjoyable, more economical and more respectful of people and the environment.

I am delighted to launch our first Michelin Guide to Hong Kong and Macau 2009. I hope it will give you a great hotel and dining experience and that it will become your favorite restaurant and hotel reference guide.

Bon voyage and bon appétit!

Michel Rollier
Michelin Chief Executive Officer

行政總裁的話

為甚麼一間世界輪胎生產業界先鋒會想出版一本香港及澳門餐廳酒店指南？說來話長 …

1900年，米芝蓮創辦人 Édouard 和 André Michelin 在法國首次出版米芝蓮指南，為駕車人士提供實用資訊，包括汽車維修及旅遊提示等。1921年，米芝蓮指南採用特定的評分系統，引入餐廳資訊，並介紹一系列的酒店。

1926年，米芝蓮開始採用著名的星級評分系統，為一流的餐廳評分。多年來，星級評分一直是信譽和品質的指標，涵蓋二十多個歐洲國家，近年包括美國，而去年更進軍日本東京。今時今日，米芝蓮指南是世界頂尖的美食指南。指南吸引大量讀者是因為他涵蓋米芝蓮三星餐廳，以及其他物有所值的餐廳、豪華住宅及迷人的酒店。因此這本指南適用於任何場合，包括二人晚餐、家庭午餐等。

延續亞洲市場的開拓，進一步是了解香港飲食傳統，我們全力以赴，選出優質的餐廳及酒店，務求切合香港和澳門多姿多彩的餐飲住宿文化。

在細心與高度保密的評估過程中，米芝蓮評審員到訪餐廳和酒店時是不會透露身份，因比能確保與任何其他客人都會享有相同待遇。

米芝蓮酒店餐廳指南系列，展現著我們對卓越和「更高流動性」的追求：米芝蓮總是提供更佳的方法，使旅程更安全輕鬆、樂趣無窮、經濟實惠，令人和環境更能和諧共融。

很高興首次推出《米芝蓮指南 香港及澳門2009》，希望此書會為您可盡享最佳的餐飲住宿體驗，成為您最喜愛的餐飲住宿指南。

祝您旅途愉快！ *Bon appétit!*

米芝蓮行政總裁

Michel Rollier

COMMITMENTS

This foreword to the very first edition of the MICHELIN Guide, written in 1900, has become famous over the years and the Guide has lived up to the prediction. It is read across the world and the key to its popularity is the consistency of its commitment to its readers, which is based on the following promises.

Anonymous inspections: Our inspectors make regular and anonymous visits to restaurants and hotels to gauge the quality of products and services offered to an ordinary customer. They settle their own bill and may then introduce themselves and ask for more information about the establishment. Our readers' comments are also a valuable source of information, which we can then follow up with another visit of our own.

Independence: Our choice of establishments is a completely independent one, made for the benefit of our readers alone. The decisions to be taken are discussed around the table by the inspectors and the editor. Inclusion in the Guide is completely free of charge.

Selection and choice:

The Guide offers a selection of the best restaurants and hotels. This is only possible because all the inspectors rigorously apply the same methods.

Annual updates:

All the practical information, the classifications and awards are revised and updated every single year to give the most reliable information possible.

Consistency:

The criteria for the classifications are the same in every country covered by the Michelin Guide.

...And our aim:

to do everything possible to make travel, holidays and eating out a pleasure, as part of Michelin's ongoing commitment to improving travel and mobility.

承諾

「這冊書於世紀交替時創辦，亦將繼續傳承下去。」

這是1900年米芝蓮首冊指南的前言，多年來享負盛名，並如預期般一直傳承下去。指南在世界各地均大受歡迎，關鍵在其秉承一貫宗旨，履行對讀者的承諾。

匿名評審：

我們的評審員以匿名方式定期到訪餐廳和酒店，以一般顧客的身份對其產品和服務質素作出評估。評審員自行結賬後，有時可能會介紹自己，並詢問更多關於餐廳的資料。讀者的評語和推薦也是寶貴的資訊來源，我們隨後會根據讀者的推薦親身到訪。

獨立性：

餐廳的挑選完全是基於我們獨立的決定，純以讀者的利益為依歸。經評審員和編輯一同討論後才作出決定，被指南收錄的餐廳完全不會被收取任何費用。

選擇：

全賴所有評審員都使用相同的嚴謹方法，指南才能提供一系列的最佳餐廳和酒店。

每年更新：

所有實用資訊、分類及評級每年都會修訂和更新，務求為讀者提供最可靠的資料。

一致性：

米芝蓮指南涉及的每個國家都用相同的分類準則。

…至於我們的目標：

盡全力令旅遊、放假及外出用膳成為一大樂事，實踐米芝蓮一貫優化旅遊和外出的承諾。

CONTENTS

目錄

THE MICHELIN GUIDE
OVER THE YEARS

Today the Michelin Guide with its famous red cover is known around the world. But who really knows the story behind this "travellers' bible" that has served people in so many countries for such a long time? After winning over Europe and the United States, Bibendum – "The Michelin Man" – is now in Asia, and will continue the fantastic adventure that started in France, a long time ago...

The first steps

Everything began one fine day in 1900, when André and Édouard Michelin published a guide to be offered free of charge to motorists. It included information to help these pioneers (barely 3,500 automobiles were on the road) to travel around France: location of garages, town plans, sights to see, lodgings and restaurants, and so forth. The guide was an instant success and became the indispensable companion to all drivers and travellers.

On the strength of this success and driven on by the development of the motor car, the *Manufacture française* extended the scope of "the little book with the red cover" to other European countries, beginning in 1904. A few years later (1908) the *Guide France* was published in English.

A star is born

As of 1920, the guide was no longer free, but marketed for sale. Little by little, the practical information gave way to a wider selection of hotels and restaurants.

The mysterious, daunting "Michelin inspector" was, however, not in the picture at first. It was touring clubs and readers who contributed to the selection of establishments.

In 1926 the *Étoile de Bonne Table* – the first Michelin star – was awarded to places where "one dines well" and was later followed by two and three-star establishments (1931 for the provinces and 1933 for Paris). The focus was

now on gastronomy and the quest for good restaurants became its real driving force.

A European journey

The guide flourished until the outbreak of war in 1939, when all guide activity was suspended. But it was revived in 1945 and, from 1950, a new generation of guides appeared – from Spain in 1952 to Switzerland in 1994. In 1982 Michelin's European credentials were confirmed with the publication of the *Main Cities of Europe* guide.

100 years young...

2000 was a winning year for Michelin: the Guide celebrated its 100th anniversary and Bibendum was voted best corporate logo of the century!

More dynamic than ever, the "little red guide" took on new challenges and set off for the United States. The guide New York not only lived up to expectations, but also the first edition was crowned "Best Restaurant Guide in the World". Next off the presses: San Francisco in 2006, Los Angeles and Las Vegas in 2007.

The newest challenge? Discovering the best restaurants in Asia. In autumn 2007, we published Michelin Tokyo guide which had a big topic. Tokyo is well known as one of the world's great capitals of fine cuisine.

Twenty countries covered in Europe, four guides to US cities and one guide to Japan: as the third millennium begins, the Michelin Guide confirms its truly international standing.

Just a gleam in the eyes of the founders more than a century ago, Bibendum is now an international star to be proud of, carrying the Michelin tradition into the 21st century.

米芝蓮指南的歷史

今時今日，米芝蓮享譽國際，它的紅色封面家傳戶曉。多年來，這本「旅遊聖經」為很多國家的人提供寶貴資訊，但又有多少人知道它背後的故事呢？

必比登「米芝蓮車胎人」(Bibendum, "The Michelin Man")，在歐洲和美國駐足後，現在終於來臨亞洲，將會延續當年在法國展開的探險旅程 …

旅程的開始

1900年晴朗的一天，André 和 Édouard Michelin 出版了一本指南，免費贈予駕車人士。當時法國只有約3,500部汽車行駛。指南涵蓋環遊法國的資訊：車房位置、城市地圖、觀光景點、住宿、餐廳等等。指南的出版取得空前成功，成為所有駕駛者和旅客的必需品。

適逢指南的空前成功和當時汽車業的迅速發展，米芝蓮公司便乘勝追擊，於1904年把這本「紅色指南」帶到其他歐洲國家。1908年，這本「法國指南」更開始以英文出版。

星的誕生

自1920年起，指南開始在市面上發售，不再是免費贈閱。除了實用資訊外，指南日漸覆蓋更多酒店及餐廳資料。

在神秘的米芝蓮評審員出現之前，餐飲推介與選擇的訊息都是來自旅遊俱樂部和讀者。

直至1926年，米芝蓮首次引入星級評分制度，得到一星 (Étoile de Bonne Table) 的餐廳為最為美味的餐廳；其後，各省份和巴黎更分別於1931年和1933年實行二星及三星評分。此後指南便集中評選美食，致力搜羅一流餐廳的資訊。

歐洲之旅

指南業務蒸蒸日上，直至1939年戰爭爆發，一切運作暫停。1945年業務回復正常，從1950年起，新一代指南陸續面世：由1952年的西班牙到1994年的瑞

士指南，期間更於不同的歐洲國家出版。1982年，米芝蓮出版歐洲主要城市指南 (Main Cities of Europe guide)，確立其歐洲主導地位。

長青一百歲

2000年是米芝蓮的勝利年，不但是指南出版的百週年紀念，「米芝蓮車胎人」必比登更獲選為世紀最佳公司標誌！這本「紅色小指南」比以往更顯積極，不斷迎接新挑戰，並進軍美國市場。紐約指南不但不負眾望，更於初版被譽為「世界上最佳餐廳指南」。其後，米芝蓮在美國大展拳腳，2006年出版三藩市指南，及推出洛杉磯和拉斯維加斯2007指南，成績驕人。

米芝蓮面臨的最新挑戰是甚麼呢？就是尋找亞洲的最佳餐廳。2007年秋季，米芝蓮東京2008指南隆重面世。於世界美食之都出版飲食指南，米芝蓮東京指南成為一時佳話。

踏入二十一世紀，米芝蓮指南已涵蓋二十個歐洲國家、四個美國城市，以及日本，其國際地位實在毋庸置疑。

一個多世紀前，始創人的一絲靈感造就了米芝蓮車胎人-必比登的誕生。今天，必比登是令人引以為榮的國際巨星，引領米芝蓮於二十一世紀與時並進。

HOW TO USE
THIS RESTAURANT GUIDE
如何使用餐廳指南

Map number / coordinates
地圖號碼 / 座標

Cuisine type
菜式種類

Name of restaurant
餐廳名稱

Stars for good food
美食星級

🏵 to 🏵🏵🏵

Bib Gourmand
(Inspectors' favourite
for good value)
Bib Gourmand
(評審員的推介榜)

😋

Restaurant classification
according to comfort
餐廳 — 以舒適程度分類

🍴 Simple shop
serving local food
供應本地美食的食店

✗ Quite comfortable
頗舒適

✗✗ Comfortable
舒適

✗✗✗ Very comfortable
十分舒適

✗✗✗✗ Top class comfort
高級舒適

✗✗✗✗✗ Luxury
豪華

Particularly pleasant if in red
紅色代表上佳

Cantonese/粵菜   MAP/地圖 4/D-2

Lei Garden (Tsim Sha Tsui)
利苑酒家 (尖沙咀)

🏵

✗✗

🍴30 🕐

The entrance takes you past an intricately carved wooden
wall and a series of large fish tanks into a big, bustling,
traditional dining room that's brightly lit and comfortable.
There's pagoda detailing on the ceiling, bare red-brick walls
and an army of staff in attendance. The varied Cantonese
menu reiterates what's on offer at the other Lei Gardens using fine quality ingredients and cooking them respectfully.

要進入這家餐廳，你要先經過雕刻精緻的木質牆壁和一列大魚缸，最後來到寬
敞熱鬧的傳統客廳。餐廳燈光明亮，座位亦十分舒適；天花上畫有精美寶塔圖
案，牆壁上也鋪有紅磚，侍應生就如軍隊一般隨時候命。這裡的廣東菜單與其
他利苑分店相若，而同一轍的就是一級的材料和廚師認真的烹調態度。

■ ADDRESS/地址
TEL.2722 1636
B2F, Houston Centre, 63 Mody Road,
Tsim Sha Tsui East, Kowloon
九龍尖沙咀東部麼地道63號好時中心地庫
2樓

● OPENING HOURS, LAST ORDER
營業時間, 最後點菜時間
Lunch/午膳 11:30-15:00 (L.O.)
Dinner/晚膳 18:00-23:30 (L.O.)

● PRICE/價錢
Lunch/午膳 carte/點菜 $ 160-750
Dinner/晚膳 carte/點菜 $ 160-750

126

18

Les Célébrités
名仕餐廳

⚒ ⚒

◻👆 ⬒10 🅲🍴●

This elegant dining room is very much in the classic European manner and is smartly lit with some beautiful contemporary chandeliers; you're also allowed a good view of the wine cellar behind a plate glass window. The cuisine mixes classic French techniques with Mediterranean flourishes and other contemporary touches on dishes such as caramel foie gras with seared sushi cake. Hors d'oeuvres and desserts are selected from an extensive buffet.

格調高雅的餐廳極具傳統歐陸風情，外形美觀時尚的吊燈照亮餐室，你還能透過玻璃窗戶清楚看見酒窖。食物方面融合了傳統法國廚藝、地中海風情和其他現代烹調變化，如焦糖鵝肝伴煎壽司飯餅。前菜和甜品以選擇繁多的自助餐形式提供。

■ ADDRESS/地址
TEL.2313 4221
1F, Nikko Hotel, 72 Mody Road, Tsim Sha Tsui East, Kowloon
九龍尖沙咀東部麼地道72號日航酒店1樓
www.hotelnikko.com.hk

■ ANNUAL AND WEEKLY CLOSING
休息日期
Closed Sunday dinner and Public Holidays
週日及公眾假期休息

■ OPENING HOURS, LAST ORDER
營業時間，最後點菜時間
Lunch/午膳 12:00-14:30 (L.O.)
Dinner/晚膳 18:30-21:30 (L.O.)

■ PRICE/價錢
Lunch/午膳　menu/套餐 $ 220-260
　　　　　　carte/點菜 $ 420-720
Dinner/晚膳　menu/套餐 $ 480
　　　　　　carte/點菜 $ 420-720

127

Restaurant symbols
餐廳標誌

💲　Cash only
　　只收現金

♿　Wheelchair access
　　輪椅適用

🛋　Terrace dining
　　陽台用餐

≼　With a view
　　有景觀

◻👆　Valet parking
　　代客泊車

🅿　Car park
　　停車場

⬒25　Private room with maximum capacity
　　私人房間及容納人數

🍽　Counter
　　櫃檯式

🅲🍴　Reservation required
　　需訂座

🍇　Interesting wine list
　　供應優良的酒類

HOW TO USE
THIS HOTEL GUIDE
如何使用酒店指南

Map number / coordinates
地圖號碼 / 座標

Name of hotel
酒店名稱

Hotel classification
according to comfort
酒店 — 根據舒適程度分類

⌂ Quite comfortable
颇舒適

⌂⌂ Comfortable
舒適

⌂⌂⌂ Very comfortable
十分舒適

⌂⌂⌂⌂ Top class comfort
高級舒適

⌂⌂⌂⌂⌂ Luxury
豪華

Particularly pleasant if in red
紅色代表上佳

●MAP/地圖 1/B-2

●**Langham Place**
郎豪

⌂⌂⌂

Not only is this 42-storey glass tower filled with every gadget a technophile could want, it also functions as a wonderfully airy showcase for Chinese Modern Art. Over 1,500 paintings, sculptures and installations are dotted impressively round the building. Bedrooms are crisply contemporary and there are several restaurants including the innovative Portal - Work & Play. Equally clever are walking tours of the neighbourhood markets daily at 6pm.

254

RESTAURANTS/ 餐廳

Recommended/推薦			Also/其他
Ming Court/明閣	⚙	✕✕✕	Portal - Work and Play
Tokoro		✕✕	The Place

Restaurant information
餐廳資料

Hotel symbols
酒店標誌

玻璃塔般的大樓樓高42層，不僅有每個科技發燒友夢寐以求的電子產品，亦是個空間廣闊的中國現代美術展覽場。超過1,500 幅畫作、雕塑與裝置藝術品分佈於整棟大樓之內。客房的設計極富現代感，酒店內亦有不少高級餐廳，包括概念創新的Portal - Work & Play。每天下午6時更設有本地市場導賞團，服務值得一讚。

■ ADDRESS/地址
TEL. 3552 3388
FAX. 3552 3322
555 Shanghai Street, Mongkok
九龍旺角上海街555號
www.hongkong.langhamplacehotels.
com

■ ROOMS AND SUITES/客房及套房
Rooms/客房 =615
Suites/套房 =50

■ PRICE/價錢
    $ 2,600-3,550
👫 $ 2,600-3,550
Suites/套房 $ 4,300-15,000
🛏 $ 120

255

♿	Wheelchair access 輪椅適用
⬿	With a view 有景觀
🔑	Valet parking 代客泊車
🅿	Car park 室外停車場
🚗	Garage 室內停車場
🚭	No smoking bedrooms 非吸煙臥室
🧑‍🤝‍🧑450	Conference rooms 會議室
🏊 🏊	Outdoor/Indoor Swimming pool 室外 / 室內游泳池
Spa	Spa 水療
🏋	Exercise room 健身室

HONG KONG
香港

RESTAURANTS
餐廳

STARRED RESTAURANTS

Within this selection, we have highlighted a number of restaurants for their particularly good cooking. When awarding one, two or three Michelin Stars there are a number of factors we consider: the quality and compatibility of the ingredients, the technical skill and flair that goes into their preparation, the clarity and combination of flavours, the value for money and above all, the taste. Equally important is the ability to produce excellent cooking not once but time and time again. Our inspectors make as many visits as necessary, so that you can be sure of the quality and consistency.

A two or three star restaurant has to offer something very special that separates it from the rest. Three stars – our highest award – are given to the very best.

Cuisines in any style of restaurant and of any nationality are eligible for a star. The decoration, service and comfort levels have no bearing on the award.

星級餐廳

在這系列的選擇裡，我們特意指出菜式上佳的餐廳。給予一、二或三粒米芝蓮星時，我們考慮到以下因素:材料的質素和相容性、烹調技巧和特色、氣味濃度和組合、價錢是否相宜，以及味道。同樣重要的是能夠持續提供美食。我們的評審員會因應需要而多次到訪，所以讀者可肯定食物品質和一致性。二或三星餐廳必有獨特之處，比其他餐廳更出眾。最高評級-三星-只會給予最好的餐廳。

不論餐廳的風格如何，供應哪個國家的菜式，都可獲星級。餐廳陳設、服務及舒適程度亦不會影響評級。

✿✿✿

Exceptional cuisine, worth a special journey.
出類拔萃的菜餚，值得專程到訪。

One always eats here extremely well, sometimes superbly.
Distinctive dishes are precisely executed, using superlative
ingredients.

食客可在這裡享用美味的菜餚，有時令人更讚不絕口。獨特的菜式以最高級的
材料精密地烹調。

Lung King Heen 龍景軒	✗✗✗	134	MAP/地圖 6/C-1

✿✿

Excellent cuisine, worth a detour.
傑出美食，值得繞道前往。

Skilfully and carefully crafted dishes of outstanding quality.
有技巧地精心烹調菜餚，品質優秀。

Amber	✗✗✗✗	54	MAP/地圖 6/C-3
Bo Innovation	✗✗	61	MAP/地圖 9/B-3
Caprice	✗✗✗✗✗	63	MAP/地圖 6/C-1
L'Atelier de Joël Robuchon	✗✗	118	MAP/地圖 6/D-3
Shang Palace 香宮	✗✗✗	171	MAP/地圖 4/D-2
Summer Palace 夏宮	✗✗✗	179	MAP/地圖 8/A-2
T'ang Court 唐閣	✗✗✗✗	184	MAP/地圖 3/B-2

A very good restaurant in its category.
同類別中出眾的餐廳。

A place offering cuisine prepared to a consistently high standard.

持續高水準菜式的地方。

Fook Lam Moon (Wanchai) 福臨門 (灣仔)	XxX	83	MAP/地圖 9/B-3
Forum 富臨	XX	84	MAP/地圖 11/B-2
Hutong 胡同	XX	105	MAP/地圖 3/B-2
Lei Garden (IFC) 利苑酒家 (國際金融中心)	XX	122	MAP/地圖 6/C-2
Lei Garden (Tsim Sha Tsui) 利苑酒家 (尖沙咀)	XX	126	MAP/地圖 4/D-2
Ming Court 明閣	XxX	142	MAP/地圖 1/B-2
Petrus 珀翠	XxXxX	159	MAP/地圖 8/A-2
Pierre	XxXX	160	MAP/地圖 6/D-3
Regal Palace 富豪金殿	XxX	162	MAP/地圖 12/D-3
Shanghai Garden 紫玉蘭	XxX	172	MAP/地圖 8/A-1
The Golden Leaf 金葉庭	XX	190	MAP/地圖 8/B-2
The Square 翠玉軒	XX	193	MAP/地圖 6/D-2
Tim's Kitchen 桃花源小廚	X	195	MAP/地圖 5/B-2
Yung Kee 鏞記	XX	219	MAP/地圖 7/B-2

BIB GOURMAND

This symbol indicates our inspector's favourites for good value. Restaurants offering good quality cooking for $ 300 or less (price of a 3 course meal excluding drinks).

這標誌表示評審員認為價錢合理而美味的餐廳。300 元或以下便可享用優質美食（三道菜式的價錢，不包括飲料）。

Café Siam	🍴	62	MAP/地圖 7/A-1
Cheung Kee 祥記飯店	🍴	67	MAP/地圖 9/B-2
Crystal Jade La Mian Xiao Long Bao (TST) 翡翠拉麵小籠包 (尖沙咀)	🍴	73	MAP/地圖 3/A-2
Farm House 農圃飯店	🍴🍴	81	MAP/地圖 12/C-3
Golden Bauhinia 金紫荊	🍴🍴	90	MAP/地圖 9/B-1
Gunga Din's 金家美食	🍴	94	MAP/地圖 7/B-2
Ho Hung Kee 何洪記	🍴	99	MAP/地圖 11/B-3
Jashan	🍴🍴	110	MAP/地圖 7/A-1
Kin's Kitchen 留家廚房	🍴	115	MAP/地圖 15/A-3
Lei Garden (Elements) 利苑酒家 (圓方)	🍴🍴	121	MAP/地圖 1/A-3
Lei Garden (Mong Kok) 利苑酒家 (旺角)	🍴🍴	124	MAP/地圖 1/B-1
Le Soleil	🍴🍴	128	MAP/地圖 4/D-2
Lian 蓮	🍴	129	MAP/地圖 6/C-2
Luk Yu Tea House 陸羽茶室	🍴	132	MAP/地圖 7/B-1
Naozen なお膳	🍴	147	MAP/地圖 7/B-2
1/5 Nuevo	🍴	150	MAP/地圖 9/A-3
Tandoor	🍴🍴	183	MAP/地圖 7/A-1
Tasty (Happy Valley) 正斗粥麵專家 (跑馬地)	🍴	185	MAP/地圖 14/A-3

RESTAURANTS BY AREA
餐廳 — 以地區分類

Hong Kong Island/香港島

Admiralty/金鍾

Jiang Shan Xiao 江山笑		X	112	MAP/地圖 8/A-2
Lippo Chiuchow 力寶軒		X	130	MAP/地圖 8/A-2
Man Ho 萬豪殿		XX	137	MAP/地圖 8/B-2
Nicholini's 意寧谷		XxxX	148	MAP/地圖 8/B-2
Ruth's Chris Steak House (Admiralty)		XX	166	MAP/地圖 8/A-2
The Golden Leaf 金葉庭	✿	XX	190	MAP/地圖 8/B-2
Yè Shanghai (Admiralty) 夜上海 (金鍾)	⊕	XX	215	MAP/地圖 8/B-2
Zen 采蝶軒		XxX	221	MAP/地圖 8/B-2

Causeway Bay/銅鑼灣

At Corner		X	58	MAP/地圖 11/B-2
Chee Kei 池記		ᵇ⌐	65	MAP/地圖 11/B-3
Farm House 農圃飯店	⊕	XX	81	MAP/地圖 12/C-3
Forum 富臨	✿	XX	84	MAP/地圖 11/B-2
Ho Hung Kee 何洪記	⊕	ᵇ⌐	99	MAP/地圖 11/B-3
Hunan Garden (Causeway Bay) 洞庭樓 (銅鑼灣)		XxX	103	MAP/地圖 11/B-3
Jade Garden (Causeway Bay) 翠園 (銅鑼灣)		X	109	MAP/地圖 11/B-2
Kiriyaki 桐燒		X	116	MAP/地圖 11/B-2
Lawry's The Prime Rib		XxX	120	MAP/地圖 12/C-3
Manor 富瑤		XX	138	MAP/地圖 11/A-2
Modern China (Causeway Bay) 金滿庭 (銅鑼灣)		X	143	MAP/地圖 11/B-3
Regal Palace 富豪金殿	✿	XxX	162	MAP/地圖 12/D-3
Rice Paper (Causeway Bay)		X	164	MAP/地圖 11/B-2

Spring Autumn 春秋		ⅩⅩ	176	MAP/地圖 11/B-3
Tai Woo (Causeway Bay) 太湖海鮮城（銅鑼灣）		ⅩⅩ	182	MAP/地圖 11/B-2
Tott's Talk of the Town		ⅩⅩⅩ	198	MAP/地圖 12/C-2
Tycoon Hotpot 聚豪軒		ⅩⅩ	203	MAP/地圖 11/B-3
Wasabisabi 山葵		Ⅹ	206	MAP/地圖 11/B-3
Water Margin 梁山泊		Ⅹ	207	MAP/地圖 11/B-3
West Villa 西苑酒家	🏮	ⅩⅩ	208	MAP/地圖 12/C-3
Xinjishi Shanghai 新吉士		Ⅹ	210	MAP/地圖 12/C-3
Yee Tung Heen 怡東軒	🏮	ⅩⅩⅩ	213	MAP/地圖 12/C-2

Central/中環

Amber	❀❀	ⅩⅩⅩⅩ	54	MAP/地圖 6/C-3
Au Belge		ⅩⅩ	59	MAP/地圖 7/A-2
Beo		Ⅹ	60	MAP/地圖 7/A-3
Café Siam	🏮	Ⅹ	62	MAP/地圖 7/A-1
Caprice	❀❀	ⅩⅩⅩⅩⅩ	63	MAP/地圖 6/C-1
Chez Patrick (Soho)		ⅩⅩ	68	MAP/地圖 5/B-2
Chilli Fagara 麻辣燙		Ⅹ	70	MAP/地圖 5/B-2
Cuisine Cuisine 国金軒		ⅩⅩⅩ	75	MAP/地圖 6/C-2
Dot Cod		ⅩⅩ	78	MAP/地圖 6/D-3
Gaia		ⅩⅩⅩ	87	MAP/地圖 5/B-2
Goccia		ⅩⅩ	89	MAP/地圖 7/A-2
Gunga Din's 金家美食	🏮	Ⅹ	94	MAP/地圖 7/B-2
Hakka Yé Yé 客家爺爺		Ⅹ	95	MAP/地圖 7/A-2
Harlan's		ⅩⅩ	97	MAP/地圖 6/C-2
Harvey Nichols		ⅩⅩ	98	MAP/地圖 6/C-3
H One		ⅩⅩⅩ	101	MAP/地圖 6/C-2
Hunan Garden (Central) 洞庭樓（中環）		ⅩⅩⅩ	104	MAP/地圖 6/C-2
Inagiku (IFC) 稻菊（國際金融中心）		ⅩⅩ	106	MAP/地圖 6/C-1
Isola		ⅩⅩ	108	MAP/地圖 6/C-2
Jashan	🏮	ⅩⅩ	110	MAP/地圖 7/A-1
Jasmine Place 怡翠軒		ⅩⅩⅩ	111	MAP/地圖 6/D-2
L'Atelier de Joël Robuchon	❀❀	ⅩⅩ	118	MAP/地圖 6/D-3

| Zuma | | ✗✗ | 222 | MAP/地圖 6/C-3 |

Happy Valley/跑馬地

| Dim Sum 譽滿坊 | | 🥢 | 76 | MAP/地圖 14/B-3 |
| Tasty (Happy Valley) 正斗粥麵專家 (跑馬地)🍜 | ✗ | 185 | MAP/地圖 14/A-3 |

North Point/北角

| Lei Garden (North Point) 利苑酒家 (北角) | ✗✗ | 125 | MAP/地圖 15/A-2 |
| Sushi Kato 加藤壽司 | ✗ | 180 | MAP/地圖 15/B-2 |

Quarry Bay/鰂魚涌

| Palki (Quarry Bay) 皇轎 (鰂魚涌) | ✗ | 152 | MAP/地圖 17/A-1 |

Sai Wan Ho/西灣河

| Palki (Sai Wan Ho) 皇轎 (西灣河) | ✗ | 153 | MAP/地圖 17/C-2 |

Sheung Wan/上環

| Tim's Kitchen 桃花源小廚 | ✿ | ✗ | 195 | MAP/地圖 5/B-2 |

Tai Koo Shing/太古城

Peking Garden (Tai Koo Shing)

| 北京樓 (太古城) | ✗✗✗ | 158 | MAP/地圖 17/B-1 |

The Peak/山頂

| Pearl on the Peak | ✗✗✗ | 155 | MAP/地圖 13/A-2 |

Tin Hau/天后

| Kin's Kitchen 留家廚房 | 🍜 | ✗ | 115 | MAP/地圖 15/A-3 |
| Palki (Tin Hau) 皇轎 (天后) | ✗ | 154 | MAP/地圖 15/A-3 |

Wanchai/灣仔

| Bo Innovation | ✿✿ | ✗✗ | 61 | MAP/地圖 9/B-3 |
| Cheung Kee 祥記飯店 | 🍜 | ✗ | 67 | MAP/地圖 9/B-2 |

Chez Patrick (Wanchai)	XX	69	MAP/地圖 9/A-3
Cinecitta	XxX	72	MAP/地圖 9/A-3
Eighteen Brook 十八溪	XX	80	MAP/地圖 9/B-2
Fook Lam Moon (Wanchai) 福臨門 (灣仔) ❀	XxX	83	MAP/地圖 9/B-3
Fu Sing 富聲	XxX	85	MAP/地圖 10/D-2
Golden Bauhinia 金紫荊 ⊕	XX	90	MAP/地圖 9/B-1
Grissini	XxX	92	MAP/地圖 9/B-1
JJ's	XX	113	MAP/地圖 9/B-1
1/5 Nuevo ⊕	X	150	MAP/地圖 9/A-3
One Harbour Road 港灣壹號	XxxX	151	MAP/地圖 9/B-1
Sukho Thai 崇都	XX	178	MAP/地圖 10/C-2
Wing Wah 永華雲吞麵家	🥢	209	MAP/地圖 9/B-3
Yeung's Noodle 楊記麵家	🥢	217	MAP/地圖 10/C-2

Kowloon/九龍

East Tsim Sha Tsui/尖沙咀東

Dong Lai Shun 東來順	XX	77	MAP/地圖 4/D-2
Inagiku (Kowloon) 稻菊 (九龍)	XX	107	MAP/地圖 4/D-2
Lei Garden (Tsim Sha Tsui)			
利苑酒家 (尖沙咀) ❀	XX	126	MAP/地圖 4/D-2
Les Célébrités 名仕餐廳	XX	127	MAP/地圖 4/D-2
Le Soleil ⊕	XX	128	MAP/地圖 4/D-2
Sabatini	XxX	167	MAP/地圖 4/D-2
Sagano 嵯峨野	XX	168	MAP/地圖 4/D-2
The Mistral 海風餐廳	XX	191	MAP/地圖 4/D-2
The Royal Garden 帝苑軒	XX	192	MAP/地圖 4/D-2
Toh Lee 桃季	XX	196	MAP/地圖 4/D-2

Hung Hom/紅磡

Harbour Grill	XxX	96	MAP/地圖 2/D-3
Hoi Yat Heen 海逸軒	XxX	100	MAP/地圖 2/D-3
Robatayaki 炉端燒	XX	165	MAP/地圖 2/D-3

Senzuru 千鶴	🍴	169	MAP/地圖 2/C-3
Tasty (Hung Hom) 正斗粥麵專家 (九龍) ⓐ	🍜	186	MAP/地圖 2/D-3

Jordan/佐敦

Yat Tung Heen 逸東軒	🍴🍴	212	MAP/地圖 1/B-2

Kwun Tong/觀唐

Lei Garden (Kwun Tong) 利苑酒家 (觀唐)	🍴🍴	123	MAP/地圖 19/C-1

Mong Kok/旺角

Guangzhou Garden 粵江春	🍴🍴	93	MAP/地圖 1/B-1
Lei Garden (Mong Kok) 利苑酒家 (旺角) ⓐ	🍴🍴	124	MAP/地圖 1/B-1
Ming Court 明閣 ✿	🍴🍴🍴	142	MAP/地圖 1/B-2
Tokoro	🍴🍴	197	MAP/地圖 1/B-2

Olympian City/奧海城

Modern China (Kowloon) 金滿庭 (九龍)	🍴	144	MAP/地圖 1/A-2

Tsim Sha Tsui/尖沙咀

Angelini	🍴🍴🍴	55	MAP/地圖 4/D-2
Aqua	🍴🍴	56	MAP/地圖 3/B-2
Aspasia	🍴🍴🍴	57	MAP/地圖 4/C-1
Celestial Court 天寶閣	🍴🍴	64	MAP/地圖 4/C-3
Chesa 瑞樵閣	🍴	66	MAP/地圖 3/B-3
Crystal Jade La Mian Xiao Long Bao (TST) 翡翠拉麵小籠包 (尖沙咀) ⓐ	🍴	73	MAP/地圖 3/A-2
Cucina	🍴🍴	74	MAP/地圖 3/A-3
Dynasty 滿福樓	🍴🍴	79	MAP/地圖 4/C-3
Fook Lam Moon (Kowloon) 福臨門 (九龍)	🍴🍴	82	MAP/地圖 4/C-1
Gaddi's 吉地士	🍴🍴🍴🍴	86	MAP/地圖 3/B-3
Ginza 銀座	🍴🍴	88	MAP/地圖 4/C-3
Golden Bull (Ocean Terminal) 金牛苑 (海運大廈)	🍴	91	MAP/地圖 3/A-3
House of Jasmine 八月居	🍴🍴	102	MAP/地圖 3/A-3

RESTAURANTS BY CUISINE TYPE
餐廳 — 以菜式分類

American / 美式

Lobster Bar and Grill 龍蝦吧		ⅩⅩ	131	MAP/地圖 8/A-2

Asian and western / 亞洲/西式

Cucina		ⅩⅩ	74	MAP/地圖 3/A-3

Belgian / 比利時菜

Au Belge		ⅩⅩ	59	MAP/地圖 7/A-2

Cantonese / 粵菜

Celestial Court 天寶閣		ⅩⅩ	64	MAP/地圖 4/C-3
Cuisine Cuisine 国金軒		ⅩⅩⅩ	75	MAP/地圖 6/C-2
Dynasty 滿福樓		ⅩⅩ	79	MAP/地圖 4/C-3
Eighteen Brook 十八溪		ⅩⅩ	80	MAP/地圖 9/B-2
Farm House 農圃飯店	✿	ⅩⅩ	81	MAP/地圖 12/C-3
Fook Lam Moon (Kowloon) 福臨門 (九龍)		ⅩⅩ	82	MAP/地圖 4/C-1
Fook Lam Moon (Wanchai) 福臨門 (灣仔)	✿	ⅩⅩⅩ	83	MAP/地圖 9/B-3
Forum 富臨	✿	ⅩⅩ	84	MAP/地圖 11/B-2
Fu Sing 富聲		ⅩⅩⅩ	85	MAP/地圖 10/D-2
Golden Bauhinia 金紫荊	✿	ⅩⅩ	90	MAP/地圖 9/B-1
Guangzhou Garden 粵江春		ⅩⅩ	93	MAP/地圖 1/B-1
Hoi Yat Heen 海逸軒		ⅩⅩⅩ	100	MAP/地圖 2/D-3
House of Jasmine 八月居		ⅩⅩ	102	MAP/地圖 3/A-3
Jade Garden (Causeway Bay) 翠園 (銅鑼灣)		Ⅹ	109	MAP/地圖 11/B-2
Jasmine Place 怡翠軒		ⅩⅩⅩ	111	MAP/地圖 6/D-2

Jiang Shan Xiao 江山笑		ⅹ	112	MAP/地圖 8/A-2
Kin's Kitchen 留家廚房	🕭	ⅹ	115	MAP/地圖 15/A-3
Lei Garden (Elements) 利苑酒家 (圓方)	🕭	ⅹⅹ	121	MAP/地圖 1/A-3
Lei Garden (IFC) 利苑酒家 (國際金融中心)	❀	ⅹⅹ	122	MAP/地圖 6/C-2
Lei Garden (Kwun Tong) 利苑酒家 (觀唐)		ⅹⅹ	123	MAP/地圖 19/C-1
Lei Garden (Mong Kok) 利苑酒家 (旺角)	🕭	ⅹⅹ	124	MAP/地圖 1/B-1
Lei Garden (North Point) 利苑酒家 (北角)		ⅹⅹ	125	MAP/地圖 15/A-2
Lei Garden (Tsim Sha Tsui) 利苑酒家 (尖沙咀)	❀	ⅹⅹ	126	MAP/地圖 4/D-2
Lippo Chiuchow 力寶軒		ⅹ	130	MAP/地圖 8/A-2
Luk Yu Tea House 陸羽茶室	🕭	ⅹ	132	MAP/地圖 7/B-1
Lung King Heen 龍景軒	❀❀❀	ⅹⅹⅹ	134	MAP/地圖 6/C-1
Man Ho 萬豪殿		ⅹⅹ	137	MAP/地圖 8/B-2
Manor 富瑤		ⅹⅹ	138	MAP/地圖 11/A-2
Man Wah 文華廳		ⅹⅹ	139	MAP/地圖 6/D-3
Ming Court 明閣	❀	ⅹⅹⅹ	142	MAP/地圖 1/B-2
One Harbour Road 港灣壹號		ⅹⅹⅹⅹ	151	MAP/地圖 9/B-1
Regal Palace 富豪金殿	❀	ⅹⅹⅹ	162	MAP/地圖 12/D-3
Shang Palace 香宮	❀❀	ⅹⅹⅹ	171	MAP/地圖 4/D-2
Spring Autumn 春秋		ⅹⅹ	176	MAP/地圖 11/B-3
Spring Moon 嘉麟樓		ⅹⅹⅹ	177	MAP/地圖 3/B-3
Summer Palace 夏宮	❀❀	ⅹⅹⅹ	179	MAP/地圖 8/A-2
Tai Woo (Causeway Bay) 太湖海鮮城 (銅鑼灣)		ⅹⅹ	182	MAP/地圖 11/B-2
T'ang Court 唐閣	❀❀	ⅹⅹⅹⅹ	184	MAP/地圖 3/B-2
The Folks 樂意居		ⅹⅹⅹ	189	MAP/地圖 13/B-1
The Golden Leaf 金葉庭	❀	ⅹⅹ	190	MAP/地圖 8/B-2
The Royal Garden 帝苑軒		ⅹⅹ	192	MAP/地圖 4/D-2
The Square 翠玉軒	❀	ⅹⅹ	193	MAP/地圖 6/D-2
Tim's Kitchen 桃花源小廚	❀	ⅹ	195	MAP/地圖 5/A-2
Toh Lee 桃季		ⅹⅹ	196	MAP/地圖 4/D-2
Tsui Hang Village 翠亨邨		ⅹⅹ	202	MAP/地圖 6/C-3
West Villa 西苑酒家	🕭	ⅹⅹ	208	MAP/地圖 12/C-3

Yan Toh Heen 欣圖軒		ⅩⅩⅩ	211	MAP/地圖 4/C-3
Yat Tung Heen 逸東軒		ⅩⅩ	212	MAP/地圖 1/B-2
Yee Tung Heen 怡東軒	🛞	ⅩⅩⅩ	213	MAP/地圖 12/C-2
Yung Kee 鏞記	❀	ⅩⅩ	219	MAP/地圖 7/B-2
Zen 采蝶軒		ⅩⅩⅩ	221	MAP/地圖 8/B-2

Chinese / 中式

Crystal Jade La Mian Xiao Long Bao (TST) 翡翠拉麵小籠包 (尖沙咀)	🛞	Ⅹ	73	MAP/地圖 3/A-2
Hunan Garden (Causeway Bay) 金滿庭 (銅鑼灣)		ⅩⅩⅩ	103	MAP/地圖 11/B-3
Hunan Garden (Central) 洞庭樓 (中環)		ⅩⅩⅩ	104	MAP/地圖 6/C-2
Modern China (Causeway Bay) 金滿庭 (銅鑼灣)		Ⅹ	143	MAP/地圖 11/B-3
Modern China (Kowloon) 金滿庭 (九龍)		Ⅹ	144	MAP/地圖 1/A-2
Shanghai Garden 紫玉蘭	❀	ⅩⅩⅩ	172	MAP/地圖 8/A-1
Shui Hu Ju 水滸居		ⅩⅩ	173	MAP/地圖 5/B-3
Yellow Door Kitchen 黃色門廚房		Ⅹ	214	MAP/地圖 7/A-1
Yun Fu 雲府		ⅩⅩ	218	MAP/地圖 7/B-2

Chinese contemporary / 時尚中式

Hutong 胡同	❀	ⅩⅩ	105	MAP/地圖 3/B-2
Prince 王子飯店		ⅩⅩⅩ	161	MAP/地圖 3/B-2

Dim sum / 點心

Dim Sum 譽滿坊		🍴	76	MAP/地圖 14/B-3

European contemporary / 時尚歐陸式

Harlan's		ⅩⅩ	97	MAP/地圖 6/C-2

French / 法式

Caprice	❀❀	ⅩⅩⅩⅩ	63	MAP/地圖 6/C-1
Chez Patrick (Soho)		ⅩⅩ	68	MAP/地圖 5/B-2
Chez Patrick (Wanchai)		ⅩⅩ	69	MAP/地圖 9/A-3
Gaddi's 吉地士		ⅩⅩⅩⅩ	86	MAP/地圖 3/B-3

Italian / 意式

Cinecitta	✗✗✗	72	MAP/地圖 9/A-3
Gaia	✗✗✗	87	MAP/地圖 5/B-2
Goccia	✗✗	89	MAP/地圖 7/A-2
Grissini	✗✗✗	92	MAP/地圖 9/B-1
Isola	✗✗	108	MAP/地圖 6/C-2
Sabatini	✗✗✗	167	MAP/地圖 4/D-2
Spasso	✗✗	174	MAP/地圖 3/A-3
The Mistral 海風餐廳	✗✗	191	MAP/地圖 4/D-2
Va Bene	✗✗	205	MAP/地圖 7/B-2

Italian and Japanese / 意式及日式

Aqua	✗✗	56	MAP/地圖 3/B-2

Italian contemporary / 時尚意式

Angelini	✗✗✗	55	MAP/地圖 4/D-2
Joia	✗✗	114	MAP/地圖 1/A-3
Nicholini's 意寧谷	✗✗✗✗	148	MAP/地圖 8/B-2

Japanese / 日式

At Corner	✗	58	MAP/地圖 11/B-2
Ginza 銀座	✗✗	88	MAP/地圖 4/C-3
Inagiku (IFC) 稻菊（國際金融中心）	✗✗	106	MAP/地圖 6/C-1
Inagiku (Kowloon) 稻菊（九龍）	✗✗	107	MAP/地圖 4/D-2
Kiriyaki 桐燒	✗	116	MAP/地圖 11/B-2
Nadaman (Kowloon) 灘萬（九龍）	✗✗	146	MAP/地圖 4/D-2
Naozen なお膳	✗	147	MAP/地圖 7/B-2
Rei Sushi 鮨	✗	163	MAP/地圖 6/C-2
Robatayaki 炉端燒	✗✗	165	MAP/地圖 2/D-3
Sagano 嵯峨野	✗✗	168	MAP/地圖 4/D-2
Senzuru 千鶴	✗	169	MAP/地圖 2/C-3
Sushi Kato 加藤壽司	✗	180	MAP/地圖 15/B-2
Sushi Kuu 壽司喰	✗	181	MAP/地圖 7/B-2

Tokoro		XX	197	MAP/地圖 1/B-2
Unkai 雲海		XX	204	MAP/地圖 4/C-3

Japanese contemporary / 時尚日式

Megu		XX	141	MAP/地圖 1/A-3
Nobu		XX	149	MAP/地圖 4/C-3
Wasabisabi 山葵		X	206	MAP/地圖 11/B-3
Zuma		XX	222	MAP/地圖 6/C-3

Mediterranean / 地中海菜

Aspasia		XXX	57	MAP/地圖 4/C-1
1/5 Nuevo	⊛	X	150	MAP/地圖 9/A-3

Noodle / 麵食

Mak's Noodle 麥奀雲吞麵世家		🍜	135	MAP/地圖 7/A-1
Wing Wah 永華雲吞麵家		🍜	209	MAP/地圖 9/B-3
Yeung's Noodle 楊記麵家		🍜	217	MAP/地圖 10/C-2

Noodle and congee / 粥麵

Chee Kei 池記		🍜	65	MAP/地圖 11/B-3
Ho Hung Kee 何洪記	⊛	🍜	99	MAP/地圖 11/B-3
Law Fu Kee 羅富記		🍜	119	MAP/地圖 7/A-1
Tasty (Happy Valley) 正斗粥麵專家 (跑馬地)	⊛	X	185	MAP/地圖 14/A-3
Tasty (Hung Hom) 正斗粥麵專家 (九龍)	⊛	🍜	186	MAP/地圖 2/D-3
Tasty (IFC) 正斗粥麵專家 (國際金融中心)	⊛	🍜	185	MAP/地圖 6/C-2
Tsim Chai Kee (Connaught Rd) 沾仔記 (干諾道)		🍜	200	MAP/地圖 6/C-2
Tsim Chai Kee (Wellington St) 沾仔記 (威靈頓街)		🍜	201	MAP/地圖 7/A-1

Pekingese / 京菜

Cheung Kee 祥記飯店	⊛	X	67	MAP/地圖 9/B-2
Dong Lai Shun 東來順		XX	77	MAP/地圖 4/D-2
Peking Garden (Central) 北京樓 (中環)		XXX	156	MAP/地圖 6/D-3

Peking Garden (Kowloon) 北京樓（九龍）		XX	157	MAP/地圖 3/B-3
Peking Garden (Tai Koo Shing) 北京樓（太古城）		XXX	158	MAP/地圖 17/B-1
Water Margin 梁山泊		X	207	MAP/地圖 11/B-3

Seafood / 海鮮

Chuen Kee Seafood 全記海鮮菜館		XX	71	MAP/地圖 20/B-2
Dot Cod		XX	78	MAP/地圖 6/D-3

Shanghainese / 上海菜

Xinjishi Shanghai 新吉士		X	210	MAP/地圖 12/C-3
Yè Shanghai (Admiralty) 夜上海（金鐘）	⌂	XX	215	MAP/地圖 8/B-2
Yè Shanghai (Kowloon) 夜上海（九龍）		XXX	216	MAP/地圖 3/A-3

Sichuan / 川菜

Chilli Fagara 麻辣燙		X	70	MAP/地圖 5/B-2
Lumiere 亮明居		XX	133	MAP/地圖 6/C-2
Yunyan 雲陽閣	⌂	XX	220	MAP/地圖 4/C-1

Steakhouse / 扒房

Lawry's The Prime Rib		XXX	120	MAP/地圖 12/C-3
Mandarin Grill		XXX	136	MAP/地圖 6/D-3
Morton's of Chicago		XX	145	MAP/地圖 4/C-3
Ruth's Chris Steak House (Admiralty)		XX	166	MAP/地圖 8/A-2
The Bostonian 美岸海鮮廳		XX	188	MAP/地圖 3/B-2
The Steak House		XX	194	MAP/地圖 4/C-3

Swiss / 瑞士菜

Chesa 瑞樵閣		X	66	MAP/地圖 3/B-3

Thai / 泰式

Café Siam	⌂	X	62	MAP/地圖 7/A-1
JJ's		XX	113	MAP/地圖 9/B-1
Sukho Thai 崇都		XX	178	MAP/地圖 10/C-2

Thai and Vietnamese / 泰國/越南菜

Lian 蓮	⊕	X	129	MAP/地圖 6/C-2
Tru		X	199	MAP/地圖 7/B-2

Vietnamese / 越南菜

Golden Bull (Ocean Terminal)

金牛苑 (海運大廈)		X	91	MAP/地圖 3/A-3
Le Soleil	⊕	XX	128	MAP/地圖 4/D-2

Vietnamese contemporary / 時尚越式

Rice Paper (Causeway Bay)		X	164	MAP/地圖 11/B-2

RESTAURANTS PARTICULARLY PLEASANT
上佳的餐廳

Amber	✿✿	XxXX	54	MAP/地圖 6/C-3
Caprice	✿✿	XxXXX	63	MAP/地圖 6/C-1
Chesa 瑞樵閣		X	66	MAP/地圖 3/B-3
Cucina		XX	74	MAP/地圖 3/A-3
Harlan's		XX	97	MAP/地圖 6/C-2
Hutong 胡同	✿	XX	105	MAP/地圖 3/B-2
Inagiku (IFC) 稻菊 (國際金融中心)		XX	106	MAP/地圖 6/C-1
L'Atelier de Joël Robuchon	✿✿	XX	118	MAP/地圖 6/D-3
Lobster Bar and Grill 龍蝦吧		XX	131	MAP/地圖 8/A-2
Lung King Heen 龍景軒	✿✿✿	XxX	134	MAP/地圖 6/C-1
Mandarin Grill		XxX	136	MAP/地圖 6/D-3
Man Wah 文華廳		XX	139	MAP/地圖 6/D-3
Megu		XX	141	MAP/地圖 1/A-3
Nobu		XX	149	MAP/地圖 4/C-3
Petrus 珀翠	✿	XxXXX	159	MAP/地圖 8/A-2
Pierre	✿	XxXX	160	MAP/地圖 6/D-3
Shang Palace 香宮	✿✿	XxX	171	MAP/地圖 4/D-2
Spoon by Alain Ducasse		XX	175	MAP/地圖 4/C-3
Summer Palace 夏宮	✿✿	XxX	179	MAP/地圖 8/A-2
Tasty (IFC) 正斗粥麵專家 (國際金融中心)	⊕	끼	187	MAP/地圖 6/C-2
The Square 翠玉軒	✿	XX	193	MAP/地圖 6/D-2
The Steak House		XX	194	MAP/地圖 4/C-3
Wasabisabi 山葵		X	206	MAP/地圖 11/B-3
Water Margin 梁山泊		X	207	MAP/地圖 11/B-3
Zuma		XX	222	MAP/地圖 6/C-3

RESTAURANTS
WITH PRIVATE ROOMS
具備私人房間的餐廳

Amber	✿✿	✗✗✗	54	MAP/地圖 6/C-3
Aqua		✗✗	56	MAP/地圖 3/B-2
Aspasia		✗✗✗	57	MAP/地圖 4/C-1
At Corner		✗	58	MAP/地圖 11/B-2
Bo Innovation	✿✿	✗✗	61	MAP/地圖 9/B-3
Caprice	✿✿	✗✗✗✗	63	MAP/地圖 6/C-1
Celestial Court 天寶閣		✗✗	64	MAP/地圖 4/C-3
Chez Patrick (Soho)		✗✗	68	MAP/地圖 5/B-2
Chez Patrick (Wanchai)		✗✗	69	MAP/地圖 9/A-3
Cinecitta		✗✗✗	72	MAP/地圖 9/A-3
Crystal Jade La Mian Xiao Long Bao (TST) 翡翠拉麵小籠包 (尖沙咀)	🅐	✗	73	MAP/地圖 3/A-2
Cuisine Cuisine 国金軒		✗✗✗	75	MAP/地圖 6/C-2
Dong Lai Shun 東來順		✗✗	77	MAP/地圖 4/D-2
Dot Cod		✗✗	78	MAP/地圖 6/D-3
Dynasty 滿福樓		✗✗	79	MAP/地圖 4/C-3
Eighteen Brook 十八溪		✗✗	80	MAP/地圖 9/B-2
Farm House 農圃飯店	🅐	✗✗	81	MAP/地圖 12/C-3
Fook Lam Moon (Kowloon) 福臨門 (九龍)		✗✗	82	MAP/地圖 4/C-1
Fook Lam Moon (Wanchai) 福臨門 (灣仔)	✿	✗✗✗	83	MAP/地圖 9/B-3
Forum 富臨	✿	✗✗	84	MAP/地圖 11/B-2
Fu Sing 富聲		✗✗✗	85	MAP/地圖 10/D-2
Gaddi's 吉地士		✗✗✗✗	86	MAP/地圖 3/B-3
Gaia		✗✗✗	87	MAP/地圖 5/B-2
Ginza 銀座		✗✗	88	MAP/地圖 4/C-3
Golden Bauhinia 金紫荊	🅐	✗✗	90	MAP/地圖 9/B-1
Golden Bull (Ocean Terminal) 金牛苑 (海運大廈)		✗	91	MAP/地圖 3/A-3

Guangzhou Garden 粵江春	✕✕	93	MAP/地圖 1/B-1
Harlan's	✕✕	97	MAP/地圖 6/C-2
Hoi Yat Heen 海逸軒	✕✕✕	100	MAP/地圖 2/D-3
H One	✕✕✕	101	MAP/地圖 6/C-2
House of Jasmine 八月居	✕✕	102	MAP/地圖 3/A-3
Hunan Garden (Causeway Bay) 洞庭樓 (銅鑼灣)	✕✕✕	103	MAP/地圖 11/B-3
Hutong 胡同 ✿	✕✕	105	MAP/地圖 3/B-2
Inagiku (IFC) 稻菊 (國際金融中心)	✕✕	106	MAP/地圖 6/C-1
Inagiku (Kowloon) 稻菊 (九龍)	✕✕	107	MAP/地圖 4/D-2
Isola	✕✕	108	MAP/地圖 6/C-2
Jade Garden (Causeway Bay) 翠園 (銅鑼灣)	✕	109	MAP/地圖 11/B-2
Jashan ⊕	✕✕	110	MAP/地圖 7/A-1
Jasmine Place 怡翠軒	✕✕✕	111	MAP/地圖 6/D-2
JJ's	✕✕	113	MAP/地圖 9/B-1
Kiriyaki 桐燒	✕	116	MAP/地圖 11/B-2
La Brasserie 林柏軒	✕✕	117	MAP/地圖 3/A-2
L'Atelier de Joël Robuchon ✿✿	✕✕	118	MAP/地圖 6/D-3
Lawry's The Prime Rib	✕✕✕	120	MAP/地圖 12/C-3
Lei Garden (Elements) 利苑酒家 (圓方) ⊕	✕✕	121	MAP/地圖 1/A-3
Lei Garden (IFC) 利苑酒家 (國際金融中心) ✿	✕✕	122	MAP/地圖 6/C-2
Lei Garden (Kwun Tong) 利苑酒家 (觀唐)	✕✕	123	MAP/地圖 19/C-1
Lei Garden (Mong Kok) 利苑酒家 (旺角) ⊕	✕✕	124	MAP/地圖 1/B-1
Lei Garden (Tsim Sha Tsui) 利苑酒家 (尖沙咀) ✿	✕✕	126	MAP/地圖 4/D-2
Les Célébrités 名仕餐廳	✕✕	127	MAP/地圖 4/D-2
Lippo Chiuchow 力寶軒	✕	130	MAP/地圖 8/A-2
Luk Yu Tea House 陸羽茶室 ⊕	✕	132	MAP/地圖 7/B-1
Lumiere 亮明居	✕✕	133	MAP/地圖 6/C-2
Lung King Heen 龍景軒 ✿✿✿	✕✕✕	134	MAP/地圖 6/C-1
Mandarin Grill	✕✕✕	136	MAP/地圖 6/D-3
Manor 富瑤	✕✕	138	MAP/地圖 11/A-2
Man Wah 文華廳	✕✕	139	MAP/地圖 6/D-3
Modern China (Causeway Bay) 金滿庭 (銅鑼灣)	✕	143	MAP/地圖 11/B-3

RESTAURANTS WITH A VIEW
有景觀的餐廳

Amber

❀ ❀   ✗✗✗✗

        ♿ ☞♪ ⊡20 ☎♨ ⸙

A tasteful mix of contemporary and Art Deco styling greets diners here. There's much ebony on show, complemented by the original ceiling decoration comprising 3,500 copper tubes: none of it is too fancy. Tables are laid with fresh flowers every day, but the food presented here is the real treat. Seriously prepared French classical cuisine is based on well-sourced seasonal produce. The wine list is comprehensive, the service near flawless.

迎接顧客的是有品味的當代和Art Deco設計。這裡充斥著黑檀木，以天花板原形襯托，包括3,500條銅管-任何部分都不是太花巧。餐桌上擺放著每天更換的新鮮花卉，而食物確實是十分美味。古典法國菜烹調認真，採用了不同原產地的季節性產品。酒類選擇很全面，服務更近乎完美。

■ ADDRESS/地址
TEL.2132 0066
7F, The Landmark Mandarin Oriental Hotel, 15 Queen's Road, Central
中環皇后大道中15號置地文華東方酒店7樓
www.mandarinoriental.com

■ OPENING HOURS, LAST ORDER
營業時間, 最後點菜時間
Lunch/午膳 12:00-14:30 (L.O.)
Dinner/晚膳 18:00-23:00 (L.O.)

■ PRICE/價錢
Lunch/午膳 menu/套餐 $450
           carte/點菜 $550-980
Dinner/晚膳 menu/套餐 $1,180
           carte/點菜 $550-980

Angelini

There are few distinguishing features to this restaurant other than the view (a window seat is desirable) and the food which is straightforward and allows the natural flavours to shine. Although other Italian regions are represented, it is the cooking of Campania that gets the upper hand with specialities such as Amalfi-style scialatielli with clams, zucchini and basil. Here is a chef who is extremely passionate about the dishes he produces.

餐廳最具特色的地方可説是其優美景觀(窗口座位尤其能飽覽美景)，以及簡單的菜式和天然的食材。雖然其他意大利地區的菜式亦有提供，但這裡以坎帕尼亞區的菜式最為突出，阿瑪菲海岸風味蜆配短扁身麵伴青瓜及羅勒香草是當中的表表者。此外，這裡更有一位極其熱愛烹飪的廚帥。

■ ADDRESS/地址
TEL.2733 8750
Mezzanine Level, Kowloon Shangri-La Hotel, 64 Mody Road, Kowloon
九龍尖沙咀麼地道64號九龍香格里拉酒店閣樓
www.shangri-la.com

■ OPENING HOURS, LAST ORDER
營業時間，最後點菜時間
Lunch/午膳　12:00-15:00 (L.O.)
Dinner/晚膳　18:30-22:30 (L.O.)

■ PRICE/價錢
Lunch/午膳　menu/套餐 $ 218
　　　　　　carte/點菜 $ 570-1,100
Dinner/晚膳　menu/套餐 $ 690
　　　　　　carte/點菜 $ 650-1,300

Aqua

This duplex penthouse operation sits on the 29th and 30th floors offering not only mesmerising views but also two distinct cuisines served in tandem: Japanese and Italian. Thus, sashimi and sushi rub up against pasta and risotto dishes. Setting aside the more soothing tatami rooms, space is precious in this vibrant, bustling atmosphere and the banquette seating is quite narrow. Booking, especially at dinner, is advised.

這家複式閣樓餐廳座落於29樓及30樓，不但可飽覽醉人美景，更同時提供兩種風格迥異的異國佳餚：日本菜和意大利菜。因此，不論是刺身、壽司，還是意大利粉、意大利飯，可謂應有盡有。不過，除了舒適寬敞的榻榻米房間外，在活躍繁忙的氣氛下空間亦分外寶貴，長凳座位頗為狹窄。建議預約訂位，尤其在晚餐時段。

■ ADDRESS/地址

TEL.3427 2288

29F, One Peking Road, Tsim Sha Tsui, Kowloon

九龍尖沙咀北京道1號29樓

www.aqua.com.hk

■ OPENING HOURS, LAST ORDER

營業時間, 最後點菜時間

Lunch/午膳 12:00-15:00 L.O. 14:30
Dinner/晚膳 18:00-23:00 L.O. 22:30

■ PRICE/價錢

Lunch/午膳   menu/套餐 $ 198-238
            carte/點菜 $ 400-1,200
Dinner/晚膳 carte/點菜 $ 400-1,200

Aspasia

This unusually elegant room is softly lit and furnished in a highly eclectic way that mixes Louis XV with wild animal prints. Filigree screens are used to break up the room and provide privacy. Apart from some flourishes round the edges, the menu is solidly Italian with its sophisticated roll-call of antipasti, soups, risotti, pastas, fish and meat. Cooking is done with care and shows great promise; the service is charming but slow.

美輪美奐的餐廳格調不凡，柔和的燈光融和了路易十五世風格及野生動物印花。金絲屏風分隔餐室，讓顧客保留一點私人空間。除了華麗裝飾外，餐單亦具有濃烈意式風情：意式什錦頭盤、 湯、意大利燴飯、意大利麵、魚類、肉類等應有盡有。烹調手法亦甚見心思，服務質素甚佳，惟速度較慢。

■ ADDRESS/地址

TEL.3763 8800

1F, The Luxe Manor Hotel, 39 Kimberley Road, Tsim Sha Tsui, Kowloon

九龍尖沙咀金巴利道39號帝樂文娜公館1樓
www.aspasia.com.hk

■ OPENING HOURS, LAST ORDER
營業時間, 最後點菜時間
Lunch/午膳 12:00-14:30 (L.O.)
Dinner/晚膳 18:30-23:30 (L.O.)

■ PRICE/價錢
Lunch/午膳   menu/套餐 $ 168-268
              carte/點菜 $ 490-690
Dinner/晚膳   menu/套餐 $ 688
              carte/點菜 $ 490-690

At Corner

      ✗

      & ⪇ 💻10

Elevator doors open onto a giant TV screen, setting the tone for a trendy, fashionable restaurant. The tables along the wall offer great window views over Kowloon; the ones further in are more secluded for intimacy. There's minimalist understatement here, though it's of a more Western style than Japanese. The menus, though, could only come from one country: classics such as sushi, sashimi and tempura are served without fuss or experimentation.

餐廳電梯門前的巨型電視屏幕,與這所時尚入流餐廳的格調融為一體。近牆邊的餐桌坐擁美麗維港景色,其他位置則讓人有較多私人的空間。餐廳環境氣氛似是西式多於日式,這樣說只是流於表面,因為餐牌上的菜式全是來自同一個國家:日本,如壽司、刺身、天婦羅等經典菜式,毫不造作,恰到好處。

■ ADDRESS/地址

TEL.2576 6777

9F, World Trade Centre, 280 Gloucester Road, Causeway Bay

銅鑼灣告士打道280號世界貿易中心9樓

www.heaplace.com

■ OPENING HOURS, LAST ORDER

營業時間, 最後點菜時間

Lunch/午膳 12:00-15:00 (L.O.)

Dinner/晚膳 18:00-23:00 (L.O.)

■ PRICE/價錢

Lunch/午膳　carte/點菜 $ 340-540

Dinner/晚膳　carte/點菜 $ 340-540

Au Belge

XX

©♨

Cosy restaurant offering a rare chance to enjoy Belgian cuisine in Hong Kong. It makes up in elegance what it lacks in size: smartly laid tables complement a classical European-style bar. Chef specials include cassoulet Ostendais (with salmon, shrimp, mussels and scallops), and waterzooi Gantoise (chicken in creamy broth with vegetables). Most diners, though, go dewy-eyed over the imported mussels in casserole, accompanied by strong Belgian beer.

這家舒適的餐廳地方雖然不算寬敞，但可讓你在風格優雅的環境下，品嚐香港罕見的比利時美食。古典歐洲風格的酒吧，與排列恰當的餐桌配合得天衣無縫。廚師推介包括「Cassoulet Ostendais」（三文魚、 蝦、青口和扇貝砂鍋）及「Waterzooi Gantoise」（雞肉蔬菜忌廉湯）。烹調砂鍋的青口均是新鮮進口，深深吸引著大部分食客，配上濃烈的比利時啤酒，美酒佳餚相映成趣。

■ ADDRESS/地址

TEL.2524 1818

Shop B, GF, 11 Old Bailey Street, Soho, Central

中環奧卑利街11號地下B舖

www.aubelge.com.hk

■ OPENING HOURS, LAST ORDER

營業時間, 最後點菜時間

Lunch/午膳 11:30-14:30 (L.O.)

Dinner/晚膳 18:00-23:00 (L.O.)

■ PRICE/價錢

Lunch/午膳   menu/套餐 $ 125

                       carte/點菜 $ 255-370

Dinner/晚膳   menu/套餐 $ 270

                       carte/點菜 $ 255-370

Beo

Enhanced by the warm, fresh touch of indoor plants, Beo is a simple organic restaurant which conveniently looks out onto swaying trees. The chef sources his ingredients from a farm in New Territories. Innovation and creativity are behind his every move, and specials include the likes of broiled halibut carpaccio with oregano, fennel seed, balsamic reduction and mustard seed tuile. As you might expect, vegetarians are handsomely catered for, too.

Beo 是一家簡單的有機食品餐廳，室內植物給人溫暖清新的感覺，餐廳外的樹木更搖曳生姿。廚師從新界的一個農場採購食材，每個烹飪步驟都是革新和創意之舉。廚師推介包括烤比目魚片配比薩草、茴香籽、意大利陳醋汁和芥籽等等。一如所料，素食者的需要亦照顧周全。

■ ADDRESS/地址

TEL.2868 0625

16 Arbuthnot Road, Central
中環亞畢諾道16號

■ ANNUAL AND WEEKLY CLOSING
　　休息日期
Closed Sunday dinner
週日晚膳休息

■ OPENING HOURS, LAST ORDER
　　營業時間，最後點菜時間
Lunch/午膳　12:00-15:00 (L.O.)
Dinner/晚膳　18:30-23:00 (L.O.)

■ PRICE/價錢
Lunch/午膳　menu/套餐 $ 180
　　　　　　carte/點菜 $ 280-500
Dinner/晚膳　carte/點菜 $ 280-500

Bo Innovation

✿ ✿　　　　　　　　　　　　　　　　　　　🍴

♳ 🛏 💺12 ☎🍴

"X-treme Chinese cuisine" is how this modern fusion restaurant describes itself. Owner-chef Alvin Leung and his team in the open kitchen create dishes that are highly innovative, delicate and inventive. He also deconstructs recognisable Chinese flavour combinations in a playful way. For the full experience, try the small tasting plates of the Chef's Menu. The lift on Ship Street takes you up to a glass-encased room with a terrace.

以「X-treme Chinese cuisine」自居的現代餐廳,主力是中菜但同時融合了其他地方的菜式。餐廳老闆兼廚師梁經倫(Alvin)和他的團隊滿腦子新主意,在開放式廚房炮製極其創新精緻、獨一無二的菜式。另一方面,他打破了中菜味道的定義,以大膽的方式創造新的組合。品嚐主廚套餐的推薦小菜,享受全面的美食體驗。這家設有露台的玻璃外牆餐廳,在船街乘搭升降機即可到達。

■ ADDRESS/地址

TEL.2850 8371

2F, J Residence, Ship Street, Wanchai
灣仔船街嘉薈軒2樓
www.boinnovation.com

■ ANNUAL AND WEEKLY CLOSING
　休息日期

Closed 3 days Lunar New Year
農曆新年休息3天

■ OPENING HOURS, LAST ORDER
　營業時間, 最後點菜時間
Lunch/午膳　12:00-14:00 (L.O.)
Dinner/晚膳　19:00-22:00 (L.O.)

■ PRICE/價錢
Lunch/午膳　menu/套餐 $ 200-1,080
Dinner/晚膳　menu/套餐 $ 600-1,080

Café Siam

This simple no-nonsense Thai operation packs in a loyal following on a daily basis. So get there early, sit upstairs by the window and order yourself a Mekong Margarita while you decide what to eat. The key elements of the authentic menu are the curries and the seafood which are bursting with flavour and freshness. You'll emerge afterwards feeling very well looked after by the young, diligent team.

這家簡單的泰國餐廳每天都熟客滿座。因此，請提早到達。在樓上雅座近窗邊位置坐低，在點菜的同時，不妨享用一杯Mekong Margarita。菜餚原汁原味，主打菜式包括各種咖哩和海鮮，既新鮮又味美。餐廳的年輕侍應幹勁十足，服務令人賓至如歸。

■ ADDRESS/地址
TEL.2851 4803
40-42 Lyndhurst Terrace, Central
中環擺花街40-42號
www.cafesiam.com.hk

■ OPENING HOURS, LAST ORDER
營業時間, 最後點菜時間
12:00-22:30 (L.O.)

■ PRICE/價錢
Lunch/午膳   menu/套餐 $ 88
              carte/點菜 $ 200-400
Dinner/晚膳   menu/套餐 $ 188
              carte/點菜 $ 200-400

Caprice

❀ ❀　　　　　　　　　　　　　　✕✕✕✕✕

♿ ⟨ ☞ 🅿 ⟷16 🍇

Lamb from Sisteron, duck from Challans and chicken from Bresse highlight straightaway that much superb quality produce used here is imported directly from France: the resulting dishes demonstrate great finesse and imagination. Every aspect of the spacious dining room displays strong interest. There are lovely views of the harbour, of the wine cellar and of the open kitchen with its jewelled canopy. The service shows great attention to detail.

Sisteron地區的羊肉、Challans地區的鴨肉和Bresse地區的雞肉充分反映這家餐廳從法國直接進口名貴材料、炮製優質法國菜的特色。所有菜式均以高超手藝與無窮巧思炮製而成，寬敞的飯廳每個角度都顯示著獨特的風格。環視四周可見維港兩岸美景、酒櫃和帳蓬鑲滿寶飾的開放式廚房。服務周到細心。

■ ADDRESS/地址
TEL.3196 8860
6F, Four Seasons Hotel, 8 Finance Street, Central
中環金融街8號四季酒店平臺6樓
www.fourseasons.com

■ OPENING HOURS, LAST ORDER
營業時間, 最後點菜時間
Lunch/午膳　12:00-14:30 (L.O.)
Dinner/晚膳　18:00-22:30 (L.O.)

■ PRICE/價錢
Lunch/午膳　menu/套餐 $ 420
　　　　　　carte/點菜 $ 800-1,260
Dinner/晚膳　menu/套餐 $ 880-1,280
　　　　　　carte/點菜 $ 800-1,260

Celestial Court
天寶閣

Although this traditional Chinese restaurant is of grand proportions, it's common for diners to queue for a table. The refinement of the silk and wood decoration is offset by the noisy reality, courtesy of a low ceiling. A large range of Cantonese and Chinese specialities includes hand-prepared dim sum, skilfully served at lunch; their steamed shrimp dumpling with bamboo shoot is renowned. Particular attention is paid to seasonal creations.

雖然這家傳統中國餐廳地方龐大，但食客排隊候座亦是見怪不怪。由於樓底較淺，絲綢和木材裝飾的優雅被嘈雜的環境抵消了。粵菜和中國菜的選擇很多，包括午飯時間供應的人手製點心。筍尖鮮蝦餃王是這裡的名菜。特別留意季節性菜式。

■ ADDRESS/地址
TEL.2369 1111
2F, Sheraton Hotel, 20 Nathan Road,
Kowloon
九龍尖沙咀彌敦道20號喜來登店2樓
www.sheraton.com/hongkong

■ OPENING HOURS, LAST ORDER
營業時間, 最後點菜時間
Lunch/午膳 11:30-15:00 (L.O.)
Dinner/晚膳 18:00-23:30 (L.O.)

■ PRICE/價錢
Lunch/午膳   menu/套餐 $ 450-838
              carte/點菜 $ 250-550
Dinner/晚膳   menu/套餐 $ 450-838
              carte/點菜 $ 250-550

Chee Kei
池記

The only problem to overcome here is getting in and out of the place: the word has spread about Chee Kei and space is tight. Noise levels are high, with staff in headscarves joining in the general merriment. An extensive menu includes a choice between five types of noodle and a selection of congee. The congee with crab is a best seller, while wonton are generously filled and flavoursome. The big hit for dessert is red bean soup with sweet tofu.

這裡唯一不方便之處是出入問題，池記一向以地方細小但食客多而受注目。戴著頭巾的員工，為嘈雜環境更添一份歡鬧氣氛。菜式選擇繁多，包括五類麵線和多種款式的粥。最熱賣的包括金衣蟹皇粥，而雲吞更是皮薄餡多，味道濃郁。甜品方面，最受歡迎的甜品是紅豆沙豆腐花。

■ ADDRESS/地址
TEL.2890 8616
84 Percival Street, Causeway Bay
銅鑼灣波斯富街84號

■ OPENING HOURS, LAST ORDER
營業時間，最後點菜時間
11:00-23:30 (L.O.)

■ PRICE/價錢
Lunch/午膳　carte/點菜 $ 27-34
Dinner/晚膳　carte/點菜 $ 52-92

Chesa
瑞樵閣

For over forty years, the cuisine of Switzerland has found a charming niche here. An imposing wood door leads you into an intimate Swiss-style chalet with wooden objects left, right and centre. The experienced chef is proud of his cheese specialities: fondue Vaudoise (traditional fondue), or raclette du Valais (hot melted cheese with potatoes, pickled onions and gherkins). For dessert, chocolate fondue or Swiss chocolate mousses are de rigueur!

瑞士美食在香港穩佔一席位超過四十年。壯觀的木門帶領你到親切的瑞士農舍，裡面四處都有木製的裝飾。經驗豐富的廚師對他的芝士作品十分自豪：沃州芝士火鍋(傳統芝士火鍋)或瓦萊州烤芝士(熱熔的芝士配馬鈴薯、醃洋蔥及青瓜)。至於甜品，巧克力火鍋或瑞士巧克力慕絲是兩大必吃！

■ ADDRESS/地址
TEL.2920 2888
1F, The Peninsula Hotel, Salisbury Road, Kowloon
九龍尖沙咀梳士巴利道半島酒店1樓
www.peninsula.com

■ OPENING HOURS, LAST ORDER
營業時間, 最後點菜時間
Lunch/午膳 12:00-14:30 (L.O.)
Dinner/晚膳 18:30-22:30 (L.O.)

■ PRICE/價錢
Lunch/午膳   menu/套餐 $ 260
　　　　　　　carte/點菜 $ 415-705
Dinner/晚膳 carte/點菜 $ 415-705

Cheung Kee
祥記飯店

Things almost seem to spill out onto the colourful street at this compact establishment spread over two small rooms. As they've been going since 1948 and have quite a local following, you'd better book to ensure a place. The extremely good-value menu features honest and earthy dishes that include seafood, casseroles and chicken. But it's the Peking duck that remains the must-have dish. Keep some room for the banana fritters too.

這家設有兩間餐室設備俱全的餐館食客如雲，擁擠情況有如把人客擠瀉於多彩多姿的街道上。這家自1948年創業的老店一向有不少忠實食客，如欲前往，最好先行預約，以免向隅。菜餚價錢超值，菜式樸實地道，包括海鮮、砂鍋、雞，而北京填鴨更是不可不吃的招牌菜。注意別吃太飽，留點胃口嚐嚐高力豆沙！

■ ADDRESS/地址
TEL.2529 0707
1F, 75 Lockhart Road, Wanchai
灣仔駱克道75號1樓

■ OPENING HOURS, LAST ORDER
營業時間, 最後點菜時間
12:00-23:00 (L.O.)

■ PRICE/價錢
Lunch/午膳   carte/點菜 $ 150-200
Dinner/晚膳   carte/點菜 $ 150-200

Chez Patrick (Soho)

XX

⊡14 ⓒ¶ℓ

Tucked away in a characterful pedestrianised street where the local market takes place, this is a little corner of France. The restaurant is neatly decorated throughout in black and white although the service can, at times, be a little hesitant. A short set-price menu is supplemented by suggestions of the day that might include a smoked foie gras and smoked salmon terrine. Monsieur Patrick in fact prepares the smoked ingredients himself.

在熙來攘往的街市行人尊用區街角裡暗藏着法國風情。餐廳裝潢以黑白為主色，整潔雅觀；不過服務有時略嫌效率欠佳。定價餐單菜式不多，但附有每日精選菜式，有時包括煙燻鵝肝或煙三文魚批。事實上，煙燻食材均由法籍主人Patrick親自烹煮。

■ ADDRESS/地址

TEL.2541 1401
26 Peel Street, Soho, Central
中環卑利街26號
www.chezpatrick.hk

■ ANNUAL AND WEEKLY CLOSING
   休息日期
Closed Sunday
週日休息

■ OPENING HOURS, LAST ORDER
   營業時間, 最後點菜時間
Lunch/午膳 12:00-14:30 (L.O.)
Dinner/晚膳 18:45-22:30 (L.O.)

■ PRICE/價錢
Lunch/午膳   menu/套餐 $ 199-279
Dinner/晚膳   menu/套餐 $ 499-599

Chez Patrick (Wanchai)

XX

⌂10

Located in a discreet little street with an upstairs entrance, Chez Patrick's elegant black and white decor attempts to bring the atmosphere of a typical Parisian apartment to Wanchai. Waiters crying "bon appétit" as glasses of Cognac, Armagnac and Calvados chink to the sound of French music helps complete a successful Gallic transplant. The romantic ambience is enhanced with a red candle on each table; the cuisine is reassuringly traditional.

Chez Patrick位處一條不顯眼的小街的樓上舖，優雅的黑白裝飾嘗試為灣仔帶來典型巴黎公寓的味道。背景播著法國音樂，襯托著盛載著干邑、雅馬邑、和蘋果酒的酒杯碰杯聲，服務員並同時大喊「bon appétit」，營造完美的法國氣氛。每張怡上都有一枝紅蠟燭，增添餐廳的浪漫情調。餐廳供應的絕對是傳統的菜餚。

■ ADDRESS/地址
TEL.2527 1408
8-9 Sun Street, Wanchai
灣仔日街8-9號
www.chezpatrick.hk

■ ANNUAL AND WEEKLY CLOSING
休息日期
Closed 4 days Lunar New Year and Sunday except Public Holidays
農曆新年4天及週日休息 (公眾假期除外)

■ OPENING HOURS, LAST ORDER
營業時間, 最後點菜時間
Lunch/午膳 12:00-14:30 (L.O.)
Dinner/晚膳 19:00-22:00 (L.O.)

■ PRICE/價錢
Lunch/午膳 menu/套餐 $ 199-279
Dinner/晚膳 menu/套餐 $ 499-599

Chilli Fagara
麻辣燙

Chillies are a passion here! The window's filled with them, as well as orange flames, which act as a forewarning! Rich red walls create an intimate atmosphere. The heat is turned up as you progress from mild 'natural' dishes through to the likes of red hot chilli prawn – only for the very brave. Caramelized banana and chrysanthemum tea cool things down at the end. A sweet ambience prevails as the small team ensures all runs smoothly.

這裡充滿辣椒的激情！窗口充滿著辣椒，而橙色的火焰就像是預警！濃豔的紅牆營造親切的氣氛，當你從溫和的「普 通」菜式吃到辣椒蝦之類的菜餚時，便會渾身發熱！當然，只有夠膽的人才會一嚐後者。最後可用拔絲香蕉及菊花茶涼快下來。為數不多的員工，和諧的團隊合作，令餐廳運作順暢，更顯溫馨。

■ ADDRESS/地址

TEL.2893 3330

Shop E, GF, 51A Graham Street, Soho, Central

中環嘉咸街51A地下E輔

www.chillifagara.com

■ ANNUAL AND WEEKLY CLOSING
   休息日期

Closed 8 days Lunar New Year and Sunday

農曆新年8天及週日休息

■ OPENING HOURS, LAST ORDER
   營業時間, 最後點菜時間

Lunch/午膳 11:30-14:00 (L.O.)
Dinner/晚膳 17:00-23:00 (L.O.)

■ PRICE/價錢

Lunch/午膳   carte/點菜 $ 230-450
Dinner/晚膳 carte/點菜 $ 230-450

Chuen Kee Seafood
全記海鮮菜館

Two family-run restaurants overlook a pleasant harbour to distant islands; choose the one with the rooftop terrace and the quayside (plastic) seats. An extraordinary range of seafood is available from adjacent fishmongers': cuttlefish, bivalve, crab and lobster, mollusc, shrimps, prawns... Go to the tank, select your meal, and minutes later it appears in front of you, steamed, poached, or wok fried. Then settle back and watch the boats go by.

這兩家餐廳是家族生意，位置優越，可觀賞海港及離島。天台陽台那一家，以及碼頭邊的塑膠座位備受推介。這裡海鮮種類繁多，包括墨魚、貝殼、蟹、龍蝦、賴尿蝦、大蝦小蝦等等。你可以到魚缸挑選你的海鮮， 蒸、 燉、炒也好，幾分鐘後便會奉到餐桌上，成為你的食物。然後你便可輕鬆地細賞船艇來往往。

■ ADDRESS/地址
TEL.2791 1195
53 Hoi Pong Street, Sai Kung
西貢海傍街53號

■ OPENING HOURS, LAST ORDER
營業時間，最後點菜時間
11:00-23:00 L.O. 22:30

■ PRICE/價錢
Lunch/午膳　carte/點菜 $ 130-300
Dinner/晚膳　carte/點菜 $ 130-300

Cinecittà

🍴🍴🍴

🚋16 🚏 🍇

This big, modern restaurant has one outstanding feature: a big screen showing Italian movies - well, it's not called Cinecitta for nothing! And if you tire of the films, there's always the food - Roman specialities and traditional Italian dishes are respected here, accompanied by warm, smiley service. Taglioni, green ravioli and tortelloni are bases for tasty specialities, while many Italian wines appear from a spectacular glass cellar.

播著意大利電影的闊螢幕是這家寬闊的現代餐廳令人注目的特徵一名副其實的Cinecitta！如果你對電影沒甚興趣，這裡還有美食-羅馬特色菜及意大利菜餚備受喜愛。此外，這裡的服務親切，服務員笑面迎人。美食首推Taglioni(意大利麵條)、嫩菜雲吞及其他自製雲吞，而壯觀的玻璃酒窖提供的意大利酒更是目不暇給。

■ ADDRESS/地址

TEL.2529 0199

GF, Starcrest Building, 9 Star Street, Wanchai

灣仔星街9號星域軒地下

www.elite-concept.com

■ ANNUAL AND WEEKLY CLOSING
　　休息日期

Closed Saturday lunch and Sunday lunch

週六、日午膳休息

■ OPENING HOURS, LAST ORDER
　　營業時間, 最後點菜時間

Lunch/午膳 12:00-15:00 (L.O.)

Dinner/晚膳 18:00-23:30 (L.O.)

■ PRICE/價錢

Lunch/午膳　menu/套餐 $ 138-168
　　　　　　carte/點菜 $ 250-500

Dinner/晚膳　carte/點菜 $ 250-500

Crystal Jade La Mian Xiao Long Bao (TST)
翡翠拉麵小籠包 (尖沙咀)

👻 ✗

♿ ⌨14

Could this be Harbour City Mall's most popular eatery? Very probably. It's a modern cafeteria that buzzes all day - if your party is less than four strong, you'll be eating communally with strangers. The food – a mix of Northern Chinese and Sichuan, prepared in a sizzling semi-open kitchen – is very fresh, aromatic and tasty. Signature dishes include steamed pork dumpling with warm soup, or la Mian hand-made noodles with shrimp and cashew nuts.

這裡是海港城裡最受歡迎的食肆嗎？很可能是。這是家整天繁忙的餐廳，如果同行少於四人，你們很可能要和人併桌而坐。食物混合了中國北方菜式和四川菜，在熱烘烘的半開放式廚房烹調，非常新鮮，既香又美味。招牌菜包括上海小籠包、四川擔擔拉麵。

■ ADDRESS/地址
TEL.2622 2699
Shop 3328, 3F, Gateway Arcade, Harbour City, Tsim Sha Tsui
九龍尖沙咀廣東道17號海港城3樓332號輔

■ OPENING HOURS, LAST ORDER
營業時間, 最後點菜時間
11:00-23:00 L.O. 22:30

■ PRICE/價錢
Lunch/午膳 carte/點菜 $ 100-250
Dinner/晚膳 carte/點菜 $ 100-250

Cucina

XX X

A chill-out atmosphere, great views and design focusing on beautiful natural materials all add up to a relaxed but fashionable interior. Factor in an extremely diverse menu that includes Chinese noodles, pan Asian combinations and a hefty dollop of Italian dishes, and you end up with something uniquely interesting. Not only do the chefs dazzle you with their technique, they also suggest wines to go with what they're cooking.

餐廳氣氛輕鬆，景色壯麗，設計更採用美麗的自然素材，交織成輕鬆而時尚的室內空間。餐單讓人目不暇給，菜式極為多樣化，囊括中式麵點、亞洲菜和多不勝數的意大利菜式，食客定能選擇獨特迷人的美食。主廚烹調技巧出色，讓你大開眼界，亦會推介配搭佳餚的美酒。

■ ADDRESS/地址
TEL.2113 0808
6F, Marco Polo Hotel, Harbour City, Tsim Sha Tsui
九龍尖沙咀海港城馬哥孛羅酒店6樓
www.cucinahk.com

■ OPENING HOURS, LAST ORDER
營業時間, 最後點菜時間
Lunch/午膳 12:00-15:00 L.O. 14:30
Dinner/晚膳 18:00-23:00 L.O. 22:30

■ PRICE/價錢
Lunch/午膳　menu/套餐 $ 220
　　　　　　carte/點菜 $ 250-500
Dinner/晚膳　carte/點菜 $ 600-2,500

Cuisine Cuisine
国金軒

XXX

14

Sharing space with the adjacent Lumiere, this large fashionably decorated room easily seats 200 people. Before you're escorted to your table with its fine harbour view, there's time to select a fish from the tank and then have it served with their very own specially-brewed soy sauce. This place is light and airy at lunchtime but more intimately lit at night. Cantonese specialities include stewed whole Yoshima abalone with premium oyster sauce.

國金軒毗鄰亮明居，裝潢極盡奢華，且能輕易容納約200人。你可以從容地先在魚缸挑選鮮魚，然後國金軒會用自製醬油清蒸，再在侍應帶領下施然走到飽覽醉人海景的餐桌。午飯時間的氣氛輕鬆悠閒，晚上則燈光璀璨。粵菜精選包括原隻皇冠吉品鮑魚。

■ ADDRESS/地址
TEL.2393 3933
Shop 3101, Podium Level 3, IFC Mall, 8 Finance Street, Central
中環金融街8號國際金融中心商場第2期3樓 3101號舖
www.cuisinecuisine.hk

■ OPENING HOURS, LAST ORDER
營業時間, 最後點菜時間
Lunch/午膳 12:00-14:30 (L.O.)
Dinner/晚膳 18:00-22:30 (L.O.)
■ PRICE/價錢
Lunch/午膳   menu/套餐 $ 298-398
           carte/點菜 $ 250-1,300
Dinner/晚膳 carte/點菜 $ 250-1,300

Dim Sum
譽滿坊

Get here early to beat the loyal Happy Valley following. There's a cosy and homely charm here defined by closely set tables: peek across at nearby diners to see what they've ordered. Start with the steamed dumplings, Leong Har Gao and Siu Mai. Top three dim sums in the luxury section are Yu Chee Gao, abalone Siu Mai and Koon Yin Gao. Also worth trying are Loong Har Tong (lobster bisque) and Goon Tong Gao (soup with giant Chinese dumpling).

早一點抵埗，在跑馬地的信眾到來前搶先入座。這裡餐桌排列緊密，既舒適又有在家中的感覺：你可以偷偷看鄰座的食客點了甚麼。先試燕液蝦餃、竹笙龍蝦餃和鮑翅燒賣，而比較昂貴的有最受歡迎的三大點心—鮮蝦魚翅餃、BB鮑燒賣和官燕鮮蝦餃。此外，竹笙龍蝦湯和鮑翅灌湯餃亦值得一試。

■ ADDRESS/地址
TEL.2834 8893
63 Shing Woo Road, Happy Valley
跑馬地成和道63號

■ ANNUAL AND WEEKLY CLOSING
　休息日期
Closed Lunar New Year
年初一休假

■ OPENING HOURS, LAST ORDER
　營業時間, 最後點菜時間
Lunch/午膳　11:00-16:30 (L.O.)
Dinner/晚膳　18:00-22:30 (L.O.)

■ PRICE/價錢
Lunch/午膳　carte/點菜 $ 105-240
Dinner/晚膳　carte/點菜 $ 135-280

Dong Lai Shun
東來順

XX

☞♟ ⊡20 ☎⊠

The first Dong Lai Shun was founded over a hundred years ago in Peking, and has been successfully transplanted to the basement of the Royal Garden hotel. Its décor is contemporary with distinct Asian nuances, such as panels and paintings; there's a water feature which creates a relaxing atmosphere. The mix of Beijing and Huaiyang recipes includes hot pot, Peking duck and 'shuan yang rou': paper thin slices of inner Mongolian black-headed mutton.

享譽百載的東來順始創於北京，其後成功遷移到帝苑酒店地庫層。餐廳的裝修揉合了現代和傳統格調；鮮明細緻的亞洲特色，從牆板和壁畫便可略窺一二。這裡的人工噴泉更營造了輕鬆的氣氛。食物方面，餐廳的北京和淮陽菜共冶一爐，包括火鍋、北京填鴨，以及「涮羊肉」：採用內蒙黑頭白羊的上乘部分，肉質薄如紙，軟如棉。

■ ADDRESS/地址
TEL.2733 2020
B2F, The Royal Garden Hotel, 69 Mody Road, Tsim Sha Tsui East, Kowloon
九龍尖沙咀東部麼地道69號帝苑酒店地庫2樓
www.rghk.com.hk

■ OPENING HOURS, LAST ORDER
營業時間, 最後點菜時間
Lunch/午膳 11:30-14:30 (L.O.)
Dinner/晚膳 18:00-22:30 (L.O.)

■ PRICE/價錢
Lunch/午膳 carte/點菜 $ 200-600
Dinner/晚膳 carte/點菜 $ 200-600

Dot Cod

XX

🍽20 ☎🍴

That this is owned by the Hong Kong Cricket Club has some bearing on the atmosphere which can get quite raucous, especially if you end up sitting near the bar when there's a match on. If you're after a more genteel time, ask for a table in the back room. The menu here of course majors on seafood but there are salads, grills and pasta dishes as well. Anyone concerned about fish sustainability should consult the menu or ask the staff.

Dot Cod是香港木球會旗下對外開放的會所餐廳，因此氣氛有時頗為狂熱，尤其是球賽舉行期間，愈近酒吧區，愈是喧鬧。如果你想享受寧靜時光，建議要求廳後面的座位。餐單主要是海鮮菜式，此外還有沙律、烤肉和意大利麵可供選擇。如果你關注海鮮的新鮮程度，可以參考餐單或向餐廳職員查詢。

■ ADDRESS/地址

TEL.2810 6988

B4F, Prince's Building, 10 Charter Road Central
中環遮打道10號太子大廈地庫4樓

■ ANNUAL AND WEEKLY CLOSING
休息日期
Closed Sunday and Public Holidays
週日及公眾假期休息

■ OPENING HOURS, LAST ORDER
營業時間, 最後點菜時間
07:30-22:30 (L.O.)

■ PRICE/價錢
Lunch/午膳　menu/套餐 $ 228
　　　　　　carte/點菜 $ 340-530
Dinner/晚膳　carte/點菜 $ 340-530

Dynasty
滿福樓

✕✕

🍽·20

Suckling pig and barbecued pork are the highlights of the traditionally Cantonese menu that also incorporates other specialities, including braised sliced abalone with goose webs and mango and pomelo sago sweet soup. The restaurant's interior is themed to recreate the charms of a Chinese tea house and has interesting crockery to match. However, it is beginning to look somewhat tired in places.

乳豬和叉燒是滿福樓的名菜，但這傳統的廣東菜譜上亦不乏其他精選菜色，包括鮮鮑扣鵝掌與楊枝甘露。餐館的裝潢以突出中國茶樓的魅力為主，並配以精美餐具，可惜有些地方稍顯殘舊。

■ ADDRESS/地址
TEL.2734 6688
4F, Renaissance Kowloon Hotel, 22 Salisbury Road, Tsim Sha Tsui
九龍尖沙咀梳士利道22號九龍萬麗酒店 4樓

■ OPENING HOURS, LAST ORDER
營業時間, 最後點菜時間
Lunch/午膳 11:30-14:30 (L.O.)
Dinner/晚膳 18:30-23:00 (L.O.)

■ PRICE/價錢
Lunch/午膳   carte/點菜 $ 180-1,200
Dinner/晚膳   carte/點菜 $ 210-1,200

Eighteen Brook
十八溪

♿ 🛏12

Handily placed if you want to reach Wanchai from mainland Hong Kong, the restaurant is close to the Star Ferry pier. An elevator brings you to the eighth floor of the hotel, where you will find an aquarium at the door but, alas, an absence of good views inside. Well-distanced tables; a gourmet destination, with specialities like sliced prawn with green crab and egg white, or steamed conpoy rice with sliced chicken, yunnan ham and mushroom.

餐廳毗鄰灣仔天星碼頭，從九龍半島到這裡十分便利。乘搭電梯直達酒店八樓，便可看見大門的魚缸，但可惜餐廳內沒有景觀。餐桌間距離適中，提供的美食包括珊瑚貴妃鮮蝦片、或者竹籠蟹子瑤柱麒麟雞飯。

■ ADDRESS/地址
TEL.2827 8802
8F, Convention Plaza (Renaissance Harbour View Hotel), 1 Harbour Road, Wanchai
灣仔港灣道1號(萬麗海景酒店)會展廣場8樓

■ OPENING HOURS, LAST ORDER
營業時間, 最後點菜時間
Lunch/午膳 11:30-15:00 (L.O.)
Dinner/晚膳 17:30-23:30 (L.O.)

■ PRICE/價錢
Lunch/午膳   menu/套餐 $ 136
             carte/點菜 $ 300-450
Dinner/晚膳   menu/套餐 $ 415
             carte/點菜 $ 300-450

Farm House
農圃飯店

XX

 ♿ 🍽20

Surrounded by chic fashion boutiques, this contemporary-style dining room has private rooms leading off as well as a huge aquarium running the length of one entire wall. The Cantonese menu uses exceedingly fresh ingredients and includes such specialities as shark's fin soup, abalone and chicken wings all of which are exceedingly tasty and well-priced. The staff are very courteous and professional.

這家飯店附近滿是時裝名店，裝潢具時代感，並備有獨立餐室和沿著牆身一路延伸的巨型水族箱。粵菜選用特級新鮮材料炮製而成，名菜有魚翅羹、鮑魚和雞翼，味道超凡，價錢相宜。員工非常專業有禮。

■ ADDRESS/地址
TEL.2881 1331
1F, Phase 1, Ming An Plazza, 8 Sunning Road, Causeway Bay
銅鑼灣新寧道民安廣場1期1樓
www.farmhouse.com.hk

■ OPENING HOURS, LAST ORDER
　營業時間, 最後點菜時間
Lunch/午膳 11:00-15:00 L.O. 14:45
Dinner/晚膳 18:00-24:00 L.O. 23:00

■ PRICE/價錢
Lunch/午膳　carte/點菜 $ 210-600
Dinner/晚膳　carte/點菜 $ 210-1,000

Fook Lam Moon (Kowloon)
福臨門 (九龍)

✕✕

🍽20

This restaurant is situated in a busy tourist area halfway between Kowloon Park and the Hong Kong Museum of History: a huge blue signpost over the road means you can't fail to miss it. Traditional Cantonese specialities such as abalone, birds nest with seafood and mango pudding are highly recommended and, at lunchtime, the menu features a Dim Sum dish of sharks fin dumpling with kim wa ham stock.

餐廳位處九龍公園和香港歷史博物館的中間點，座落於繁華遊客區之中；路上的巨型藍色招牌，你絕對不會看不見。強烈推薦傳統粵菜美食，如鮑魚、海鮮燕窩及芒果布甸。午市時段點心餐單更設金華火腿上湯魚翅餃。

■ ADDRESS/地址
TEL.2366 0286
53-59 Kimberley Road, Tsim Sha Tsui, Kowloon
九龍尖沙咀金巴利道53-59號
www.fooklammoon-grp.com

■ ANNUAL AND WEEKLY CLOSING
   休息日期
Closed Lunar New Year
年初一休息

■ OPENING HOURS, LAST ORDER
   營業時間, 最後點菜時間
Lunch/午膳 11:30-15:00 (L.O.)
Dinner/晚膳 18:00-22:30 (L.O.)

■ PRICE/價錢
Lunch/午膳 carte/點菜 $ 300-2,000
Dinner/晚膳 carte/點菜 $ 300-2,000

Fook Lam Moon (Wanchai)
福臨門 (灣仔)

Newly renovated and spread over three floors, this has been owned by the same family for several generations. The care and attention they've invested is clearly visible in the refinement of the Cantonese cooking. Ingredients don't come any more natural or fresher, there's complete respect for seasonality and a ban on artificial flavourings. Subtle cooking is matched by fine wines on this well-selected list.

全新裝潢的店面佔地三層，由同一家族數代相傳。提供極盡精緻的廣東菜色，背後付出的心血可見一斑。選用最當造(時 令)的新鮮材料，更嚴禁使用人工添加劑，確保原汁原味。巧思妙手的菜式配上特選美酒，可謂一絕。

■ ADDRESS/地址
TEL.2866 0663
35-45 Johnston Road, Wanchai
灣仔莊中敦道35-45號
www.fooklammoon-grp.com

■ ANNUAL AND WEEKLY CLOSING
　休息日期
Closed 3 days Lunar New Year
農曆新年休息3天

■ OPENING HOURS, LAST ORDER
　營業時間, 最後點菜時間
Lunch/午膳　11:30-14:30 (L.O.)
Dinner/晚膳　18:00-22:30 (L.O.)

■ PRICE/價錢
Lunch/午膳　menu/套餐 $ 380-2,750
　　　　　　carte/點菜 $ 800-2,750
Dinner/晚膳　menu/套餐 $ 380-2,750
　　　　　　carte/點菜 $ 800-2,750

Cantonese/粵菜   MAP/地圖   11/B-2

Forum
富臨

🌸   ✕✕

🚐·40 ☎🍴

You cannot fail to notice the pictures of owner-chef Yeung
Koon Yat. For over thirty years he's been attracting everyone
from world leaders to locals to his Forum restaurant, thanks
largely to his celebrated speciality: abalone. His fried bird's
nest and shark's fin soup are noteworthy too but it is for the
abalone cooked in a clay pot that many come. The restaurant
is spread over three floors, with seating for around 150.

你肯定會留意到世界御廚楊貫一的照片。三十多年來，光顧他的客人從世界領
導人到本地食客包羅萬有，這大概應歸功於他的拿手名菜：阿一鮑魚。大部分
客人都為其砂鍋鮑魚慕名而來，而皇冠燕盞及紅燒翅也相當不俗。飯店佔地三
層，可容納約一百五十人。

■ ADDRESS/地址
TEL.2891 2555
485 Lockhart Road, Causeway Bay
銅鑼灣駱克道485號

■ OPENING HOURS, LAST ORDER
    營業時間, 最後點菜時間
Lunch/午膳 11:00-15:00 (L.O.)
Dinner/晚膳 18:00-23:00 (L.O.)

■ PRICE/價錢
Lunch/午膳   menu/套餐 $ 1,400-2,600
              carte/點菜 $ 200-2,000
Dinner/晚膳   menu/套餐 $ 1,400-2,600
              carte/點菜 $ 600-2,000

Fu Sing
富聲

✗✗✗

🍴20 ☎🍴

Taking the lift up in this stylish modern building will bring you out directly into the plush spacious restaurant with its smart carpeting and wall plates. The service is very attentive and the cooking is equally precise with its broad range of Cantonese dishes. Among the recommendations are stewed abalone and goose web as well as braised cow tail in red wine. Plenty of fresh juices are available and there's a fine collection of cognacs.

進入設計時尚、富現代感的大樓後，升降機帶你直達富麗堂皇、佔地寬廣的餐廳，牆紙和地毯的鋪設均見心思。服務非常周到，烹調方法亦獨具特色，備有一系列粵菜可供選擇。推介菜式包括炆鮑魚鵝掌和紅酒炆牛腩。除了各種鮮榨果汁，店內亦提供精選法國干邑白蘭地。

■ ADDRESS/地址
TEL.2893 0881
1F, 353 Lockhart Road, Sunshine Plaza, Wanchai
灣仔駱克道353號三湘大廈1樓

■ OPENING HOURS, LAST ORDER
營業時間, 最後點菜時間
Lunch/午膳　11:00-15:00 (L.O.)
Dinner/晚膳　18:00-23:00 (L.O.)

■ PRICE/價錢
Lunch/午膳　menu/套餐 $ 480
　　　　　　 carte/點菜 $ 250-450
Dinner/晚膳　menu/套餐 $ 480
　　　　　　 carte/點菜 $ 250-450

Gaddi's
吉地士

XXXXX

🖐 · ⛄16 📞🍴 🐝

Gaddi's is truly an institution in the city. A private lift whisks you to this legend celebrating over fifty years of fine dining. Live music and old-style British formality accompanies the French classical cuisine. If you want to make an evening of it you should try the tasting menu. Others settle for seasonal specials from the efficient staff. Gaddi's celebrates a bygone elegance where the proper meaning of dining is taken very seriously.

吉地士是城內有名的食府。私人電梯迅速把你把帶到這個超過五十年的優質餐飲傳奇。現場音樂和服務員的傳統英式招待配襯著經典法國菜。如果想享受美好的晚餐,便要試試品嚐菜單。一些人會點由高效率的服務員即時送上的季節性特選。吉地士保留著一種昔日的典雅,餐飲的真正意義得以尊重。

■ ADDRESS/地址
TEL.2920 2888
1F, The Peninsula Hotel, Salisbury Road, Tsim Sha Tsui
九龍尖沙咀梳士巴利道半島酒店1樓
www.peninsula.com

■ OPENING HOURS, LAST ORDER
營業時間, 最後點菜時間
Lunch/午膳 12:00-14:30 (L.O.)
Dinner/晚膳 19:00-22:30 (L.O.)

■ PRICE/價錢
Lunch/午膳   menu/套餐 $ 480
             carte/點菜 $ 1,000-1,200
Dinner/晚膳 menu/套餐 $ 1,388-2,388
             carte/點菜 $ 1,400-1,500

Gaia

Classy Italian restaurant with a subdued and sober atmosphere enhanced by ambient music and, in the evening, the romantic addition of a glowing candle at each table. The welcoming manager is everywhere, ensuring that you have a meal to remember. Fresh ingredients from Italy help create memorable dishes such as homemade pasta tossed in a rabbit-stew style ragout, or sautéed veal chop with truffle cheese, porcini mushrooms and goose liver sauce.

這優質的意大利餐廳，在音樂陪襯下，氣氛典雅而莊嚴。尤其在傍晚時分，每張桌上點起蠟燭，增添浪漫氣氛。好客的經理隨時候命，確保客人對這一餐留下深刻印象。餐廳採用從意大利運來的新鮮材料，烹調令人難忘的菜餚。例如蔬菜雜燴拌自製意大利麵，或嫩煎小牛扒配芝士磨菇及鵝肝醬。

■ ADDRESS/地址
TEL.2167 8200
GF, Grand Millennium Plaza, 181 Queen's Road, Central
中環皇后大道中181號新紀元廣場地下

■ ANNUAL AND WEEKLY CLOSING
　休息日期
Closed Lunar New Year
年初一休息

■ OPENING HOURS, LAST ORDER
　營業時間, 最後點菜時間
Lunch/午膳 12:00-15:00 (L.O.)
Dinner/晚膳 18:30-23:30 (L.O.)

■ PRICE/價錢
Lunch/午膳   menu/套餐 $ 248
　　　　　　　carte/點菜 $ 300-730
Dinner/晚膳   carte/點菜 $ 330-750

Ginza
銀座

One of the attractions is that this is more or less at eye-level with the harbour, and large windows behind the sushi counter provide a ring-side seat for watching the boats go by. It's named after a neighbourhood of Tokyo and offers a full range of menus including sushi, teppanyaki and tempura, in both the main room and tatami rooms. Ignore the limited wine selection as there's a good list of different sakes to choose from.

這家餐廳的其中一個賣點是與海港差不多同一水平線，坐在壽司吧後面的巨型玻璃前，你可以靜靜欣賞千帆過盡的海景。餐廳以東京地區為名，菜式包括壽司、鐵板燒和天婦羅，更設有主餐室和榻榻米房間。琳瑯滿目多種日本酒的選擇，令人對其他酒的選擇不多不會介懷。

■ ADDRESS/地址
TEL.2368 6138
Shop L057, New World Centre, 18-24 Salisbury Road, Tsim Sha Tsui, Kowloon
九龍尖沙咀梳士巴利道18-24號新世界中心地下L057號舖

■ OPENING HOURS, LAST ORDER
營業時間, 最後點菜時間
Lunch/午膳 12:00-14:30 (L.O.)
Dinner/晚膳 18:30-22:30 (L.O.)

■ PRICE/價錢
Lunch/午膳   menu/套餐 $ 110-280
              carte/點菜 $ 500-800
Dinner/晚膳 menu/套餐 $ 500-1,000
              carte/點菜 $ 560-2,100

Goccia

Stairs from the stylish ground floor bar lead up to an impressive dining room with its dramatic contemporary artwork and clubby atmosphere. A lovely terraced area is where you'll find the pizza oven. Most ingredients are imported directly from Italy including seasonal specialities such as asparagus and Alba truffles. A lot of effort has been taken with a good-value healthy option set menu at lunchtime.

位於地下的酒吧散發著時尚的味道,拾級而上就會進入風格鮮明的飯廳,擁有現代藝術品裝飾,氣氛猶如俱樂部。宜人的戶外陽台更設有薄餅爐。絕大部分食材均從意大利空運而來,包括季節佳餚如蘆筍和白松露。餐廳更別出心裁,設計健康午市套餐,物超所值。

■ ADDRESS/地址

TEL.2167 8181

73 Wyndham Street, Central
中環雲咸街73號

■ ANNUAL AND WEEKLY CLOSING
  休息日期

Closed Saturday lunch, Sunday lunch and Public Holidays
週六、日午膳及公眾假期休息

■ OPENING HOURS, LAST ORDER
  營業時間, 最後點菜時間

Lunch/午膳 12:00-14:30 (L.O.)
Dinner/晚膳 18:00-23:00 (L.O.)

■ PRICE/價錢

Lunch/午膳   menu/套餐 $ 115-178
Dinner/晚膳 carte/點菜 $ 265-625

Golden Bauhinia
金紫荊

🦷 ☞📍 **P** ▭14

Easily located for visitors to the Hong Kong Convention and
Exhibition Centre (and not far from the ferry pier either),
this large dining room may be monochrome in tone but
has some of the best-value traditional Cantonese cooking
around. Specialities include steamed bean curd with shrimp
and scallop in fish soup, and crab claw wrapped in sliced
watermelon and egg white. Great care is taken with the service.

前往香港會議展覽中心的人士可輕易找到這家餐廳，離碼頭亦是咫尺之遙。偌
大的餐廳配色可能較為單一，但物有所值的傳統粵菜是這裡的過人之處。特色
小菜包括：海皇魚湯浸豆腐及西施百花蟹拑。服務非常細心。

■ ADDRESS/地址
TEL.2582 7728
Hong Kong Convention and Exhibition
Centre, Golden Bauhinia Square, Expo
Drive East, Wanchai
灣仔博覽道1號金紫荊廣場香港會議展覽中
心地下

■ OPENING HOURS, LAST ORDER
　營業時間, 最後點菜時間
Lunch/午膳 12:00-14:45 (L.O.)
Dinner/晚膳 18:30-22:45 (L.O.)

■ PRICE/價錢
Lunch/午膳　carte/點菜 $ 250-800
Dinner/晚膳　carte/點菜 $ 250-800

Golden Bull (Ocean Terminal)
金牛苑 (海運大廈)

This charmingly discreet restaurant has fine views over the ferry pier plus very crisp white interior design aided by elegant chandeliers, framed mirrors and plenty of flowers. The menu hovers between Chinese and Vietnamese but sticks rigidly to the seasons. One particular speciality is the barbecued eel in honey sauce with black pepper. Prices are very reasonable and the restaurant team is friendly and cooperative.

這家迷人又樸素的餐廳飽覽碼頭的景色，室內設計以清爽的白色為主，輔以雅緻的吊燈、框鏡和大量鮮花。餐單設計以時令食材為主，兼容中越特色，蜜椒燒鱔球是其招牌菜式。價錢非常合理，而且服務員亦友善親切。

■ ADDRESS/地址
TEL.2730 4866
3F, Ocean Terminal, 5 Canton Road, Tsim Sha Tsui
九龍尖沙咀廣東道5號海運大廈3樓LCX

■ OPENING HOURS, LAST ORDER
營業時間, 最後點菜時間
Lunch/午膳 11:30-15:00 L.O. 14:30
Dinner/晚膳 17:30-23:00 L.O. 22:00

■ PRICE/價錢
Lunch/午膳　menu/套餐 $ 90-284
　　　　　　　carte/點菜 $ 150-300
Dinner/晚膳　menu/套餐 $ 284
　　　　　　　carte/點菜 $ 250-500

Grissini

If you fancy a romantic dinner with views to match, then this smart Italian restaurant with its candle-lit tables is just the job. The range of authentic dishes captures the length and breadth of Italy's regions and manages to be both traditional and imaginative. Equal space is given to pasta, risotto, meat and fish. You'll find it hard restricting yourself to just one of the exquisite grissini that lend the place its name.

假如你嚮往在醉人夜景下享受燭光晚餐，這家時尚的餐廳定是必然之選。真材實料的菜式囊括意大利不同地域的尊長，兼具傳統特色和創意。意大利麵，意大利燴飯，肉類和魚類菜式均有不少選擇。這店的名詞來自意大利一種長條麵包，也是餐廳裡忍不住要吃的美食。

■ ADDRESS/地址
TEL.2588 1234
Grand Hyatt Hotel, 1 Harbour Road, Wanchai
灣仔港灣道1號君悅酒店
www.hongkong.grand.hyatt.com

■ OPENING HOURS, LAST ORDER
營業時間, 最後點菜時間
Lunch/午市 12:00-14:30 (L.O.)
Dinner/晚市 19:00-23:00 (L.O.)

■ PRICE/價錢
Lunch/午膳　carte/點菜 $ 640-850
Dinner/晚膳　carte/點菜 $ 640-850

Guangzhou Garden
粵江春

🚌·96 📞🍴

The office workers of Mongkok flock to this huge restaurant in a bustling mall. There are four dining rooms: the first looks attractive enough with its urban vistas, but the others are rather ordinary, with tired looking chairs and tables. It's the food that draws everyone in. The tasty Cantonese cuisine features lots of dim sum, shark's fin soup in golden glass, and sizzling honey-glazed BBQ pork. Another plus? It comes at a keen price.

佔地甚寬的餐廳位於繁忙的商場內，吸引了旺角區的藍領白領。餐廳內設四個中菜廳，其中一間坐擁城市景觀，環境相當吸引；其他則較為普通，椅子和餐桌似已使用多時。這裡真正的誘人之處其實是令人垂涎欲滴的菜式，美味的粵菜包括大量點心、金杯翅，以及鐵板蜜味叉燒。還要說餐廳的其他優點嗎？那便是菜式價錢相當平民化！

■ ADDRESS/地址

TEL.3542 5768
Shop 35, Level 3, Langham Place, 8 Argyle Street, Mongkok
九龍旺角亞皆老街8號朗豪坊3樓35號鋪

■ OPENING HOURS, LAST ORDER
營業時間, 最後點菜時間
08:00-24:00 L.O. 23:00

■ PRICE/價錢
Lunch/午膳 carte/點菜 $ 120-250
Dinner/晚膳 carte/點菜 $ 120-250

Gunga Din's
金家美食

This compact restaurant has just celebrated its 30th anniversary, although it's beginning to look a little worn. Old sepia photographs line the walls and there's also the reassuring presence of idols of the Hindu Gods Shiva and Ganesh. However, the subtly spiced traditional cooking remains sharp, with fresh ingredients and strong flavours all served up at a very reasonable price. Better to book, especially towards the end of the week.

這家餐廳佔地不多，剛邁入三十週年，稍有歷史痕跡。牆上貼滿了泛黃舊照，並同時供奉印度濕婆神(Shiva)和大象神(Ganesha)。雖然如此，辣度較溫和的傳統菜式依然突出，只需用極合理的價錢就可享受新鮮材料和強烈口味。最好先行預約，臨近週末時座位供應較為緊張。

■ ADDRESS/地址
TEL.2523 1276
Lower GF, 57-59 Wyndham Street, Central
中環雲咸街57-59號地庫1樓
www.gundadins.com

■ ANNUAL AND WEEKLY CLOSING
　休息日期
Closed Saturday lunch and Sunday lunch
週六、日午膳休息

■ OPENING HOURS, LAST ORDER
　營業時間, 最後點菜時間
Lunch/午市 11:45-14:30 (L.O.)
Dinner/晚市 18:00-23:00 (L.O.)

■ PRICE/價錢
Lunch/午膳 menu/套餐 $ 98
　　　　　 carte/點菜 $ 140-250
Dinner/晚膳 carte/點菜 $ 140-250

Hakka Yé Yé
客家爺爺

The food of the Hakka people is very much sophisticated peasant cookery, relying largely on pork and chicken. Specialities here include braised pork belly with preserved vegetables and Yé Yé drunken chicken bowl with Hakka rice wine. The small room is simply furnished but the charming team go out of their way to explain the distinctive characteristics of their authentic and reasonably-priced regional cuisine.

客家菜的特色是農家菜，大部分食材選用豬肉和雞肉。這裡的推介菜式包括西施梅菜扣肉和爺爺醉鳳凰煮客家糯米酒。地方小巧裝潢精緻，親切友善的員工用獨有方式介紹原汁原味的客家菜，且價錢合理。

■ ADDRESS/地址

TEL.2537 7060

2F, Parekh House, 63 Wyndham Street, Central

中環雲咸街63號巴力大廈2樓

www.yeyegroup.com

■ ANNUAL AND WEEKLY CLOSING
休息日期
Closed Sunday and Public Holidays
週日及公眾假期休息

■ OPENING HOURS, LAST ORDER
營業時間, 最後點菜時間
Lunch/午市 12:00-15:00 (L.O.)
Dinner/晚市 18:00-23:00 (L.O.)

■ PRICE/價錢
Lunch/午膳   menu/套餐 $ 92
               carte/點菜 $ 135-215
Dinner/晚膳 menu/套餐 $ 150-300
               carte/點菜 $ 135-215

Harbour Grill

The décor here is elegant and comfortable and suits a romantic evening just as well as a more formal business lunch. The international menu shows ambition, placing classical French dishes alongside grills incorporating Wagyu and Japanese Kobe beef. Specialities include scallops seared with pork belly and caramelised pear plus blue eye cod baked with mint yoghurt and cumin salt. An extensive wine list has been well chosen.

此處的裝修優雅舒適，不論共度醉人黃昏，或是與客人食午餐都適合不過。國際化的菜式充份表現酒店的野心：傳統法國菜佐以燒烤和牛及日本神戶牛柳。特別推介包括煎帶子伴脆極黑豬腩肉配糖燴香梨和薄荷乳酪焗鱈魚柳。酒類選擇繁多，且經精心挑選。

■ ADDRESS/地址

TEL.2996 8433

GF, Harbour Plaza Hotel, 20 Tak Fung Street, Whampoa Garden, Hung Hom, Kowloon

九龍紅磡黃埔花園德豐街20號海逸酒店地下

www.harbour-plaza.com

■ OPENING HOURS, LAST ORDER
營業時間, 最後點菜時間
Lunch/午膳 12:00-14:00 (L.O.)
Dinner/晚膳 18:00-22:00 (L.O.)

■ PRICE/價錢
Lunch/午膳   carte/點菜 $ 450-800
Dinner/晚膳 carte/點菜 $ 450-800

Harlan's

XX

← 🚌16 ☎🍴 🍇

"Please try another dining experience" says the sign on the door and, inside, not only do all tables have lovely harbour views, but there's also a broad sweep of contemporary European influences to the cooking. The diverse menu allows pizzas and sandwiches to share space with a range of oysters and freshly sliced hams as well as more substantial dishes. Lighter lunches and afternoon teas are also served. Wines are well chosen.

門上的告示寫道：「請一嚐嶄新美食體驗」，入內一看，全場均可欣賞迷人海港景致，而且菜式充滿當代歐陸風情。令人目不暇給的餐單，從意大利薄餅、三文治到蠔、鮮切火腿片以至較具份量的菜色都應有盡有。餐廳另有提供較輕盈的午餐和下午茶餐。選酒質素一流。

■ ADDRESS/地址
TEL.2805 0566
Shop 2075, Podium level 2, IFC Mall, 8
Finance Street, Central
中環金融街8號國際金融中心商場第2期2樓
2075號舖
www.harlans.com.hk

■ OPENING HOURS, LAST ORDER
營業時間, 最後點菜時間
Lunch/午膳 11:30-14:30 (L.O.)
Dinner/晚膳 18:30-22:30 (L.O.)

■ PRICE/價錢
Lunch/午膳 menu/套餐 $ 278
carte/點菜 $ 360-950
Dinner/晚膳 menu/套餐 $ 800
carte/點菜 $ 360-950

Harvey Nichols

It's not just the shopping that's chic here. The lengthways restaurant is design-led, with a harlequin costume-style ceiling and floor, the colours illuminated by shifting beams of light. There's black leather seating and comfy imitation snakeskin armchairs. What about the food? Well, the French cuisine, in contrast to its surroundings, doesn't really embrace modernity, and sticks to simple traditions, with tasty, fresh ingredients.

這裡入時的不僅是購物。這家縱長的餐廳設計新穎，天花及地板採用了丑角服裝的風格，移動的燈光照亮顏色。餐廳內有黑色皮革座位及舒適的仿蛇皮扶手椅。至於食物又如何？跟四周環境比較，菜餚並不怎麼現代。相反地，菜式堅守簡單的傳統，食材都是既美味又新鮮的。

■ ADDRESS/地址

TEL.3695 3389

4F, The Landmark, 15 Queen's Road Central
中環皇后大道中15號置地廣場4樓

■ ANNUAL AND WEEKLY CLOSING
　休息日期
Closed Lunar New Year
年初一休息

■ OPENING HOURS, LAST ORDER
　營業時間, 最後點菜時間
Lunch/午膳 12:00-14:30 (L.O.)
Dinner/晚膳 19:00-22:30 (L.O.)

■ PRICE/價錢
Lunch/午膳　menu/套餐 $ 340
Dinner/晚膳　menu/套餐 $ 550
　　　　　　carte/點菜 $ 450-570

Ho Hung Kee
何洪記

The owner's parents opened the business in Wanchai in 1946. The restaurant's been here, near Times Square, since 1974, so Mr Ho advisedly calls it the Original Noodle Shop! His wife claims the noodles won her over before she'd even met her husband. On both sides of the entrance, two little cook stations entice you in with their aromas. Exceptional shrimp won ton boasts a decades-old recipe, while congee with fish is also of legendary status.

東主父母於1946年在灣仔開設此家餐廳。自1974年以來，餐廳一直座落於現時位置，毗鄰時代廣場。因此，何先生特意稱它為「傳統麵店」！他太太聲稱還未與丈夫第一次見面，麵就已經贏得芳心。入口兩邊都有廚師以食物香味引誘你。著名的鮮蝦雲吞以幾十年的祖傳食譜烹調，而魚粥亦是令人讚不絕口的菜式。

■ ADDRESS/地址
TEL.2577 6558
2 Sharp Street, Causeway Bay
銅鑼灣雲東街2號

■ OPENING HOURS, LAST ORDER
營業時間, 最後點菜時間
11:30-23:30 (L.O.)

■ PRICE/價錢
Lunch/午膳   carte/點菜 $ 26-38
Dinner/晚膳 carte/點菜 $ 30-99

Hoi Yat Heen

XXX

⟨ 👉 🖥12 ☎🍴

This large restaurant has great harbour views and so too do the two private rooms. With live music every night, it serves carefully prepared Cantonese cooking that has been given a contemporary twist. Specialities include oven baked crabmeat with shredded onion on the crab shell and sautéed sliced pork with pear and black vinegar. The very diligent manager heads up an attentive team.

這家餐廳不論主廳與貴賓房，都能俯瞰美麗的維港景色。每晚有現場音樂演奏，配搭大廚精美菜式，為廣東菜添上一絲現代感。特色菜包括：金牌焗釀蟹蓋、桂花　黑醋脆　。勤快的經理帶領著出色的服務團隊，這裡絕對能讓你賓至如歸。

■ ADDRESS/地址

TEL.2996 8459

2F, Harbour Plaza Hotel, 20 Tak Fung Street, Whampoa Garden, Hung Hom, Kowloon

九龍紅磡德豐街20號海逸酒店2樓

www.harbour-plaza.com

■ OPENING HOURS, LAST ORDER

營業時間, 最後點菜時間

Lunch/午膳 11:30-15:00 (L.O.)
Dinner/晚膳 18:00-23:00 (L.O.)

■ PRICE/價錢

Lunch/午膳　carte/點菜 $ 200-1,000
Dinner/晚膳　carte/點菜 $ 200-1,000

H One

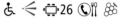

You'll be spoiled for choice here as the menu features varieties of oysters and aged hams, pastas, char-grills and what the menu nonchalantly refers to as "kick ass" curries. And then, there are the daily specials on top... Hip staff and cutting edge décor make this a fashionable destination that backs on to next door's G Bar (under the same ownership). To ensure a window table with its great harbour views, make sure you book early.

你肯定會被這裡繁多的菜式打動：蠔、火腿、意大利麵、木炭烤肉、以及餐單上稱之為「了不起」的咖哩。此外，更不能不提到每日精選！打扮時尚的服務員、前衛的裝潢都與旁邊G Bar的潮流格調非常匹配，兩家食肆均由同一東主經營。要預訂海景窗口位，請儘早預約。

■ ADDRESS/地址

TEL.2805 0638

Shop 4008-10, Podium level 4, IFC Mall, 8 Finance Street, Central
中環金融街8號國際金融中心商場第2期4樓
4008-4010號舖
www.h-one.com.hk

■ ANNUAL AND WEEKLY CLOSING
  休息日期
Closed Lunar New Year
年初一休息

■ OPENING HOURS, LAST ORDER
  營業時間, 最後點菜時間
Lunch/午膳 12:00-14:30 (L.O.)
Dinner/晚膳 18:30-22:30 (L.O.)

■ PRICE/價錢
Lunch/午膳   menu/套餐 $ 278
           carte/點菜 $ 300-600
Dinner/晚膳 menu/套餐 $ 900
           carte/點菜 $ 800-1,300

House of Jasmine
八月居

XX

 👌 🏠 ☝ **P** ⌷60

When it's not too hot outside, grab a seat on the terrace for fantastic views of the harbour and Hong Kong Island. Inside, though not so dramatic, there's an attractive, contemporary feel to this busy, three-roomed restaurant. One of the rooms, featuring a bar, is particularly pleasant and cosy. What keeps the customers coming is the Cantonese cuisine with modern twists; typically, marinated ox tendon with black vinegar, or prawn on egg custard.

天氣稍涼時，食客可以選擇露天雅座，飽覽維港及港島的璀璨美景；餐廳裡頭雖然不及戶外變化多端，不過裝潢設計富現代感，甚具吸引力，與餐廳的繁忙景象相映成趣。餐廳共分為三間餐室，其中一間設有酒吧，極其舒適愜意。這裡客似雲來的原因，在於其原味粵菜以現代方式呈現，招牌菜包括鎮江牛蹄筋脆及太雕玻璃蝦球。

■ ADDRESS/地址
TEL.2992 0232
Shop 401, Level 4, Ocean Centre, Harbour City, Tsim Sha Tsui, Kowloon
九龍尖沙咀海港城海洋中心4樓401號舖

■ OPENING HOURS, LAST ORDER
營業時間, 最後點菜時間
Lunch/午膳　11:00-15:00 L.O. 14:30
Dinner/晚膳　18:00-23:00 L.O. 22:30

■ PRICE/價錢
Lunch/午膳　menu/套餐 $ 128
　　　　　　carte/點菜 $ 120-600
Dinner/晚膳　menu/套餐 $ 200-250
　　　　　　carte/點菜 $ 200-600

Hunan Garden (Causeway Bay)
洞庭樓 (銅鑼灣)

XXX

⌨ 60

As you walk in on the 13th floor, you're welcomed near a channel of running water complete with live fish. This leads into a spacious contemporary room with bright chandeliers and painted wood panels on the walls. The Cantonese-style cooking uses well-sourced, fresh local ingredients: there's a broad selection of dim sum dishes at lunchtime appealing to shoppers and business people alike. Service could be a little sharper.

甫踏進十三樓,你就會看見水流源源不絕的活魚水槽。繼續往前走,便進入了寬敞時尚的進餐區。璀璨的吊燈點綴加上牆身的漆木板,交織成獨特的風格。粵菜選料皆採用本地新鮮食材,午飯時段設有一系列的點心,供購物及商務客人選擇。服務仍有改善空間。

■ ADDRESS/地址
TEL.2506 9288
Shop 1302, 13F, Food Forum, Times Square, Causeway Bay
銅鑼灣時代廣場食通天13樓1302號鋪

■ OPENING HOURS, LAST ORDER
營業時間, 最後點菜時間
Lunch/午膳 11:30-14:30 (L.O.)
Dinner/晚膳 18:00-23:00 (L.O.)

■ PRICE/價錢
Lunch/午膳　carte/點菜 $ 300-850
Dinner/晚膳　carte/點菜 $ 300-850

Hunan Garden (Central)
洞庭樓 (中環)

Large and luxurious restaurant in a prestigious development. Expensive carpets, floor-to-ceiling glass, huge columns decorated with flowers, and pink and white linen-clad tables announce a refined dining experience, though the rather stuffy and brusque service can be a little off-putting. As the cuisine is predominantly Hunan, expect fiery flavours with extensive use of chillies. For more conservative tastes, Cantonese dishes are also offered.

這家寬敞豪華的餐廳位處高級商業地段。價值不菲的地毯、落地玻璃、以鮮花裝飾的龐大圓柱、粉紅色白色的麻質桌布,交織成高雅的餐飲體驗,惟服務態度稍嫌傲慢。食物方面以湖南菜為主,大部分菜式都會採用辣椒,因此請做好心理準備!至於口味較為保守的食客,則可選擇粵菜。

■ ADDRESS/地址
TEL.2868 2880
3F, The Forum, Exchange Square, Central
中環交易廣場富臨閣3樓
www.maxims.com.hk

■ OPENING HOURS, LAST ORDER
營業時間, 最後點菜時間
Lunch/午膳 11:30-15:00 L.O. 14:45
Dinner/晚膳 17:30-23:30 L.O. 23:00

■ PRICE/價錢
Lunch/午膳 carte/點菜 $ 210-540
Dinner/晚膳 carte/點菜 $ 210-540

Hutong
胡同

For a fantastic vista of the harbour, this is your venue. The view inside is pretty good, too: all carved antique wood, silk curtains, red lanterns and cosy alcoves with doors from traditional Hutong houses. A hip destination, the waiters can be just too cool and trendy to smile. The menu is original (eg, red mandarin fish with peanut crust) and features a total mix of dishes, including a lot of offal and some other pretty unusual ingredients.

要觀賞維港的壯麗景色，到這裡便是最好不過。餐廳內的景觀亦不錯：全面雕刻的古式木材、絲綢布簾、紅燈籠，以及配備傳統胡同屋門的舒適餐室。餐廳位處潮流熱點，亦因此服務員可能會因太時髦或太酷而不會笑。獨創的有一見龍在田一桂花魚配酥脆花生。另一特點是將菜式完全混合，包括採用很多內臟及一些頗不尋常的食材。

■ ADDRESS/地址
TEL.3428 8342
28F, 1 Peking Road, Tsim Sha Tsui, Kowloon
九龍尖沙咀北京道1號28樓
www.aqua.com.hk

■ OPENING HOURS, LAST ORDER
營業時間, 最後點菜時間
Lunch/午膳 12:00-15:00 L.O. 14:30
Dinner/晚膳 18:00-24:00 L.O. 23:30

■ PRICE/價錢
Lunch/午膳　carte/點菜 $ 250-400
Dinner/晚膳　carte/點菜 $ 400-1,000

Inagiku (IFC)
稻菊（國際金融中心）

Adjacent to the Four Seasons Hotel in the International Finance Centre, this is a delightfully uncluttered contemporary installation with illuminated flooring and large plate glass windows affording fine views. There are separate sushi, teppanyaki and tempura bars and a whole series of specialist set menus. This is very much modern Japanese cooking that has been successfully adapted to suit the local market.

鄰靠中環國際金融中心香港四季酒店，餐廳設計極具時尚風格。射燈地板配上大型落地玻璃，怡人景觀盡收眼底。餐廳設有壽司、鐵板燒及天婦羅吧，更提供一系列的特選套餐。這可算是日式料理進軍本地市場的成功例子。

■ ADDRESS/地址

TEL.2805 0600
4F, Four Seasons Hotel, 8 Finance Street, Central
中環金融街8號四季酒店4樓
www.rghk.com.hk

■ OPENING HOURS, LAST ORDER
　營業時間, 最後點菜時間
Lunch/午膳 11:30-14:30 (L.O.)
Dinner/晚膳 18:00-22:30 (L.O.)

■ PRICE/價錢
Lunch/午膳　menu/套餐 $ 300-600
Dinner/晚膳　menu/套餐 $ 620-3,000
　　　　　　carte/點菜 $ 800-1,100

Inagiku (Kowloon)
稻菊（九龍）

☞📍 ⛊40 ⛓ ☎🍴

Inagiku has a strong pedigree: the first was established over a century ago in Japan. Décor is elegantly upscale, the Japanese influences a visual pleasure. There are several dining areas: a sushi bar with fish tank, a tempura counter, a teppanyaki area and a few tables in the centre of the room. Not only that, but five separate private rooms, too. The restaurant is renowned for its tempura and teppanyaki, though staff could show more interest.

稻菊來頭殊不簡單，早在百多年前已於日本開業。這裡的裝潢設計典雅高尚，源自日本人對美學的要求，為食客帶來視覺上的享受。餐廳共有幾個用餐區，包括設有魚缸的壽司吧、天婦羅檯、鐵板燒區，以及餐廳中心的幾張餐桌。此外，稻菊還設有五間私人餐室。這裡的天婦羅及鐵板燒享負盛名，而員工亦可為你推介更多菜式。

■ ADDRESS/地址
TEL.2733 2933
1F, The Royal Garden Hotel, 69 Mody Road, Tsim Sha Tsui East, Kowloon
九龍尖沙咀東部麼地道69號帝苑酒店1樓
www.rghk.com.hk

■ OPENING HOURS, LAST ORDER
營業時間, 最後點菜時間
Lunch/午膳 12:00-14:30 (L.O.)
Dinner/晚膳 18:00-22:30 (L.O.)

■ PRICE/價錢
Lunch/午膳   menu/套餐 $ 300-1,020
              carte/點菜 $ 230-1,500
Dinner/晚膳   menu/套餐 $ 320-1,020
              carte/點菜 $ 230-1,500

Isola

There's no rest for the staff as they dart between the main dining room with its trendy wavy white wall and the equally large outside terrace. The place is invariably packed with people ordering generous plates of pizza, pasta and grilled meats – so make sure you book. Considering the speed and volume involved, the kitchen is remarkably consistent. Should it rain outside and everyone dashes in, allow for more than a spot of chaos!

主餐室的波浪形白色牆身非常新穎，露天部份亦相當寬敞。餐廳的人流絡繹不絕，服務員繁忙地穿插店內外，替客人落著一碟又一碟的薄餅、意大利麵和烤肉的菜單；所以謹記事先訂座。考慮到速度和食物份量，廚房仍能保持一貫水準。下雨時連室外的客人也湧進店內，必須有如此速度才能避免混亂呢！

■ ADDRESS/地址

TEL.2383 8765

Shop 3071-75, 4011, Podium level 3&4, IFC Mall, 8 Finance Street, Central

中環金融街8號國際金融中心商場第2期3&4樓，3071-75, 4011號舖

www.isolabarandgrill.com

■ ANNUAL AND WEEKLY CLOSING
  休息日期

Closed Lunar New Year
年初一休息

■ OPENING HOURS, LAST ORDER
  營業時間, 最後點菜時間

Lunch/午膳 12:00-14:30 (L.O.)

Dinner/晚膳 18:30-23:00 (L.O.)

■ PRICE/價錢

Lunch/午膳   menu/套餐 $ 248-268
                         carte/點菜 $ 320-370

Dinner/晚膳 carte/點菜 $ 750-900

Jade Garden (Causeway Bay)
翠園 (銅鑼灣)

✕

🍽 12

Fancy a quiet dinner in a romantic location? Then don't come here! Jade Garden is located in a very busy street, and the restaurant is just as lively. Cantonese dishes are served in an interesting way - waiters push trolleys of food, you lift the lid to see if you like the contents, and, if you're happy, you have an instant meal. Don't be shy about stopping the waiter. Recommended: dumpling dim sum, but many other delicacies will catch your eye.

想在浪漫的地方寧靜渡過晚膳時光？這裡不會是你的選擇!翠園位處車水馬龍的繁忙街道上，餐廳本身亦同樣生氣勃勃。這家粵菜餐廳的上菜方式十分有趣：侍應會推著手推車，食客可隨時示意截停，先看食物再決定是否點菜。推介菜式包括餃子類點心，而多款其他美食亦觸目皆是。

■ ADDRESS/地址
TEL.2573 9339
3F, Causeway Bay Plaza II, 463-483 Lockhart Road, Causeway Bay
銅鑼灣駱克道463-483號銅鑼灣廣場第2期3樓

■ OPENING HOURS, LAST ORDER
營業時間, 最後點菜時間
07:00-24:00 (L.O.)

■ PRICE/價錢
Lunch/午膳 carte/點菜 $ 200-300
Dinner/晚膳 carte/點菜 $ 200-300

Jashan

🍴🍴

🪑8

Easy to find, as it's next to an escalator - in fact, sit by one of the windows here, leaning into a comfy Indian cushion, and you'll see hoards of legs roll past! The menus are quite predictable, mostly north Indian, but the kitchen delivers tasty, flavoursome dishes based on sound ingredients. At lunch there's a 'live' counter where chefs conjure up dosas and chaats in front of you. Popular with English city bankers, so it can get 'raucous'!

餐廳毗鄰扶手電梯,位置便利。事實上,你可一邊擁著印度咕臣靠窗而坐,一邊觀看窗外人來人往的景象!菜式方面偏向主流,以北印度菜為主。儘管如此,廚房採用各式食材,精心炮製美味菜餚,令人食指大動。餐廳會在午膳時間設置櫃檯,讓廚師在食客面前即時炮製印度薄餅(dosa)和多款小食(chaat)。這裡大受英國銀行家歡迎,因此會較為「喧鬧」!

■ ADDRESS/地址
TEL.3105 5300
1F, Amber Lodge, 23 Hollywood Road, Central
中環荷里活道23號金珀苑1樓
www.jashan.com.hk

■ OPENING HOURS, LAST ORDER
營業時間, 最後點菜時間
Lunch/午膳 12:00-14:30 (L.O.)
Dinner/晚膳 18:00-23:00 (L.O.)

■ PRICE/價錢
Lunch/午膳　menu/套餐 $ 108
Dinner/晚膳　carte/點菜 $ 136-241

Jasmine Place
怡翠軒

XXX

🍽️12 ☎️🍴

A total refurbishment in early 2008 has given this Cantonese restaurant an elegant aura, typified by hand paintings of birds and flowers on the walls, with embroidered tablecloths and porcelain objects inducing a feeling of 'home-from-home'. Cuisine is bursting with flavours prepared in a refreshing way. For example, there's prawn on egg white custard with "tai diao" rice liquor, or boneless chicken wing stuffed with glutinous rice.

2008年初全面翻新後，這家粵菜餐廳頓時煥然一新：典型的設計特色包括牆上的手繪花鳥圖案，瑰麗優雅；而繡花桌布和瓷器更帶來一種「家」的感覺。菜餚味道濃郁，烹調方式更令人耳目一新，例如太雕玻璃蝦球及糯米釀鳳翼。

■ ADDRESS/地址

TEL.2524 5098

Shop 5, Lower GF, Jasmine House, Central

中環怡和大廈地庫1樓5號

www.maxims.com.hk

■ OPENING HOURS, LAST ORDER

營業時間, 最後點菜時間

Lunch/午膳   11:00-15:00 (L.O.)

Dinner/晚膳   18:0-23:00 (L.O.)

■ PRICE/價錢

Lunch/午膳   menu/套餐 $ 198-228

carte/點菜 $ 150-600

Dinner/晚膳   menu/套餐 $ 198-228

carte/點菜 $ 150-600

Jiang Shan Xiao
江山笑

There's something almost unique about this first-floor restaurant: it's one of the very few in Hong Kong to offer you al fresco dining on a terrace. No, you don't get to see the sea, but the imposing towers of Admiralty can nevertheless provide their own interest. If it gets too hot, come inside to a cosy dining room, particularly friendly service, and Sichuan specialities ranging from double-boiled soups to rich spicy dishes with chilli sauce.

這家位處二樓的餐廳有其獨特之處：它是香港少有讓你在陽台上戶外用餐的地方。雖然看的不是海景，不過金鐘宏偉的高樓卻令人樂在其中。如天氣較熱，亦可以請移玉步入室內用膳，餐廳既舒適，服務又特別好。四川菜包括燉湯，也有加了辣醬的辛辣菜式，各適其適。

■ ADDRESS/地址

TEL.2810 6921

Shop 2B, 1F, Retail Podium, Lippo Centre, 89 Queensway, Admiralty
香港金鐘道89號力寶中心一樓商場2B舖
www.jiangshanxiao.com.hk

■ OPENING HOURS, LAST ORDER
營業時間, 最後點菜時間
Lunch/午膳 11:30-14:30 (L.O.)
Dinner/晚膳 18:30-23:00 (L.O.)

■ PRICE/價錢
Lunch/午膳   menu/套餐 $ 148-1,380
                   carte/點菜 $ 200-350
Dinner/晚膳   menu/套餐 $ 148-1,380
                   carte/點菜 $ 200-350

JJ's

XX

⌐☞ P ⟨⟩8 ☏⟨⟩

This has a reputation for being one of the best music venues in town with a live band playing in the evenings. With its low-level lighting, the clubby atmosphere and sparse furnishing is at once moody and minimal. You can dine in several different areas including spaces overlooking the hotel lobby and also the wine store. What is essentially a Thai menu also incorporates grilled meats and fresh seafood.

此處以其晚間現場演奏樂隊聞名，是欣賞音樂的好選擇。昏暗的燈光配合夜店氣氛，店內裝潢寬敞，簡約舒適，節奏隨心情起伏。設有不同的進餐區，其中有些可飽覽酒店大堂及酒類專賣店的景觀。泰國餐單加入了烤肉和新鮮海鮮菜式，獨具特色。

■ ADDRESS/地址

TEL.2588 1234

Grand Hyatt Hotel, 1 Harbour Road, Wanchai

灣仔港灣道1號君悅酒店地下

www.hongkong.grand.hyatt.com

■ OPENING HOURS, LAST ORDER

營業時間，最後點菜時間

Dinner/晚膳 18:00-23:00 (L.O.)

■ PRICE/價錢

Dinner/晚膳 menu/套餐 $ 380-520

carte/點菜 $ 250-1,210

Joia

Easy-going restaurant that's especially pleasant at night
if you're seated next to the floor-to-ceiling windows under dimmed lights looking out over Civic Square's attractive rooftop courtyard with palm trees. The Italian menus
specialise in a light Mediterranean cuisine: the trademark
is pasta, though the pizza, too, is very popular here. This is
backed up with a good choice of Italian wines, served by a
very friendly and attentive team.

餐廳氣氛自然悠閒，晚上坐在落地玻璃窗旁的雅座，燈光微黃；在此細看外面
的天台廣場和棕櫚樹，尤其舒適愜意。餐廳提供意大利菜式，主打為輕盈的地
中海菜。招牌菜包括各種意大利麵食，比薩薄餅也很受歡迎；佐以意大利美酒
享用。侍應招呼周到，提供賓至如歸的服務。

■ ADDRESS/地址
TEL.2382 2323
Roof Garden, 3F Elements Hall, 1
Austin Road West, Kowloon
九龍柯士甸道西1號圓方3樓花園平台
www.joia.com.hk

■ OPENING HOURS, LAST ORDER
營業時間, 最後點菜時間
Lunch/午膳 12:00-14:30 (L.O.)
Dinner/晚膳 18:00-22:30 (L.O.)

■ PRICE/價錢
Lunch/午膳   menu/套餐 $ 210-250
            carte/點菜 $ 330-690
Dinner/晚膳 carte/點菜 $ 330-690

Kin's Kitchen
留家廚房

The bad news - Kin's Kitchen is hidden away on a noisy, grubby street beneath an expressway. The good news - this buzzing single room boasts two friendly owners who are passionate about food and who eat in some of the world's best restaurants. They've made it a wonderfully informal place that serves tasty Cantonese dishes, including specials like Kin's smoked chicken (smoked in the kitchen), and stuffed duck braised with lotus seed and barley.

壞消息：留家廚房隱藏在一條嘈雜骯髒的街，位處高速公路下面。好消息：這家熱鬧的餐廳是屬於兩位熱衷美食，品嚐過世上最好一些餐廳的菜式的東主。他們為餐廳營造輕鬆的氣氛，並奉上美味的廣東菜，包括留家煙燻雞(在廚房內煙燻)，以及京酥鴨。

■ ADDRESS/地址

TEL.2571 0913
9 Tsing Fung Street, Tin Hau
天后清風街9號
www.yellowdoorkitchen.com.hk

■ ANNUAL AND WEEKLY CLOSING
    休息日期
Closed 3 days Lunar New Year
農曆新年休息3天

■ OPENING HOURS, LAST ORDER
    營業時間, 最後點菜時間
Lunch/午膳 11:00-15:00 L.O. 14:30
Dinner/晚膳 18:00-23:00 L.O. 22:30

■ PRICE/價錢
Lunch/午膳 carte/點菜 $ 146-298
Dinner/晚膳 carte/點菜 $ 146-298

Kiriyaki
桐燒

✂

⊡11

Fancy your chances as a Japanese grill chef? Well, now's your chance. Situated on a busy shopping floor, this slightly austere setting is sharply spruced up by the presence of a grill at the centre of every table. The idea is that you order your fresh fish or (largely) meat and cook it yourself. It's worth paying the extra for the meltingly-tender imported Japanese beef at this lively operation which manages to get everyone involved.

想試試當日式燒烤師傅的滋味嗎？現在就是機會了！餐廳位處繁忙的購物樓層，每張餐桌中心設有燒烤爐，將樸素的餐廳裝飾得整潔漂亮。這裡的特色是讓客人點選新鮮魚類或(更多時候是)肉類，然後自己燒烤。店內每位座上客都能動手做菜，愉快品嚐入口即溶的鮮嫩日本進口牛肉，雖然價錢略貴但絕對值回票價。

■ ADDRESS/地址
TEL.2895 1313
Shop 1302, 13F, World Trade Centre,
280 Gloucester Road, Causeway Bay
銅鑼灣告士打道280號世貿中心13樓
1302號舖

■ OPENING HOURS, LAST ORDER
營業時間, 最後點菜時間
Lunch/午膳 12:00-15:00 (L.O.)
Dinner/晚膳 18:00-24:00 (L.O.)

■ PRICE/價錢
Lunch/午膳　carte/點菜 $ 220-350
Dinner/晚膳 carte/點菜 $ 220-350

La Brasserie
林柏軒

✗✗

🍱10

This basement restaurant adopts the adage 'simply French', and so it is. There's a typically unpretentious brasserie atmosphere, with brown wooden walls, old French furniture and the reassuring aroma of garlic. Classics derive from all across France, including tartiflette from the Alps, cassoulet from the southwest and poulet aux ecrevisses from Lyon. Local staff dress as 'garcons de café' and go about their work in a quietly stylish way.

這家地庫餐廳的格言是「simply　French」，也名副其實。餐廳氣氛像法國的簡樸餐館一樣，毫不造作；採用了棕色木牆、舊法國傢具，以及大蒜的氣味，更添一點法國味道。經典菜式源自法國各地，包括阿爾卑斯山的培根芝士奶油燉菜、西南部的豆燜肉，以及里昂的螯蝦雞。當地服務員打扮成「咖啡館男生」一般，以時尚安靜的方式工作。

■ ADDRESS/地址

TEL.2113 7925
Lower lobby, Gateway, Harbour City, 17 Canton Road, Tsim Sha Tsui, Kowloon
九龍尖沙咀廣東道17號海港城港威酒店大堂下層
www.marcopolohotels.com

■ OPENING HOURS, LAST ORDER
營業時間, 最後點菜時間
Lunch/午膳 12:00-15:00 L.O. 14:30
Dinner/晚膳 18:30-23:00 L.O. 22:00

■ PRICE/價錢
Lunch/午膳　menu/套餐 $ 198
　　　　　　carte/點菜 $ 420-800
Dinner/晚膳　carte/點菜 $ 420-800

117

L'Atelier de Joël Robuchon

✿✿   ✗✗

🪑6 ⫴

The hallmark colours of red and black are once again evident at this branch of the Robuchon Empire. A relaxed salon de thé leads on to the main restaurant which is divided into two sections: Le Jardin and L'Atelier. The first is elegant and intimate with views of a roof top garden, the latter gives you a ringside seat at the show kitchen. Construct your own menu from dishes such as sea urchin in lobster jelly or the beef and foie gras burger.

紅黑色的標記清楚顯示這是世紀大廚Robuchon集團旗下的餐廳。經過氣氛優閒的法式茶館(salon de thé)後，你會來到兩間主餐室的門前：Le Jardin和L'Atelier。Le Jardin格調高雅，可飽覽天台花園的景致；L'Atelier則以弧形吧枱圍着中間的開放式廚房。菜式包括海膽龍蝦啫喱和鵝肝牛肉漢堡飽等。

■ ADDRESS/地址

TEL.2166 9000

Shop 401, 4F, The Landmark, 15 Queen's Road, Central
中環皇后大道中15號置地廣場4樓401號舖
www.robuchon.hk

■ OPENING HOURS, LAST ORDER
營業時間, 最後點菜時間
Lunch/午膳 12:00-14:30 (L.O.)
Dinner/晚膳 18:30-22:30 (L.O.)

■ PRICE/價錢
Lunch/午膳　menu/套餐 $ 390-1,850
　　　　　　carte/點菜 $ 700-1,100
Dinner/晚膳　menu/套餐 $ 390-1,850
　　　　　　carte/點菜 $ 800-1,300

Law Fu Kee
羅富記

Don't expect any frills to this popular establishment that's now been in existence for over 50 years and under several generations of the same owners: the comforts are well and truly basic. But the strength here lies in the fact that family recipes are consistently adhered to and the congee with pork is highly recommended. So too are the deep-fried fish balls with clam sauce and the noodles with sweet and hot pork slices.

這家超過五十年歷史，家族式經營數代相傳，廣受歡迎的老字號餐廳雖然沒有花巧的裝飾，但環境簡約舒適，樸實自然。當然，餐廳的制勝之道還是其家傳食譜。特別推介這裡的瘦肉粥、蜆介炸鯪魚球和炸醬麵。

■ ADDRESS/地址
TEL.2850 6756
50 Lyndhurst Terrace, Central
中環擺花街50號舖

■ ANNUAL AND WEEKLY CLOSING
　　休息日期
Closed 7 days Lunar New Year
農曆新年休息7天

■ OPENING HOURS, LAST ORDER
　　營業時間, 最後點菜時間
08:00-20:00 (L.O.)

■ PRICE/價錢
Lunch/午膳　carte/點菜 $ 21-25
Dinner/晚膳　carte/點菜 $ 21-25

Lawry's The Prime Rib

This famous chain originated in Beverley Hills in 1938 and faithful diners are always drawn by one thing only: finest American roast prime rib of beef served "au jus" and carved directly from the trolley. Here is no exception. There's lobster and shrimp to kick things off and New York cheesecake plus English trifle if you've still got room at the end. Simple as that. Uniformed staff are charming and the list of Napa Valley wines is good.

Lawry's 是著名的連鎖牛扒餐廳於1938年在比華利山創辦,忠實顧客最重視的只有一件事:原汁原味的烤肉眼牛排、在手推車上直接切肉及奉到桌上。香港分店亦秉承一貫宗旨,頭盤可以是龍蝦和鮮蝦;假如當天胃口佳,還可以品嚐紐約芝士餅和英式冧酒蛋糕作甜點。簡簡單單、並無花巧。侍應制服整齊,活力十足;餐廳亦提供不錯的各種美國加州納帕谷酒。

■ ADDRESS/地址

TEL.2907 2218

4F, The Lee Gardens, 33 Hysan Avenue, Causeway Bay
銅鑼灣希慎道33號利園4樓
www.maxconcepts.com.hk

■ OPENING HOURS, LAST ORDER
營業時間, 最後點菜時間
Lunch/午膳　11:30-14:30 (L.O.)
Dinner/晚膳　18:00-22:30 (L.O.)

■ PRICE/價錢
Lunch/午膳　menu/套餐 $ 200-250
　　　　　　 carte/點菜 $ 500-800
Dinner/晚膳　menu/套餐 $ 528
　　　　　　 carte/點菜 $ 500-800

Lei Garden (Elements)
利苑酒家 (圓方)

P ⊷20

Located in the blue-tinted "water" area of this large shopping mall, the décor is more contemporary than some of the other Lei Garden branches. It is composed of different dining rooms one of which offers the striking sight of water cascading down some crystal curtains. The cooking throughout is reliable Cantonese but excels with its broad range of interesting seafood preparations as well as some highly unusual double-boiled tonic soups.

這家裝潢華麗優雅的餐館位於巨大的購物商場中的藍色「水」區，比其他利苑分店更有時代感。它由不同的飯廳組合而成，其中一間更有流水，從水晶簾如瀑布般落下。菜色是清一色的廣東菜，但以各種方法烹調的海鮮和與別不同的燉湯，都令這裡顯得分外出色。

■ ADDRESS/地址
TEL.2196 8133
Shop 2068-70, 2F, Elements, 1 Austin Road West, Kowloon
九龍柯士甸道西1號圓方2樓2068-70號鋪

■ OPENING HOURS, LAST ORDER
營業時間, 最後點菜時間
Lunch/午膳 11:30-14:45 (L.O.)
Dinner/晚膳 18:00-22:45 (L.O.)

■ PRICE/價錢
Lunch/午膳 carte/點菜 $ 160-1,100
Dinner/晚膳 carte/點菜 $ 160-1,100

Lei Garden (IFC)
利苑酒家 (國際金融中心)

❀ 　　　　　　　　　　　　　　　　　　　　　　　✗✗

🍱 12　📞🍴

Forward planning is advisable here – not only when booking but also when selecting certain roast meat dishes which require advance notice. An extensive menu also features specialist seafood dishes and the lunchtime favourites include shrimp and flaky pastries filled with shredded turnip. All this is served up by good-natured staff in cleanly contemporary surroundings enhanced by attractive floral arrangements.

到利苑用餐，無論是預訂座位，還是食燒臘，提早預約都十分重要。這裡菜式繁多，其中以海鮮炮製的佳餚最具特色，而午市時段的美食首推的銀蘿千層酥。格局設計富時代感，潔淨雅致，且伴有花藝擺設點綴，氣氛更為迷人，服務令人賓至如歸。

■ ADDRESS/地址
TEL.2295 0238
Shop 3008-3011, Podium level 3, IFC Mall, 1 Harbour View Street, Central
中環港景街1號國際金融中心商場第2期3樓 3008-3011號舖
www.leigarden.com.hk

■ OPENING HOURS, LAST ORDER
營業時間，最後點菜時間
Lunch/午膳　11:30-15:00 (L.O.)
Dinner/晚膳　18:00-23:00 (L.O.)

■ PRICE/價錢
Lunch/午膳　menu/套餐 $ 150-300
　　　　　　carte/點菜 $ 60-80
Dinner/晚膳　menu/套餐 $ 150-300
　　　　　　carte/點菜 $ 350-550

Lei Garden (Kwun Tong)
利苑酒家 (觀唐)

XX

🍽40

Avoid the escalators and use the shuttle lift to get to the fifth floor in this confusingly arranged new shopping mall. Once there, it'll seem familiar if you've experienced other Lei Garden branches: the menu is the standard Cantonese but is reliably cooked using fresh ingredients. The place is as frantic as the others but has been partitioned into different seating areas by smart trellis. Try not to sit near the entrance – too noisy.

由於這新建商場的設計混亂且複雜,最好不要使用扶手電梯;升降機可直達5樓。假如你曾光顧利苑的其他分店,你絕不會感到陌生:依然是清一色的廣東菜與可靠的美食及新鮮的材料。當然,這裡同樣擠滿了利苑的忠實擁躉,店內設計簡潔的屏風巧妙地將餐廳分隔成不同的用餐區。入口附近太嘈吵,最好不要選擇那裡的座位。

■ ADDRESS/地址
TEL.2365 3238
Shop L5-8, Level 5 apm, Millennium City 5, 418 Kwun Tong Road, Kwun Tong
觀塘觀塘道418號創紀之城5期apm5樓L5-8號舖

■ OPENING HOURS, LAST ORDER
營業時間, 最後點菜時間
Lunch/午膳 11:30-15:00 (L.O.)
Dinner/晚膳 18:00-23:30 L.O. 23:00

■ PRICE/價錢
Lunch/午膳　carte/點菜 $ 160-750
Dinner/晚膳　carte/點菜 $ 160-750

Lei Garden (Mong Kok)
利苑酒家 (旺角)

Families, shoppers and business people continuously flock to this perennially popular good-sized restaurant so it's essential to book. The smart contemporary décor is spread across the two floors and the upper space has views out onto the busy street. The long and varied Cantonese menu certainly offers very good value and includes such excellent seafood recommendations as giant sea whelk and mantis shrimp sautéed with salt, pepper and garlic.

家庭，購物者與白領一族都對這家餐廳趨之若鶩，其受歡迎程度可見一斑。儘管餐廳已經非常寬敞，沒有事先預約的客人依然難覓座位。富時代感的餐廳共分為兩層，樓上可看到旺角繁華的街景。以廣東菜為主的菜單花樣多變令人目不暇給，菜色物有所值，特別推薦薄殼大響螺及富蝦(椒 鹽，避風塘)塘)。

■ ADDRESS/地址
TEL. 2392 5184
121 Sai Yee Street, Mong Kok, Kowloon
九龍旺角洗衣街121

■ OPENING HOURS, LAST ORDER
營業時間, 最後點菜時間
Lunch/午膳 11:30-15:00 (L.O.)
Dinner/晚膳 18:00-23:30 (L.O.)

■ PRICE/價錢
Lunch/午膳　carte/點菜 $ 160-750
Dinner/晚膳　carte/點菜 $ 160-750

Lei Garden (North Point)
利苑酒家 (北角)

Discreetly tucked away on the first floor of an office block but overlooking a pleasant courtyard garden, things at this branch of the popular chain can get frenetic: the place accommodates up to 300 people. The lengthy Cantonese mirrors what's available at other Lei Gardens with its emphasis on shark's fin, abalone and bird's nest preparations. The dim sum lunchtime selection includes excellent dumplings and deep-fried turnip pastries.

隱藏在商業大廈的一樓，從餐廳望出去可看到一個美麗的後花園—這家受歡迎的連鎖餐廳分店絕對可以滿足瘋狂的食客；寬敞的餐廳足可容納三百人！這裡的菜單與其他利苑分店相差無幾，特別推薦魚翅、鮑魚和燕窩。午市點心包括各式包點與蘿蔔絲酥餅，水準一流。

■ ADDRESS/地址
TEL.2806 0008
1F, Block 9-10, City Garden, North Point
北角城市花園9-10座1樓

■ OPENING HOURS, LAST ORDER
營業時間, 最後點菜時間
11:00-23:00 L.O. 22:30

■ PRICE/價錢
Lunch/午膳　carte/點菜 $ 160-750
Dinner/晚膳　carte/點菜 $ 160-750

Lei Garden (Tsim Sha Tsui)
利苑酒家（尖沙咀）

🍴 🍴

📷 30 📞🍴

The entrance takes you past an intricately carved wooden wall and a series of large fish tanks into a big, bustling, traditional dining room that's brightly lit and comfortable. There's pagoda detailing on the ceiling, bare red-brick walls and an army of staff in attendance. The varied Cantonese menu reiterates what's on offer at the other Lei Gardens using fine quality ingredients and cooking them respectfully.

要進入這家餐廳，你要先經過雕刻精緻的木質牆壁和一列大魚缸，最後來到寬敞熱鬧的傳統客廳。餐廳燈光明亮，座位亦十分舒適；天花上畫有精美寶塔圖案，牆壁上也鋪有紅磚，侍應生就如軍隊一般隨時候命。這裡的廣東菜單與其他利苑分店相若，而同出一轍的就是一級的材料和廚師認真的烹調態度。

■ ADDRESS/地址

TEL.2722 1636
B2F, Houston Centre, 63 Mody Road, Tsim Sha Tsui East, Kowloon
九龍尖沙咀東部麼地道63號好時中心地庫2樓

■ OPENING HOURS, LAST ORDER
營業時間, 最後點菜時間
Lunch/午膳 11:30-15:00 (L.O.)
Dinner/晚膳 18:00-23:30 (L.O.)

■ PRICE/價錢
Lunch/午膳　carte/點菜 $ 160-750
Dinner/晚膳　carte/點菜 $ 160-750

Les Célébrités
名仕餐廳

This elegant dining room is very much in the classic European manner and is smartly lit with some beautiful contemporary chandeliers; you're also allowed a good view of the wine cellar behind a plate glass window. The cuisine mixes classic French techniques with Mediterranean flourishes and other contemporary touches on dishes such as caramel foie gras with seared sushi cake. Hors d'oeuvres and desserts are selected from an extensive buffet.

格調高雅的餐廳極具傳統歐陸風情，外形美觀時尚的吊燈照亮餐室，你還能透過玻璃窗戶清楚看見酒窖。食物方面融合了傳統法國廚藝、地中海風情和其他現代烹調變化，如焦糖鵝肝伴煎壽司飯餅。前菜和甜品以選擇繁多的自助餐形式提供。

■ ADDRESS/地址
TEL.2313 4221
1F, Nikko Hotel, 72 Mody Road, Tsim Sha Tsui East, Kowloon
九龍尖沙咀東部麼地道72號日航酒店1樓
www.hotelnikko.com.hk

■ ANNUAL AND WEEKLY CLOSING
　休息日期
Closed Sunday dinner and Public Holidays
週日及公眾假期休息

■ OPENING HOURS, LAST ORDER
　營業時間, 最後點菜時間
Lunch/午膳　12:00-14:30 (L.O.)
Dinner/晚膳　18:30-21:30 (L.O.)

■ PRICE/價錢
Lunch/午膳　menu/套餐 $ 220-260
　　　　　　carte/點菜 $ 420-720
Dinner/晚膳　menu/套餐 $ 480
　　　　　　carte/點菜 $ 420-720

Le Soleil

No, not a French restaurant, but a Vietnamese one, over-looking the hotel's atrium from third floor level, which can be an interesting diversion for diners. It feels a bit like sitting on a rooftop veranda as you watch elevators glide up and down. Very friendly service backs up nicely presented dishes - sometimes with an 'Asian fusion' twist - prepared with fresh market ingredients. Prices are keen and the ambience unfailingly hits the spot.

Le Soleil並非法國餐廳，而是一家越南餐廳。餐廳位於酒店三樓，食客可一邊用餐，一邊觀看中庭景象，可算是有趣的另類體驗；看著電梯上下行駛，感覺仿如置身於頂樓露台一樣。服務態度友善，菜式賣相亦相當討好，並選用新鮮食材，有時會融入亞洲元素。價錢相宜，環境格調可謂無懈可擊。

■ ADDRESS/地址
TEL.2733 2033
3F, The Royal Garden Hotel, 69 Mody Road, Tsim Sha Tsui East, Kowloon
九龍尖沙咀東部麼地道69號帝苑酒店3樓
www.rghk.com.hk

■ OPENING HOURS, LAST ORDER
營業時間, 最後點菜時間
Lunch/午膳 11:30-14:30 (L.O.)
Dinner/晚膳 18:00-22:30 (L.O.)

■ PRICE/價錢
Lunch/午膳　menu/套餐 $ 145
　　　　　　carte/點菜 $ 250-500
Dinner/晚膳　carte/點菜 $ 250-500

Lian
蓮

With dishes like chicken soup with rice sheet noodles and green chilli sauce or braised ox cheek in red coconut curry, this establishment deftly blends hotter punchier Thai tastes to more subtle Vietnamese ones. The interior with its sweeps and curves is sleek and casual. You may like to sit at tables or at the centrepiece, the lotus pool counter with its lush leaves and lily pads. Altogether, this is a very relaxed and affordable restaurant.

這家餐廳融合了泰國菜的辛辣和越南菜的溫和，當中包括嫩雞絲清湯河粉或紅咖哩燴牛面珠。餐廳的裝修配合彎曲線條，打造時尚舒適的空間。除了獨立餐桌，你還可以選擇坐在餐廳中央的荷花池旁，花葉相映成趣。總括來說，這家餐廳環境舒適，價錢適中。

■ ADDRESS/地址

TEL.2521 1117

Shop 2004, Podium level 2, IFC Mall, Central

中環港景街 1 號國際金融中心商場 2 樓 2004號舖

www.maxims.com.hk

■ OPENING HOURS, LAST ORDER
營業時間, 最後點菜時間

Lunch/午膳 11:30-15:00 (L.O.)
Dinner/晚膳 18:00-23:30 (L.O.)

■ PRICE/價錢

Lunch/午膳　carte/點菜 $ 215-300
Dinner/晚膳　carte/點菜 $ 215-300

Lippo Chiuchow
力寶軒

One thing's for sure – you don't come to Lippo Chiuchow for the comfort. Being kind, you'd probably call it a 'brasserie' atmosphere; otherwise, you'd probably go for 'big, bold and noisy'. However, it's always full because the food's very good, and booking's essential. Chiuchow – a popular Cantonese style of cuisine – is simple and fresh: steamed chicken, braised whole abalone, deep-fried shrimp ball or crab meat ball are recommended.

有一點是可以肯定的：你來力寶軒不是為了舒適。比較寬容的人，可能會形容這裡有「簡樸餐館」的氣氛，否則便大概會說是「大、顯眼、嘈」。不過，餐廳總是滿座，因為食物實在太好吃，必須預先訂座。這裡的潮州菜(粵菜的一種)既簡單又新鮮，推介菜式包括貴妃雞、炆原隻鮑魚或酥炸蝦蟹棗。

■ ADDRESS/地址
TEL.2526 1168
Shop 4, GF, Lippo Centre, 89 Queensway, Admiralty
香港金鐘道89號力寶中心4號舖
www.lipporestaurant.com

■ OPENING HOURS, LAST ORDER
營業時間, 最後點菜時間
Lunch/午膳 11:00-15:30 (L.O.)
Dinner/晚膳 17:30-23:00 (L.O.)

■ PRICE/價錢
Lunch/午膳　carte/點菜 $ 180-550
Dinner/晚膳　carte/點菜 $ 200-700

Lobster Bar and Grill
龍蝦吧

The clubby atmosphere here derives from the British colonial furniture and décor: you can even enjoy an aperitif or single malt whisky in a cosy armchair upholstered in Scottish tartan. Specialities here are of course Maine lobsters (where you choose which one you want from the large tank) as well as a variety of oysters and grilled meats. Largely business-orientated at lunchtime but more relaxed with live music during the evening.

殖民地英式傢具和裝潢襯托出夜店般的氣氛：你可以躺在舒適的蘇格蘭格仔扶手椅上享受一杯餐前酒或單一麥芽威士忌。鎮店菜式當然少不了波士頓(緬因州)龍蝦(可以從大魚缸中挑選)，以及一系列蠔類及烤肉。午餐時段較多商務人士，晚上氣氛則較悠閒，有現場樂隊演奏。

- ADDRESS/地址
TEL.2820 8560
6F, Island Shangri-La Hotel, Pacific Place, Supreme Court Road, Central
中區法院道太古廣場港島香格里拉大酒店6樓
www.shangri-la.com

- OPENING HOURS, LAST ORDER
營業時間, 最後點菜時間
Lunch/午膳 12:00-14:30 (L.O.)
Dinner/晚膳 18:30-22:30 (L.O.)

- PRICE/價錢
Lunch/午膳   menu/套餐 $ 310
     carte/點菜 $ 400-900
Dinner/晚膳   menu/套餐 $ 588
     carte/點菜 $ 400-900

Luk Yu Tea House
陸羽茶室

🍴

📷10 📞🍴

You may have to try hard to tease a smile out of the old boys serving you at one of the few remaining authentic teahouses in this area. But persevere: it's well worth it. The dim sum here is affordable and excellent: no wonder the entire three floors fill up very quickly. Make sure you don't leave without trying the superb egg tarts which are divinely fresh. Tang Dynasty scholar and tea fanatic Luk Yuk, after whom this is named, would be proud.

在中環碩果僅存的這一間正宗茶室裡，你可能要努力一番才可能逗到年長的侍應一笑。但不要因此而卻步，留下用餐絕對不枉此行。這裡的點心價廉物美，佔地三層的茶室一早滿座亦理所當然。來到陸羽茶室，別忘記一嘗新鮮出爐的滋味蛋撻，店名中的唐代學者兼茶聖陸羽也會倍感自豪。

■ ADDRESS/地址
TEL.2523 5464
24-26 Stanley Street, Central
中環士丹利街24-26號

■ ANNUAL AND WEEKLY CLOSING
　休息日期
Closed Lunar New Year
年初一休息

■ OPENING HOURS, LAST ORDER
　營業時間, 最後點菜時間
Lunch/午膳 07:00-17:00 (L.O.)
Dinner/晚膳 18:00-22:00 (L.O.)

■ PRICE/價錢
Lunch/午膳　carte/點菜 $ 100-300
Dinner/晚膳　carte/點菜 $ 200-300

Lumiere
亮明居

🍴🍴

♿ ⍃ ⏲·14

Next door to Cuisine Cuisine, this immediately invigorates with its cascading waterfall and wood detailing. Just before entering the restaurant, you'll pass a small green glass statue of Mr Zhuge, the commander-in-chief of the army in Sichuan Province nearly 2,000 years ago. Let's hope he'd have been happy with the sharp chilli and peppercorn spicing of the dishes. A particular speciality is the Sichuan braised pigeon in a cabbage pocket.

亮明居毗鄰國金軒，與瀑布木飾相映成趣。甫踏進餐廳，你會看到一個綠色的玻璃諸葛亮像，正是劉備三顧茅廬才出山的四川統帥。餐廳的紅椒及乾胡椒辛辣菜式應該合他口味吧！特色美食首推錦簇乳鴿。

■ ADDRESS/地址
TEL.2393 3933
Shop 3101-3107, Podium 3, IFC Mall, 8 Finance Street, Central
中環金融街8號國際金融中心商場第2期3樓 3101-3107號舖
www.lumiere.hk

■ OPENING HOURS, LAST ORDER
營業時間, 最後點菜時間
Lunch/午膳　12:00-14:30 (L.O.)
Dinner/晚膳　18:00-22:30 (L.O.)

■ PRICE/價錢
Lunch/午膳　carte/點菜 $ 350-550
Dinner/晚膳　carte/點菜 $ 500-1,000

Lung King Heen
龍景軒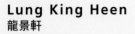

❁ ❁ ❁   ✕✕ ✕

♿ ⟨ ☞♪ ⊡16 🕐♨ 🕸

Translated as 'view of the dragon', it now offers a pan-orama of Victoria Harbour whilst the interior is smart and uncluttered, with hand-embroidered silk, columns and glass screens. Ingredients here are of the highest quality – particularly the seafood which is impeccably fresh; all dishes are expertly crafted, nicely balanced and enticingly presented. The serving team is highly professional and describe dishes with great care and obvious pride.

龍景軒名副其實，坐擁動人心弦的維港全景；餐廳內部亦時尚整潔，飾以手工刺繡絲綢、圓柱和玻璃屏幕。食材品質上等，特別是海鮮，絕對新鮮。菜式全是悉心烹調，精心雕琢，賣相一流。服務專業，侍應會細心自豪地介紹菜式。

■ ADDRESS/地址

TEL.3196 8880
4F, Four Seasons Hotel, 8 Finance Street, Central
中環金融街8號四季酒店4樓

■ OPENING HOURS, LAST ORDER
營業時間, 最後點菜時間
Lunch/午膳 12:00-14:30 (L.O.)
Dinner/晚膳 18:00-22:30 (L.O.)

■ PRICE/價錢
Lunch/午膳   menu/套餐 $ 400
                carte/點菜 $ 500-700
Dinner/晚膳   menu/套餐 $ 980
                carte/點菜 $ 1,000-1,500

Mak's Noodle
麥奀雲吞麵世家

A small place with a famous reputation: Mak Chi Ming's father opened the original Mak's Noodle in 1960, while his granddad was 'king of the won ton' in the 1930s. Fittingly, for a world-renowned name, the premises are immaculate. The staff - strict, efficient and overseen by the boss - serve nothing but noodles, with fresh, authentic recipes utilising seasonal vegetables produced to order. Most prized dish is the mouth-watering chutney pork.

地方淺窄的餐廳卻享負盛名：麥志明祖父是30年代的「雲吞麵大王」，父親則於1960年創立了麥奀記老店。作為世界知名的食店，地方亦整潔無瑕。員工由老闆監督著，既嚴謹又有效率。餐廳供應的只有麵，採用新鮮食材、正宗食譜，以及季節性蔬菜。最特別的菜式是令人垂涎欲滴的炸醬麵。

■ ADDRESS/地址
TEL.2854 3810
77 Wellington Street, Central
中環威靈頓街77號

■ OPENING HOURS, LAST ORDER
營業時間, 最後點菜時間
11:00-20:00 (L.O.)

■ PRICE/價錢
Lunch/午膳　carte/點菜 $ 28-40
Dinner/晚膳　carte/點菜 $ 30-60

Mandarin Grill

A luminous dining room - Sir Terence Conran's refurbishment has kept the Oriental references. If you want to be seen, this is the place to eat. Alternatively, if you want to see the sashimi and oyster chefs at work, sit at the bar and watch them – guaranteed freshness! Soufflé lovers adore this place as they have an embarrassment of riches to choose from. More so, oyster lovers: they can even indulge their passion in a dessert with chocolate.

明亮的餐廳經過20世紀著名的室內設計師Sir Terence Conran 的裝修後，仍然保留文華東方的味道。如果你想給人看到，這家餐廳十分適合。另一方面，如果你想看看師傅如何準備魚生和生蠔，你可以坐在吧檯觀看他們，保證新鮮！梳乎厘的愛好者鍾情於這個地方，因為這裡的選擇琳瑯滿目。再者，喜歡吃生蠔的人也可以放縱一下，品嚐巧克力甜品。

■ ADDRESS/地址

TEL.2825 4932
Mandarin Oriental Hotel, 5 Connaught Road, Central
中環干諾道中5號文華東方酒店
www.mandarinoriental.com

■ OPENING HOURS, LAST ORDER
　營業時間, 最後點菜時間
Lunch/午膳　12:00-14:30 (L.O.)
Dinner/晚膳　18:30-22:30 (L.O.)

■ PRICE/價錢
Lunch/午膳　menu/套餐 $ 988
　　　　　　carte/點菜 $ 580-1,100
Dinner/晚膳　menu/套餐 $ 988
　　　　　　carte/點菜 $ 580-1,100

Man Ho
萬豪殿

XX

You're guaranteed a warm welcome at this extremely popular operation where lacquered wood furniture and a large aquarium have been employed to create a lively, colourful atmosphere. Large family groups often return and there's a separate private room for up to 48 guests. Fresh, local ingredients are used to fine effect and the good-value dishes include double-boiled sea whelk with fish maws soup.

一直以來，餐廳的漆木傢具和大型魚缸都給人朝氣勃勃和色彩繽紛的感覺；這家大受歡迎的餐廳，服務更是熱情周到。一家大小的食客經常再次光顧。這裡設有可以容納達48人的獨立餐室。菜餚採用本地生產的新鮮食材，烹調技巧出色，物超所值的菜式包括花膠燉響螺。

■ ADDRESS/地址

TEL.2841 3853
3F, JW Marriott Hotel, Pacific Place, 88 Queensway, Admiralty
香港金鐘道88號太古廣場萬豪酒店3樓
www.jw.marriotthk.com

■ OPENING HOURS, LAST ORDER
營業時間, 最後點菜時間
Lunch/午膳 11:30-14:30 (L.O.)
Dinner/晚膳 18:30-21:30 (L.O.)

■ PRICE/價錢
Lunch/午膳   menu/套餐 $ 460-1,128
              carte/點菜 $ 300
Dinner/晚膳   menu/套餐 $ 460-1,128
              carte/點菜 $ 300

Manor
富瑤

✕✕

🍽12

Don't be put off by Manor's unappealing façade. It stands behind a rather neglected garage on Jaffe Road. Appearances, though, can be deceptive and the restaurant itself comprises a comfortable dining room and just the right number of tables for those wishing to escape the city's bigger, more crowded establishments. This is one of Hong Kong's favourite dim sum destinations; fish lovers come here too for live cooking from the room's aquariums.

不要因富瑤外表不吸引而卻步，餐廳位處謝斐道一個半空置的車房後面。不過外表容易把人騙倒，但餐廳的環境其實很舒適，餐桌的數目亦恰到好處，想避開去其他較大及擁擠的餐廳就剛剛好。這是香港其中一個點心熱點；愛吃魚的客人都到訪看廚師即場從魚缸挑選魚出來烹調。

■ ADDRESS/地址

TEL.2836 9999

Shop F-G, GF, Lockhart House, 440 Jaffe Road, Causeway Bay

銅鑼灣謝斐道440號駱克大廈地下F-G舖

■ OPENING HOURS, LAST ORDER
營業時間, 最後點菜時間
Lunch/午膳 11:00-16:00 (L.O.)
Dinner/晚膳 18:00-04:00 (L.O.)

■ PRICE/價錢
Lunch/午膳　carte/點菜 $ 250-400
Dinner/晚膳　carte/點菜 $ 250-400

Man Wah
文華廳

✗✗

◁ ☞ ⌖14

Man Wah seems to have been untouched by the hotel's modern renovation and exudes a luxuriously intimate and traditional feel. Tables just off the room entrance have the better harbour views, though everyone can appreciate the décor: brass lanterns hang from the wood ceiling and the ornate screen is from the original opening. The menu is steeped in classics, the Peking duck a veritable legend. Unhurried staff have the time to look after guests.

文華似乎沒有被酒店的現代裝修影響，這裡仍然散發著一種豪華的舒適傳統氣息。雖然近門口的餐桌享有較佳的海景，但所有人都可以欣賞這裡的裝潢：木天花板吊著黃銅燈籠，而華麗的屏幕是從開張使用至今。菜單充斥著經典菜式，這裡的北京填鴨是名副其實的美食。服務員不慌不忙，可充分照顧食客的需要。

■ ADDRESS/地址

TEL.2522 0111
25F, Mandarin Oriental Hotel, 5 Connaught Road, Central
中環于諾道中5號文華東方酒店25樓
www.mandarinoriental.com

■ OPENING HOURS, LAST ORDER
營業時間, 最後點菜時間
Lunch/午膳 12:00-14:30 (L.O.)
Dinner/晚膳 18:30-22:30 (L.O.)

■ PRICE/價錢
Lunch/午膳　carte/點菜 $ 550-1,200
Dinner/晚膳　carte/點菜 $ 550-1,200

M at the Fringe

The title? Well, M stands for Michelle, the owner, and the Fringe is an alternative art club next door. Housed in an old farm building dating back to 1913, this is decorated in a wonderful contemporary baroque style. The diverse menu features recipes picked up from around the world. Try the foie gras and the crispy suckling pig. If you've still got room, there's always M's Pavlova with passion fruit sorbet.

這裡為何以「M AT THE FRINGE」命名？M代表東主Michelle，而Fringe就是餐廳座落位置-另類藝術集中地：藝穗會。藝穗會的歷史追溯至1913年，當時是舊牛奶公司的寫字樓，以當代巴洛克風格設計，甚具藝術感。餐廳的菜式種類繁多，並從世界各地採集食譜。推介菜式包括鵝肝醬、脆皮燒豬等。吃過主菜，可一嚐招牌甜品M's Pavlova伴熱情果雪芭。

■ ADDRESS/地址
TEL.2877 4000
1F, South block, 2 Lower Albert Road, Central
中環下亞厘畢道2號南座1樓
www.m-atthefringe.com

■ ANNUAL AND WEEKLY CLOSING
　休息日期
Closed Saturday lunch and Sunday lunch
週六、日午膳休息

■ OPENING HOURS, LAST ORDER
　營業時間, 最後點菜時間
Lunch/午膳 12:00-14:30 (L.O.)
Dinner/晚膳 19:00-22:30 (L.O.)

■ PRICE/價錢
Lunch/午膳　　menu/套餐 $ 284
　　　　　　　carte/點菜 $ 380-540
Dinner/晚膳　carte/點菜 $ 320-610

Megu

Megu may be above a shopping mall, but it's well worth the trip. Not only is the two-level restaurant a superb example of contemporary design, it also serves mouth-watering Japanese cuisine. Downstairs is a sushi counter with booths; upstairs, and even more popular, the stylish main restaurant and bar. Signature dishes include delicious Australian Wagyu beef from the stone grill, while staff are happy to help you choose from over 40 sake.

Megu雖然位於商場內，但實在值得一去。兩層的餐廳不但是現代設計的完美例子，同時亦提供令人垂涎欲滴的日本料理。下層是壽司吧檯及雅座，而上層則更受歡迎的時尚主餐廳及酒吧。招牌菜包括美味的石烤澳洲和牛，此外服務員亦很樂意助你從40多種清酒中作出選擇。

■ ADDRESS/地址
TEL.3743 1421
R002 & R003, 3F Elements, 1 Austin Road West, Kowloon
九龍柯士甸道西1號圓方3樓平台R002-R003號鋪
www.megunyc.com

■ OPENING HOURS, LAST ORDER
營業時間, 最後點菜時間
Lunch/午膳　12:00-14:30 (L.O.)
Dinner/晚膳　18:00-22:30 (L.O.)

■ PRICE/價錢
Lunch/午膳　menu/套餐 $ 130-400
　　　　　　carte/點菜 $ 225-670
Dinner/晚膳　menu/套餐 $ 900-1,150
　　　　　　carte/點菜 $ 225-1,310

Ming Court
明閣

A fascinating collection of replica Ching Dynasty statues as well as some fine Chinese landscape paintings lend elegance to this already stylish interior with its curved walls and smart lighting. This is more than matched by the equally sophisticated Cantonese menu with its featured specialities of shark fin flight (4 ways with shark fin) and deep-fried lobster with cheese and simmered abalone with vinegar. The service here is also excellent.

餐廳收藏了一系列清代雕像的仿製品，以及一些筆法細緻的中國山水畫，令本已獨具風格的裝潢更顯高雅。牆身呈弧形，燈光亦經過精心設計。這樣的環境與同樣匠心獨運的粵菜菜譜配合得天衣無縫。精選菜式包括魚紅翅肆薈(四種魚翅烹調法)及脆芝士龍蝦伴醋香鮑魚天使麵。服務態度更是一流。

■ ADDRESS/地址
TEL.3552 3300
6F, Langham Place Hotel, 555 Shanghai Street, Mongkok, Kowloon
九龍旺角上海街555號朗豪酒店6樓
www.hongkong.langhamplacehotels.com

■ OPENING HOURS, LAST ORDER
營業時間, 最後點菜時間
Lunch/午膳　11:00-14:30 (L.O.)
Dinner/晚膳　18:00-22:30 (L.O.)

■ PRICE/價錢
Lunch/午膳　menu/套餐 $ 228-348
　　　　　　carte/點菜 $ 200-450
Dinner/晚膳　menu/套餐 $ 378-798
　　　　　　carte/點菜 $ 200-450

Modern China (Causeway Bay)
金滿庭 (銅鑼灣)

✕

🍽18

Two statues of ancient Chinese soldiers stand guard at the entrance to this Northern Chinese establishment housed on one of the 4 floors of a bustling food forum and with its own direct lift access. Inside, the atmosphere is lively and noisy and diners are allowed a clear view into the spotless kitchen to see good-value specialities from the areas of Shanghai, Sichuan and Beijing being prepared. Booking is essential.

兩座中國古代士兵雕像昂然屹立於門前;金滿庭位於佔地四層的食通天美食廣場,人流旺盛,設有專屬升降機供顧客使用。店內同樣是一片熙來攘往,廚房只隔一道透明玻璃,顧客可清楚看見一塵不染的廚房烹調來自上海、四川、北京等地的名菜。必須預先訂座。

■ ADDRESS/地址
TEL.2606 2525
Shop 1002, 10F, Food Forum, Times Square, 1 Matheson Street, Causeway Bay
銅鑼灣勿地臣街1號時代廣場食通天10樓1002號舖

■ ANNUAL AND WEEKLY CLOSING
　休息日期
Closed 1st January
1月1日休息

■ OPENING HOURS, LAST ORDER
　營業時間, 最後點菜時間
Lunch/午膳 11:45-14:45 (L.O.)
Dinner/晚膳 17:45-22:45 (L.O.)

■ PRICE/價錢
Lunch/午膳　menu/套餐 $ 950-1,250
　　　　　　carte/點菜 $ 200-600
Dinner/晚膳　menu/套餐 $ 1,050-1,650
　　　　　　carte/點菜 $ 200-800

Modern China (Kowloon)
金滿庭（九龍）

♿ **P** ⌂16

Set in a huge shopping mall in an area showing signs of gentrification, this spacious restaurant may lack some charm but it is clean and contemporary. Service is fast and efficient: English is not spoken, so the menu with pictures is helpful. Worth seeking out are five spice sesame chicken, Shanghai style noodle soup, and sweet and sour boneless king fish. Dishes are inexpensive, but ingredients are good quality and the cooking skill appreciable.

餐廳位於市區重建的龐大商場，有點缺乏魅力；但這裡採用當代設計，地方清潔。服務既快捷又高效率，雖然服務員不懂英語，但菜單上有照片可作參考。值得一試的菜式包括五香芝麻雞、上海湯麵、甜酸魚。菜餚價錢相宜，而食材屬上等，烹調技巧亦值得讚賞。

■ ADDRESS/地址
TEL.2910 1000
UG 06B, Olympian City 2, 18 Hoi Ting Road, West Kowloon
九龍西九龍海庭道18號奧海城第2期 UG06B舖
www.modernchinarestaurant.com

■ OPENING HOURS, LAST ORDER
營業時間, 最後點菜時間
Lunch/午膳 11:30-15:00 L.O. 14:30
Dinner/晚膳 17:30-23:00 L.O. 22:30

■ PRICE/價錢
Lunch/午膳 carte/點菜 $ 120-500
Dinner/晚膳 carte/點菜 $ 120-500

Morton's of Chicago

This buzzing outpost of the legendary Illinois steakhouse allows you to feast on all the classic dishes – only with Victoria Harbour sparkling as the backdrop. As well as old favourites such as Caesar salad and shrimp cocktail, all the prime cuts are available using both American and Australian aged beef. But beware: portions are massive and two of you may care to share a double Porterhouse steak!

這家享負盛名的美國伊利諾扒房總是鬧哄哄，在此食客可以品嘗到所有經典美食，同時飽覽維多利亞港的閃爍夜景。除了凱撒沙律和大蝦雞尾酒等招牌美食，這裡更提供美國和澳洲頂級的各種牛扒。請注意：這裡的牛扒份量十足，一塊雙份上等腰肉牛扒已足夠二人享用！

■ ADDRESS/地址

TEL.2732 2343
4F, Sheraton Hotel, 20 Nathan Road, Kowloon
九龍尖沙咀彌敦道20號喜來登酒店4樓
www.mortons.com

■ OPENING HOURS, LAST ORDER
營業時間, 最後點菜時間
Dinner/晚膳 17:30-23:00 (L.O.)

■ PRICE/價錢
Dinner/晚膳 carte/點菜 $ 600-900

Nadaman (Kowloon)
灘萬 (九龍)

A contemporary installation is divided up according to the style of culinary preparation involved. Fundamental is a sushi bar where chefs deftly prepare sushi and sashimi. Then there's the dramatic teppanyaki counter as well as separate tatami rooms and the main dining area where bamboo partitioning offers quiet intimacy. The culinary centre point here is the series of special Kaiseki full course dinner menus.

時尚的餐廳根據菜式風格分為不同的進餐區。師傅在主力的壽司吧熟練靈巧地製作壽司和刺身,而鐵板燒檯則充滿生氣;餐廳更設有獨立的榻榻米房間,至於主餐室則以竹子分隔,寧靜親切。晚膳的特色美食首推是一系列的特別懷石料理套餐。

■ ADDRESS/地址
TEL.2733 8751
B2, Kowloon Shangri-La Hotel, 64 Mody Road, Tsim Sha Tsui, Kowloon
九龍尖沙咀麼地道64號九龍香格里拉酒店地庫2樓
www.shangri-la.com

■ OPENING HOURS, LAST ORDER
營業時間, 最後點菜時間
Lunch/午膳 12:00-15:00 (L.O.)
Dinner/晚膳 18:00-22:30 (L.O.)

■ PRICE/價錢
Lunch/午膳　menu/套餐 $ 180-400
　　　　　　carte/點菜 $ 200-500
Dinner/晚膳　menu/套餐 $ 440-1,300
　　　　　　carte/點菜 $ 440-1,300

Naozen
なお膳

A simple, sober Japanese restaurant in an easy-to-find location. There are two rooms, one at the front and one at the back; as you enter, you can watch the chef in front of you preparing sushi and sashimi. Upstairs are three tatami rooms for private dining (take off your shoes when you come up here). Specialities are offered in half portions to widen your dining experience. Friendly service, sake in abundance, and very tasty, well-priced dishes.

這是一家簡單沉著的日本餐廳，位置容易尋找。餐廳包括兩個房間，一間在前面，另一間在後面。進入餐廳時，可以看到師傅在你面前準備壽司和魚生。樓上有三間榻榻米房間供私人用餐，到這裡時便要脫鞋。菜式以半份的分量奉上，讓你享用更多不同的食物。服務態度良好，並提供豐富的清酒，菜餚十分美味，價錢適中。

■ ADDRESS/地址
TEL.2877 6668
21-25 Wellington Street, Central
中環威靈頓街21-25號
www.naozen.com

■ ANNUAL AND WEEKLY CLOSING
  休息日期
Closed Lunar New Year and Sunday lunch
年初一及週日午膳休息

■ OPENING HOURS, LAST ORDER
  營業時間，最後點菜時間
Lunch/午膳 11:30-15:00 (L.O.)
Dinner/晚膳 18:00-23:00 (L.O.)

■ PRICE/價錢
Lunch/午膳   menu/套餐 $ 90-400
              carte/點菜 $ 250-650
Dinner/晚膳 menu/套餐 $ 320-780
              carte/點菜 $ 250-650

Nicholini's
意寧谷

🍴🍴🍴🍴

← 👆🔑 🚪12 📞🍴

This stylish circular room has large windows that offer a peak between the adjoining tower blocks allowing views over the bay. At the back of the room, there's a large Venetian scene and some intriguing glass sculptures lending a sumptuous formal air. The cooking is contemporary Italian and whilst the pastas are excellent, many dishes are deemed a little too elaborate. Service is over-eager but well meaning.

時尚的圓形餐廳擁有寬大的窗戶，於鄰近摩天大樓中鶴立雞群，坐擁維港美景。餐廳後方的巨型威尼斯布景和迷人的玻璃塑像，散發著豪華莊重的氣息。餐廳提供時尚意大利菜，意大利粉味道一流，不過很多菜式都似乎有點花巧。服務或許太熱切，但出自好意。

■ ADDRESS/地址
TEL.2521 3838
8F, Conrad Hotel, Pacific Place, 88 Queensway, Admiralty
香港金鐘道88號太古廣場港麗酒店8樓
www.conradhotels.com

■ ANNUAL AND WEEKLY CLOSING
　　休息日期
Closed Saturday lunch
週六午膳休息

■ OPENING HOURS, LAST ORDER
　　營業時間, 最後點菜時間
Lunch/午膳 12:00-15:00 (L.O.)
Dinner/晚膳 18:30-23:00 (L.O.)

■ PRICE/價錢
Lunch/午膳　carte/點菜 $ 670-1,260
Dinner/晚膳　carte/點菜 $ 670-1,260

Nobu

XX

♿ ✉ 🚩 📷14 🚌 🍽 🎐

The ceiling here has patterns of undulating sea urchin spines and behind the bar, there are views of cherry blossoms at this branch of the über-fashionable Nobu brand. Sadly, the service is not so spot on. At lunch, bento boxes are very popular. At dinner, Mr. Matsuhisa's beguiling blend of Japanese and South American tastes continues to work its fashionable magic by featuring sushi and sashimi, excellent quality seafood and fine salsas.

天花板有呈波浪狀的海膽刺，而酒吧後面則有櫻花美景—走在時代尖端的設計盡在享譽國際的NOBU餐廳，然而服務尚有改善空間。午餐時間的便當盒非常受歡迎，而晚餐方面，主廚松久信幸融合日本和南美風味，炮製的嶄新口味更是迷人。菜式包括壽司、刺身、頂級海鮮及辛香番茄醬。

■ ADDRESS/地址
TEL.2313 2323
2F, Intercontinental Hotel, 18 Salisbury Road, Tsim Sha Tsui, Kowloon
九龍尖沙咀梳士巴利道18號洲際酒店2樓

■ OPENING HOURS, LAST ORDER
營業時間, 最後點菜時間
Lunch/午膳　12:00-14:30 (L.O.)
Dinner/晚膳　18:00-23:00 (L.O.)

■ PRICE/價錢
Lunch/午膳　menu/套餐 $ 130-588
　　　　　　　carte/點菜 $ 250-1,200
Dinner/晚膳　menu/套餐 $ 888-1,188
　　　　　　　carte/點菜 $ 250-1,200

1/5 Nuevo

Behind the modern glass façade you'll find a stylish bar but head beyond, to the rear dining room. Here, red drapes and arty nude photos add to the sensual and intimate feel. The open-plan kitchen delivers very good value international cooking at lunch which is geared towards local business types. The dinner à la carte menu offers more Mediterranean influences, especially from France and Italy. The cooking is crisp, light, fresh and satisfying.

1/5 Nuevo擁有時尚的玻璃外觀，型格酒吧的後面便是餐室，這裡的紅色窗簾和藝術性的裸照營造了感性的氣氛。這間開放式廚房的餐廳在午市時段供應物有所值的國際菜式，食客亦以本地商務客人為主。晚餐散叫的菜單涵蓋較多地中海菜式，尤其是法國菜和意大利菜。菜餚清新輕盈，既新鮮又豐足。

- ADDRESS/地址
TEL.2529 2300
9 Star Street, Wanchai
灣仔星街9號
www.elite-concepts.com

- ANNUAL AND WEEKLY CLOSING
  休息日期
Closed Sunday lunch
週日午膳休息

- OPENING HOURS, LAST ORDER
  營業時間, 最後點菜時間
Lunch/午膳 12:00-14:30 L.O. 14:00
Dinner/晚膳 18:00-24:00 L.O. 22:45

- PRICE/價錢
Lunch/午膳　menu/套餐 $ 118-168
Dinner/晚膳　carte/點菜 $ 220-300

One Harbour Road
港灣壹號

XXXX

♿ ‹ ☞ **P** 📽14 ☎🍽

One Harbour Road may be set in a hotel, but its beautifully refined ambience will make you think you're on the terrace of an elegant 1930s Taipan mansion. The bright and airy feel comes courtesy of split-level dining offering views of the harbour. A profusion of plants, large lotus pond and sound of running water soften the bold statement of the huge pillars. Renowned Cantonese menus offer a wide variety of well-prepared meat and fish dishes.

雖然港灣壹號位於酒店內，但這裡的優雅氣氛，令你恍如置身於30年代的優雅大班府第。分層用餐讓你同時飽覽海景，享受明亮又通風的環境。茂盛的植物、大型蓮花池，以及潺潺的流水聲，軟化了龐大柱子給人的感覺。這裡的著名粵菜包括準備妥當、種類繁多的肉類和魚類菜式。

■ ADDRESS/地址
TEL.2588 1234
8F, Grand Hyatt Hotel, 1 Harbour Road, Wanchai
灣仔港灣道一號君悅酒店8樓
www.hongkong.grand.hyatt.com

■ OPENING HOURS, LAST ORDER
營業時間, 最後點菜時間
Lunch/午膳　12:00-14:30 (L.O.)
Dinner/晚膳　18:00-23:00 (L.O.)

■ PRICE/價錢
Lunch/午膳　　menu/套餐 $ 400
　　　　　　　carte/點菜 $ 330-990
Dinner/晚膳　 menu/套餐 $ 770
　　　　　　　carte/點菜 $ 330-990

Palki (Quarry Bay)
皇轎 (鰂魚涌)

Recently opened, this is the latest arrival for the small chain and has a timber-style façade and the familiar large red sign. Inside, the installation is fairly traditional with Moghul-style décor and, as elsewhere, the cooking is firmly rooted in the Punjab. Some vegetarian items are featured but the strength of the cooking here is the section of tandoori-related dishes as well as the very authentic home-made breads.

鰂魚涌分店剛開張不久，是其連鎖店的最新一份子。餐廳擁有木質橫樑前門，以及為人熟悉的大型紅色標誌。內部裝修頗為傳統，以莫　兒風格設計。至於菜餚方面，主打是旁遮普地區的菜式，亦有提供一些素食選擇。而鎮店至寶則包括唐杜里菜式及原汁原味的自家製麵包。

■ ADDRESS/地址
TEL.2561 2968
Shop 1, GF, Hoi Kwong Court, 13-15
Hoi Kwong Street, Quarry Bay
鰂魚涌海光街13-15號海光苑地下1號舖
www.palki.com.hk

■ OPENING HOURS, LAST ORDER
營業時間, 最後點菜時間
Lunch/午膳 11:00-15:00 L.O. 14:45
Dinner/晚膳 18:00-23:00 L.O. 22:45

■ PRICE/價錢
Lunch/午膳　carte/點菜 $ 125-250
Dinner/晚膳　carte/點菜 $ 125-250

Palki (Sai Wan Ho)
皇轎 (西灣河)

It's quite easy to drive straight past this tiny little operation despite the big red sign. However, if you make a point of stopping and going in, you'll find a delightfully intimate room seating no more than 20 people and enlivened by some Moghul-style windows. Otherwise, everything is kept simple and the menus make a feature of correctly prepared seafood curries as well as a number of authentic vegetarian items.

雖然有大大的紅色招牌，駕駛時還是很容易錯過這家小店。不過，只要你駐足停留，進內就會發現只能容納約二十人的細小空間，在蒙兀兒風格的窗戶妝點下生色不少。除此以外，一切從簡，而菜單裡包括精心烹調的海鮮咖哩及一系列素食菜色。

■ ADDRESS/地址

TEL.3579 8278
GF, Rear Block, Hoi Fu Building, 240 Shau Kei Wan Road, Sai Wan Ho
西灣河筲箕灣道240號海富樓地下後座
www.palki.com.hk

■ OPENING HOURS, LAST ORDER
營業時間, 最後點菜時間
Lunch/午膳 11:00-15:00 L.O. 14:45
Dinner/晚膳 18:00-23:00 L.O. 22:45

■ PRICE/價錢
Lunch/午膳　carte/點菜 $ 115-200
Dinner/晚膳　carte/點菜 $ 115-200

Palki (Tin Hau)
皇轎 (天后)

There's a large red neon sign making sure this doesn't get lost in this bustling street partly hidden under a flyover. Inside, everything's fairly basic but the kitchen does produce a very authentic range of Punjabi preparations from Northern India including a very good butter chicken and rogan josh. Efforts are made to import the necessary spices as well as Indian beers. The Indian manager heads up a friendly, obliging team.

店前大大的霓虹燈告示牌確保你不會迷失在天橋下的繁華街道。餐廳一切從簡，但廚房毫不馬虎，提供原汁原味的北印度菜式，包括美味的牛油雞和咖喱番茄燉(羊)肉(Rogan Josh)。餐廳亦花了不少心思引入不同食品及印度啤酒。由印籍經理帶領的服務團隊親切專業。

■ ADDRESS/地址
TEL.2566 8411
GF, Fook Wah Mansion, 2 Tsing Fung Street, Tin Hau
天后清風街2號福華大廈地下
www.palki.com.hk

■ OPENING HOURS, LAST ORDER
營業時間, 最後點菜時間
Lunch/午膳 11:00-15:00 L.O. 14:45
Dinner/晚膳 18:00-23:00 L.O. 22:45

■ PRICE/價錢
Lunch/午膳   carte/點菜 $ 125-250
Dinner/晚膳 carte/點菜 $ 125-250

Pearl on the Peak

Huge plate glass windows allow for stunning panoramic views: you have (literally) the whole of Hong Kong and Kowloon at your feet! Inside, black marble floors and gold columns only add to the sense of occasion whilst at night, the lights are turned down low for a romantic experience. An intriguing menu makes regular nods to Australia both in terms of its ingredients (such as kangaroo and barramundi) and its eclectic, fusion style.

餐廳每個角落都有大片落地玻璃窗，盡收寬廣景緻：香港九龍皆在腳下！黑色大理石地板配上金色圓柱，與餐廳的獨特風格相得益彰，入夜後更會調暗燈光，營造浪漫氣氛。引人入勝的餐單，不論食材(如袋鼠肉和金目鱸)還是精挑細選、融合百家之長的烹調特色，都可見其澳洲風格。

■ ADDRESS/地址

TEL.2849 5123

1F, The Peak Tower, 128 Peak Road, The Peak

山頂山頂道128號凌霄閣1樓

www.maxims.com.hk

■ OPENING HOURS, LAST ORDER

營業時間, 最後點菜時間

Lunch/午膳 12:00-15:00 L.O. 14:30

Dinner/晚膳 18:00-24:00 L.O. 22:30

■ PRICE/價錢

Lunch/午膳   menu/套餐 $ 198

                carte/點菜 $ 365-1,930

Dinner/晚膳   carte/點菜 $ 365-1,930

Peking Garden (Central)
北京樓 (中環)

At the end of a corridor, you'll find two massive wooden doors, each leading into a brightly lit dining room where the tables are neatly arranged and you're looked after by a team of chicly dressed hostesses. The signature item on the menu is Peking duck, prepared with great precision at the table by the chef. Beware when ordering as portions are generous. Mainly business customers at lunchtime and large family groups at night.

走廊盡頭有兩道巨型的木門,每道門都能將你帶到一間明亮的餐室;裡面的餐桌排列整齊,侍應穿著時尚的制服,服務更是十分周到。招牌菜是北京填鴨,由廚師在餐桌旁為食客細心準備。因為食物份量豐富,點菜時要小心衡量。午市時段的食客主要是商務客人,而晚上則較多為一家大小。

■ ADDRESS/地址
TEL.2526 6456
Alexandra House, 7-15 Des Voeux Road Central, Central
中環德輔道中7-15號歷山大廈
www.maxims.com.hk

■ OPENING HOURS, LAST ORDER
營業時間, 最後點菜時間
Lunch/午膳 11:00-15:00 (L.O.)
Dinner/晚膳 18;00-23:30 (L.O.)

■ PRICE/價錢
Lunch/午膳　carte/點菜 $ 200-600
Dinner/晚膳　carte/點菜 $ 200-600

Peking Garden (Kowloon)
北京樓 (九龍)

XX

Lit by faux-crystal chandeliers, this is a huge, boisterous Peking restaurant with eight rooms and 500 seats. In the most spacious room (200 seats) diners are lucky indeed to get a table with a view onto the ferry pier. The well-structured staff are either supervising with calm deliberation, or pushing trolleys and serving. The hallmark is the barbecued Peking duck with pancake, or braised sliced perch with minced pork and salted cabbage.

人造水晶吊燈，燃亮著這家龐大熱鬧的北京餐廳。這裡共有8間餐室及500個座位，最大的餐室有200個座位，食客可在此觀賞碼頭海景。員工分工合作，或沉靜地監督著，或推餐車奉上食物。招牌菜是北京烤鴨配烙餅，或炆切片鱸魚配豬肉泡菜。

■ ADDRESS/地址
TEL.2735 8211
3F, Star House, 3 Salisbury Road, Tsim Sha Tsui, Kowloon
九龍尖沙咀梳士巴利道3號星光行3樓

■ OPENING HOURS, LAST ORDER
營業時間, 最後點菜時間
Lunch/午膳 11:00-15:00 L.O. 14:30
Dinner/晚膳 14:30-22:30 L.O. 22:00

■ PRICE/價錢
Lunch/午膳   menu/套餐 $ 105
             carte/點菜 $ 300-1,200
Dinner/晚膳   menu/套餐 $ 105
             carte/點菜 $ 300-1,200

Peking Garden (Tai Koo Shing)
北京樓 (太古城)

Head for the City Plaza's indoor ice rink to find this ultra-smart restaurant. The interior hits the gold standard, its glitter an ornately ubiquitous statement - just what's required to draw in all those shoppers. The accomplished cuisine is mostly Peking, and the hallmark dish is Peking duck, but spice is nice here too: tuck in to fried prawns with chilli sauce. Sichuan and Shanghai elements are also on the menu, though dim sum is low key.

向太古城溜冰場的方向走，便會找到這家超時尚的餐廳。餐廳的內部實在金壁輝煌：發出閃閃生輝、無所不在的光芒，如此華麗的氣派正正吸引了購物者到此用餐。餐廳的菜式大部分是北京菜，招牌菜是北京填鴨，而這裡的香料亦頗美味：不仿試試京爆明蝦球。有些菜式含四川和上海元素，但點心則較少。

■ ADDRESS/地址
TEL.2884 4131
2F, Cityplaza II, Tai Koo Shing
太古城中心第2期2樓
www.maxims.com.hk

■ OPENING HOURS, LAST ORDER
營業時間, 最後點菜時間
Lunch/午膳 11:30-15:00 L.O. 14:30
Dinner/晚膳 18:00-23:30 L.O. 23:00
■ PRICE/價錢
Lunch/午膳   carte/點菜 $ 135-290
Dinner/晚膳 carte/點菜 $ 135-290

Petrus
珀翠

Perched on the 56th floor with dramatic views, this is firmly in the classical European style with moulded ceilings, chandeliers, elegantly draped curtains and refined table settings. The professional service blends in perfectly and demonstrates great attention to detail. All this is matched by very proficient French cooking that relies on a roll-call of wonderfully fresh ingredients. Try the reasonable set lunch menu that includes house wine.

餐廳座落於酒店56樓，可飽覽海港美景，設計別出心裁：雕有線條的天花、高雅的窗簾、吊燈及排列優雅的餐桌，盡顯經典歐洲格調。服務十分專業，細心周到。餐廳的法國菜廚藝一流，與絕對新鮮食材，相得益彰。價錢合宜的午市套餐連餐酒, 不能不試。

■ ADDRESS/地址
TEL.2820 8590
56F, Island Shangri-La Hotel, Pacific Place, Supreme Court Road, Central
中區法院道太古廣場港島香格里拉酒店
56樓
www.shangri-la.com

■ ANNUAL AND WEEKLY CLOSING
　　休息日期
Closed Public Holidays lunch
公眾假期午膳休息

■ OPENING HOURS, LAST ORDER
　　營業時間, 最後點菜時間
Lunch/午膳　12:00-14:30 (L.O.)
Dinner/晚膳　18:30-22:30 (L.O.)

■ PRICE/價錢
Lunch/午膳　menu/套餐 $ 428
Dinner/晚膳　menu/套餐 $ 986-1,180
　　　　　　carte/點菜 $ 850-1,200

Pierre

🖐 16 🍴

Stylish restaurant, opened by celebrated French chef Pierre Gagnaire, with a rarefied air to match the Mandarin Oriental's highest floor. Picture windows frame large views of the harbour; the room itself has a contemporary flair, much like the menus on offer, which are complex but sober; the ambience is enhanced with soft lighting. High quality produce comes directly from France: Bigorre pork, Aubrac beef, Allaiton lamb, Bresse chicken.

由著名法國廚師Pierre Gagnaire開辦的時尚餐廳，位處文華東方頂層，居高臨下，氣勢不凡。透過窗戶可盡覽外面的大海景，餐廳本身散發著當代的氣息，就像這裡的菜單一樣，既複雜又沉實；加上柔和的燈光，氣氛十足。高質產品直接由法國進口：Bigorre省份的豬肉、Aubrac省份的牛肉、Allaiton省份的羊肉、Bresse省份的雞肉等等。

■ ADDRESS/地址
TEL.2825 4001
25F, Mandarin Oriental Hotel, 5 Connaught Road, Central
中環干諾道中5號文華東方酒店25樓
www.mandarinoriental.com

■ ANNUAL AND WEEKLY CLOSING
  休息日期
Closed Saturday lunch, Sunday and Public Holidays
週六午膳、週日及公眾假期休息

■ OPENING HOURS, LAST ORDER
  營業時間, 最後點菜時間
Lunch/午膳 12:00-14:30 (L.O.)
Dinner/晚膳 19:00-22:30 (L.O.)

■ PRICE/價錢
Lunch/午膳   carte/點菜 $ 450-1,000
Dinner/晚膳   menu/套餐 $ 1,888
              carte/點菜 $ 660-1,400

Prince
王子飯店

🏷 XXX

♿ ⟨ ☞ 🚗48 ☎🍴

The artistically presented cuisine in Prince goes nicely with the elegant surroundings – One Peking is a smart building, and views from the 11th floor to the harbour are equally impressive. The self-proclaimed 'Imperial cuisine' is in fact a modern approach to Chinese food with specialities like braised grouper with ginger and spring onion, or dry braised shark fin soup with crab meat. Stylish service complements a smoothly comfortable ambience.

王子飯店環境優雅，與其雅緻的菜餚一脈相承。北京道一號是一幢時尚的建築物，從11樓看出去的海景同樣令人印象深刻。餐廳稱為「御膳」的其實是現代中國菜，包括砂鍋干迫海斑和生拆蟹 扒乾燒鮑翅。時尚的服務與舒適的氣氛配合得天衣無縫。

■ ADDRESS/地址
TEL.2366 1308
11F, One Peking, Tsim Sha Tsui, Kowloon
九龍尖沙咀北京道1號11樓
www.prince-catering.com

■ OPENING HOURS, LAST ORDER
營業時間, 最後點菜時間
Lunch/午膳　11:00-16:30 L.O. 16:00
Dinner/晚膳　18:00-24:00 L.O. 23:00

■ PRICE/價錢
Lunch/午膳　menu/套餐 $ 138-398
　　　　　　carte/點菜 $ 200-2,000
Dinner/晚膳　menu/套餐 $ 480-1,380
　　　　　　carte/點菜 $ 600-2,000

Regal Palace
富豪金殿

This elegant and imposing restaurant is on the third floor of the Regal Hotel and provides a sophisticated backdrop for fine cookery that mixes new culinary concepts with established traditions: no wonder the menu is labelled as "Innovation meets Nostalgia". The basis for many of the dishes is Cantonese but this has been overlaid with finely judged imagination and sharp technique to create a very contemporary dining experience.

位於富豪酒店三樓的富豪金殿裝潢瑰麗，精雕細琢的烹調手法獨具特色，融合最新餐飲概念和多年傳統；難怪餐牌題名為「創新中的懷舊」。不少菜式都以粵菜為基調，配合無窮創意，經過精心考慮和高巧技法渾成時尚的餐飲體驗。

■ ADDRESS/地址
TEL.2837 1773
3F, Regal Hotel, 88 Yee Wo Street, Causeway Bay
銅鑼灣怡和街88號富豪酒店3樓
www.regalhotel.com

■ OPENING HOURS, LAST ORDER
營業時間, 最後點菜時間
Lunch/午膳 12:00-14:30 (L.O.)
Dinner/晚膳 18:30-23:00 (L.O.)

■ PRICE/價錢
Lunch/午膳   menu/套餐 $ 144-390
                carte/點菜 $ 250-420
Dinner/晚膳   menu/套餐 $ 144-390
                carte/點菜 $ 250-420

Rei Sushi
礼鮨

As you leave the shopping opportunities behind and crouch down under a traditional white banner to enter, the team offer up an equally traditional welcoming chant. Sit at the sushi counter and watch the deft preparation of classic dishes in the sleek, minimal surroundings. The service is unfailingly polite as you get served sushi and sashimi set lunches with more stewed and deep-fried preparations in the evenings.

當您暫停購物，經過傳統的白色簾子進入餐廳的時候，服務員便即時送上傳統的日本歡迎語。坐在壽司檯可看到師傅巧手製作經典菜式，與雅致簡單的環境相映成趣。服務員非常有禮，餐廳提供壽司及刺身午市套餐，而晚市則有較多煮和炸的菜式。

■ ADDRESS/地址
TEL.3188 1900
Shop 1103, Podium 1, IFC Mall, 8 Finance Street, Central
中環金融街8號國際金融中心商場第2期1樓1103號舖

■ OPENING HOURS, LAST ORDER
營業時間, 最後點菜時間
Lunch/午膳 11:30-15:00 (L.O.)
Dinner/晚膳 18:00-22:00 (L.O.)

■ PRICE/價錢
Lunch/午膳　menu/套餐 $ 168-298
Dinner/晚膳　carte/點菜 $ 300-500

Rice Paper

X

⊞10

Take the escalators up to the 4th floor of this large commer-
cial centre and you'll find a charmingly straightforward room
simply furnished in a modern style and staffed by a friendly
Vietnamese team. The cooking here is light and fragrant;
try the rice papers accompanied by different fillings or the
barbecued beef with lemongrass and basil. There's a good
choice of vegetarian plates as well as salads and curries.

餐廳座落於大型商業中心的四樓，設計時尚簡單，魅力非凡。越南裔侍應服務
親切，而菜式既清淡又香味洋溢，推介不同餡料的米紙卷或香茅烤牛肉。此
外，餐廳亦有提供不俗的素食菜式、沙律及咖喱。

■ ADDRESS/地址
TEL.2890 3975
Shop 413-8, 4F, World Trade Centre,
280 Gloucester Road, Causeway Bay
銅鑼灣告士打道280號世貿中心商場4樓
413-418號舖

■ OPENING HOURS, LAST ORDER
營業時間，最後點菜時間
11:00-23:00 (L.O.)
■ PRICE/價錢
Lunch/午膳   carte/點菜 $ 250-350
Dinner/晚膳 carte/點菜 $ 250-350

Robatayaki
炉端燒

Walking in from the main hotel lobby, you're confronted by horse-shoe shaped counters as well as an extensive range of seasonal ingredients. The concept here is a Japanese barbecue where food is selected and then cooked directly at the counter by a team of chefs. Otherwise, the installation is rustic with wood panels and beamed ceiling. Weekend lunchtimes are host to the all-you-can-eat "Sumo's Choice" that includes sashimi, sushi and tempura.

從酒店大堂進入餐廳,你會看到馬蹄形的櫃檯和形形色色的時令食材。這是一家爐端燒餐廳,食客可自選食材,然後廚師會直接在櫃檯進行烹調。裝潢方面,簡樸的餐廳設有木質壁板和架樑天花板。週末供應的相撲手任食午餐大受歡迎,包括刺身、壽司和天婦羅。

■ ADDRESS/地址

TEL.2996 8438

GF, Harbour Plaza Hotel, 20 Tak Fung Street, Whampoa Garden, Hung Hom, Kowloon
九龍紅磡黃埔花園德豐街20號海逸酒店地下
www.harbour-plaza.com/hphk

■ OPENING HOURS, LAST ORDER
營業時間, 最後點菜時間
Lunch/午膳 12:00-14:00 (L.O.)
Dinner/晚膳 18:00-22:30 (L.O.)

■ PRICE/價錢
Lunch/午膳   menu/套餐 $ 300
              carte/點菜 $ 200-600
Dinner/晚膳   carte/點菜 $ 200-600

Ruth's Chris Steak House (Admiralty)

XX X

🍽16 🚋 🐝

A mahogany-coloured dining room and Country & Western music lend atmosphere to this efficient grill operation which specialises in importing all its American prime and Australian grain-fed beef cuts. Start your meal with a salad or seafood cocktail and round things off with bread pudding and whisky sauce which, along with many of the other 'specials' is based on a traditional New Orleans recipe.

這家扒房餐廳擁有赤褐色的餐室，背景播放著西部鄉村音樂，甚具特色。侍應服務效率高，而美國頂級牛肉和澳洲穀飼牛肉均是新鮮入口。頭盤可選沙律或海鮮雞尾杯，而甜品則推介麵包布甸佐威士忌汁，與其他「特色美食」都是以新奧爾良傳統風味炮製而成。

■ ADDRESS/地址

TEL.2522 9090

GF, Lippo Centre, 89 Queensway, Admiralty

香港金鐘道89號力寶中心地下

www.hasmoreltd.com

■ ANNUAL AND WEEKLY CLOSING
  休息日期

Closed Lunar New Year

年初一休息

■ OPENING HOURS, LAST ORDER
  營業時間, 最後點菜時間

Lunch/午膳 12:00-14:45 (L.O.)

Dinner/晚膳 17:30-23:00 (L.O.)

■ PRICE/價錢

Lunch/午膳　menu/套餐 $ 180-390
　　　　　　carte/點菜 $ 420-800

Dinner/晚膳　menu/套餐 $ 650-950
　　　　　　carte/點菜 $ 420-800

Sabatini

XX X

☞📍 ▭ 20 ☎🍴

The original Sabatini is in Rome, so this version enjoys a fine pedigree and ticks all the right boxes. A comfy lounge bar sets you up nicely before your meal. The main dining room is large with a real trattoria décor comprising a wooden beam ceiling, a shiny floor made with old tiles, rustic furniture and yellow walls embellished with Italian style frescoes. The menu runs the gamut from antipasti to soup, pasta, fish, meat and dessert trolley.

首家Sabatini始創於羅馬,可見帝苑酒店的Sabatini來頭不小,美食正宗,佳釀一流。舒適的雅座酒吧是享用正餐的完美前奏。主餐室地方寬敞,天花由木橫樑組成,光滑的地板以舊磚鋪成,黃色牆壁掛著意式壁畫,加上質樸的傢具,構成真正的意大利餐廳格局。餐廳的菜單非常全面,涵蓋各種意式前菜、湯類、意大利麵食、魚類、肉類,以至甜品車。

■ ADDRESS/地址
TEL.2733 2000
3F, The Royal Garden Hotel, 69 Mody Road, Tsim Sha Tsui East, Kowloon
九龍尖沙咀東部麼地道69號帝苑酒店3樓
www.rghk.com.hk

■ OPENING HOURS, LAST ORDER
營業時間,最後點菜時間
Lunch/午膳 12:00-14:30 (L.O.)
Dinner/晚膳 18:00-23:00 (L.O.)

■ PRICE/價錢
Lunch/午膳　menu/套餐 $ 238-298
　　　　　　carte/點菜 $ 600-900
Dinner/晚膳　menu/套餐 $ 980
　　　　　　carte/點菜 $ 600-900

Sagano
嵯峨野

✕✕ ✕✕

🔑 ⛽12 🚃 ☎️🍴

Essential to understanding this restaurant is the Japanese former-imperial city of Kyoto: this is named after one of its suburbs, the chef hails from there as do some of the dishes on the menu. The installation is sober, the tatami rooms are delightful and the waitresses are elegantly dressed in kimonos. At lunchtime, set menus and bento boxes are the order of the day, whilst at night, kaiseki (tasting menus) rely heavily on seasonal ingredients.

假如你熟悉日本京都，你便不會對餐廳的名稱感到陌生—嵯峨野是京都的一個郊區，餐廳主廚和一些菜式均來自那裡。嵯峨野的裝潢沉實，榻榻米房間十分雅致舒適，而服務員更穿著和服，舉止優雅。午市套餐和便當盒大受歡迎，而晚市的懷石料理(品嚐餐單)則主要採用時令食材。

■ ADDRESS/地址
TEL.2313 4215
1F, Nikko Hotel, 72 Mody Road, Tsim Sha Tsui East, Kowloon
九龍尖沙咀東部麼地道72號日航酒店1樓
www.hotelnikko.com.hk

■ OPENING HOURS, LAST ORDER
營業時間, 最後點菜時間
Lunch/午膳 12:00-14:30 (L.O.)
Dinner/晚膳 18:00-22:30 (L.O.)

■ PRICE/價錢
Lunch/午膳   menu/套餐 $ 200-380
              carte/點菜 $ 300-900
Dinner/晚膳   menu/套餐 $ 500-980
              carte/點菜 $ 300-900

Senzuru
千鶴

This simple and straightforward restaurant focuses tightly on two styles of Japanese preparation: teppanyaki and sushi/sashimi. The first style has two counters where you can watch fish or meat being cooked directly in front of you. The second, smaller one is dedicated purely to the deft slicing of raw fish, much of which arrives daily from Japan. There's a list of over 40 different sakes to accompany the food.

這家簡樸的餐廳主力供應兩種日本菜式：天婦羅和壽司/刺身。前者設有兩張櫃檯，可面對面看廚師直接烹調魚或肉類菜式；後者則可看到廚師巧手將魚生切片，而大部分魚生均是從日本每天新鮮運抵。此外，餐廳亦供應超過40種不同的燒酒佐膳。

■ ADDRESS/地址

TEL.3160 6898
8F, Harbour Plaza Metropolis Hotel, 7 Metropolis Drive, Hunghom, Kowloon
九龍紅磡都會道7號都會海逸酒店8樓
http://fnb.hpme.harbour-plaza.com

■ OPENING HOURS, LAST ORDER
營業時間, 最後點菜時間
Lunch/午膳 12:00-15:00 (L.O.)
Dinner/晚膳 18:00-23:00 (L.O.)

■ PRICE/價錢
Lunch/午膳   menu/套餐 $ 420-480
            carte/點菜 $ 220-800
Dinner/晚膳 menu/套餐 $ 420-480
            carte/點菜 $ 220-800

Sevva

The talk of Hong Kong's dining set, this fashionable destination only opened its doors in 2008. The whole concept is sleek and sassy, comprising a U-shaped terrace with great views, mouth-watering cake shop, slinky cocktail bar, corridors part-covered in grass, and two distinct restaurants: the purple-painted Bank side and the sunny yellow Harbour side. Only average element here is the simple, rather unsurprising international cuisine.

談到香港的餐飲業，不得不提這家剛於2008年正式開幕的時尚餐廳。整個概念是豪華精緻的，包括一個坐擁美麗景觀的U形露台、令人垂涎欲滴的餅店、閃爍的雞尾酒吧、部分用草鋪設的走廊，以及兩間截然不同的餐廳：漆上紫色的Bank Side及陽光生輝的Harbour Side。這裡的國際菜肴則較爲簡單，頗無驚喜。

■ ADDRESS/地址

TEL.2537 1388

25F, Prince's Building, 10 Chater Road, Central

中環遮打道10號太子大廈25樓

www.sevvahk.com

■ ANNUAL AND WEEKLY CLOSING
　　休息日期
Closed Sunday
週日休息

■ OPENING HOURS, LAST ORDER
　　營業時間, 最後點菜時間
12:00-24:00 (L.O.)

■ PRICE/價錢
Lunch/午膳　carte/點菜 $ 410-1,300
Dinner/晚膳　carte/點菜 $ 410-1,300

Shang Palace
香宮

✿ ✿   ✗✗✗

☞♟ 💺12 ☎🍽

Two golden statues by the entrance welcome you to this sumptuous room that vividly evokes the grandeur of the Sung Dynasty. Red lacquered walls, antique paintings and classic lanterns only add to the authentic atmosphere. The same care has been lavished on the Cantonese menu which includes well chosen vegetarian items. The cooking here is finely judged and the speciality Shang Palace three-layer basket includes abalone, scallops and aubergine.

大門的兩個金色塑像歡迎你來到這家豪華的餐廳，宋朝的顯赫氣派活靈活現。紅色漆牆、古董國畫，以及傳統燈籠交織出古色古香的氣氛。這裡的粵菜亦同樣精巧，更提供不錯的素食菜式。烹調技巧出色，特色美色包括三元及第：金龍鮑、帶子及蒸茄子。

■ ADDRESS/地址
TEL.2733 8754
Lower level, Kowloon Shangri-La Hotel,
64 Mody Road, Kowloon
九龍尖沙咀麼地道64號九龍香格里拉酒店
地庫1樓
www.shangri-la.com

■ OPENING HOURS, LAST ORDER
  營業時間，最後點菜時間
Lunch/午膳 12:00-15:00 (L.O.)
Dinner/晚膳 18:00-23:00 (L.O.)

■ PRICE/價錢
Lunch/午膳   menu/套餐 $ 228-1,860
             carte/點菜 $ 220-800
Dinner/晚膳 menu/套餐 $ 590-1,860
             carte/點菜 $ 220-800

Shanghai Garden
紫玉蘭

✿   ✗✗✗

                                               ♿ 🛏6

Dining at Shanghai Garden is something special, courtesy of fine table arrangements, spotlessly attired staff unerringly eager to please, and wonderfully delicate Huai Yang and Shanghainese cuisine. Dishes arrive bursting with freshness and vibrancy; sourcing seasonal produce is paramount here. Braised mandarin fish and fresh water shrimps are typical of the superb seafood, while steamed hairy crabs in the autumn are a renowned signature dish.

在紫玉蘭用餐感覺有些特別。餐廳的餐桌編排妥善，衣著整潔的服務員提供熱誠的服務，淮陽和上海菜亦十分精細。由於餐廳著重採購季節性的產物，故此奉上的菜餚可以做到既新鮮又夠火候。典型的上等海鮮包括炆桂魚和淡水蝦，而秋天的清蒸大閘蟹是著名的招牌菜。

■ ADDRESS/地址
TEL.2524 8181
1F, Hutchison House, 10 Harcourt Road, Central
中環夏愨道10號和記大廈1樓

■ OPENING HOURS, LAST ORDER
營業時間, 最後點菜時間
Lunch/午膳 11:30-15:00 (L.O.)
Dinner/晚膳 18:00-23:30 (L.O.)

■ PRICE/價錢
Lunch/午膳　carte/點菜 $ 180-200
Dinner/晚膳　carte/點菜 $ 200-400

Shui Hu Ju
水滸居

✕✕

⏱30 ☎🍴

Arriving at this discreet location has been likened to the journey undertaken to reach the mystical mountain from where this establishment takes its name. Pushing open the heavy wooden doors reveals a set of carefully recreated interiors of old China with a limited number of seats. The cuisine is a combination of Sichuan and Northern Chinese cooking resulting in a number of quite fiery dishes. Braised meats are a speciality.

踏進這別出心裁的世外之地，有如登上水滸傳的傳奇梁山。推開一道道厚重木門後，舉目盡是古色古香的精心裝潢。座位數目不多，菜式方面融合了川菜和北方風味，口味頗為辛辣。燜肉尤其馳名。

■ ADDRESS/地址
TEL.2869 6927
68 Peel Street, Soho, Central
中環卑利街68號
www.aqua.com.hk

■ OPENING HOURS, LAST ORDER
營業時間, 最後點菜時間
Dinner/晚膳 18:00-24:00 (L.O.)

■ PRICE/價錢
Dinner/晚膳 carte/點菜 $ 300-500

Spasso

Right on Ocean Centre's top floor, this has great views, particularly from the outdoor terrace. The interior is stylish with both the wine cellar and pizza oven fully open to view. Many artisanal products are specially imported from Italy for use in such signature dishes as spaghetti with fresh sardines, pine nuts and tomato and lamb chops with sausage and Norcia black truffles. The excellent wine list includes well over 50 choices by the glass.

座落於海洋中心頂樓，Spasso坐擁壯麗景觀，露天雅座的景色特別迷人。餐廳設計時尚，設有開放式的酒櫃和意大利薄餅焗爐，食客可直擊製作過程。店內很多工藝品特地由意大利入口，用以奉上招牌菜，包括蕃茄松子鮮沙甸意粉、肉腸羊扒配諾爾察黑松露菌。餐廳更提供超過50種上等葡萄酒。

■ ADDRESS/地址

TEL.2730 8027
Shop 403, 4F, Ocean Centre, Harbour City, 17 Canton Road, Kowloon
九龍尖沙咀廣東道17號海港城海洋中心4樓403號舖
www.spassoristorante-bar.com.hk

■ OPENING HOURS, LAST ORDER
營業時間, 最後點菜時間
Lunch/午膳 12:00-15:30 L.O. 15:00
Dinner/晚膳 18:00-23:30 L.O. 23:00

■ PRICE/價錢
Lunch/午膳   menu/套餐 $ 158-208
             carte/點菜 $ 320-650
Dinner/晚膳 carte/點菜 $ 380-850

Spoon by Alain Ducasse

Great views, stylish seating and a ceiling lined with spoons – characteristics of this fashionable outpost of the Alain Ducasse empire. The cooking is divided into two sections: Original is home to dishes including spit-roast saddle of lamb with honey jus semolina and dried fruits and nuts, whilst the Classic section is just that and features items such as chicken and crayfish with marbled sauce and potato gnocchi with girolles.

優美景觀、時尚雅座、排列著匙羹的天花板一打造成名廚艾倫杜卡斯(Alain Ducasse)美食王國的香港分部，實為潮流時尚之選。菜餚分為兩部分：「原 創」菜式包括燒羊柳伴法式炒中東米，而「經 典」菜式顧名思義，較為典型，特色美食包括雙色醬雞肉小龍蝦併雞油菌薯仔麵團等。

■ ADDRESS/地址
TEL.2313 2323
GF, Intercontinental Hotel, 18 Salisbury Road, Tsim Sha Tsui, Kowloon
九龍尖沙咀梳士巴利道18號洲際酒店地下
www.hongkong-ic.intercontinental.com

■ OPENING HOURS, LAST ORDER
營業時間, 最後點菜時間
Dinner/晚膳 18:00-23:00 (L.O.)

■ PRICE/價錢
Dinner/晚膳　menu/套餐 $ 1,188-1,388
　　　　　　　carte/點菜 $ 580-1,650

Spring Autumn
春秋

XX

⊟12

Hot pots traditionally served during the cooler months are the inspiration for this pleasant, friendly operation in an otherwise bustling part of town. Aquariums with live fish line the room but the main feature is the extensive range of soups (including tomato with oxtail and spicy fish head) that are served with an equally impressive range of sauces and condiments. The tone is largely Cantonese with the addition of Japanese Matsusaka beef.

天氣清涼時，香港人一向愛吃火鍋，餐廳以此命名，座落於繁華的銅鑼灣。春秋火鍋環境舒適，氣氛親切。餐室內排列著一個個盛載游水魚的魚缸，而林林總總的湯底更是一大特色，包括鮮茄牛尾湯焗及麻辣大魚頭焗，醬汁和配料同樣也是種類繁多。食材主要是粵菜，亦有提供日本松阪牛肉。

■ ADDRESS/地址

TEL. 2878 1128
26 Leighton Road, Causeway Bay
銅鑼灣禮頓道26號
www.spring-autumn.net

■ ANNUAL AND WEEKLY CLOSING
　　休息日期
Closed 2 days Lunar New Year
元旦日及年初一休息

■ OPENING HOURS, LAST ORDER
　　營業時間, 最後點菜時間
Lunch/午膳 11:00-15:00 (L.O.)
Dinner/晚膳 17:00-02:00 (L.O.)

■ PRICE/價錢
Lunch/午膳　carte/點菜 $ 200-300
Dinner/晚膳　carte/點菜 $ 200-300

Cantonese/粵菜

Spring Moon
嘉麟樓

An elegant and luxurious Cantonese restaurant very much at home at The Peninsula. You can admire the tropical hardwood or the bamboo flower arrangements while sipping tea at the tea bar. Dine in the restaurant or on the more intimate mezzanine floor. Refined service oversees authentic dishes loaded with flavour. Different soy sauces are proposed to bring out the flavour of specialities, which include shark fin or roasted pigeon with osmanthus.

嘉麟樓位於半島酒店內，是一家優雅豪華的粵菜餐廳，令人感覺舒適。食客可以邊在"茶檔"茗茶，邊欣賞餐廳內的熱帶硬木或竹花排列。你可以選擇在餐廳內或在較隱蔽的私家房內用餐，完善的服務配合味道濃郁的原味菜餚。建議使用不同種類的豉油帶出美食的味道，包括魚翅及桂花燒乳鴿。

■ ADDRESS/地址

TEL.2315 3160

1F, The Peninsula Hotel, Salisbury Road, Kowloon
九龍尖沙咀梳士巴利道半島酒店1樓
www.peninsula.com

■ OPENING HOURS, LAST ORDER
營業時間, 最後點菜時間
Lunch/午膳　11:30-14:30 (L.O.)
Dinner/晚膳　18:00-22:30 (L.O.)

■ PRICE/價錢
Lunch/午膳　menu/套餐 $ 368-448
　　　　　　carte/點菜 $ 200-800
Dinner/晚膳　menu/套餐 $ 888-1,288
　　　　　　carte/點菜 $ 200-800

Sukho Thai
崇都

⚛ ⚛

Get off the Star Ferry, keep walking along the footbridge and you'll reach this colourful Thai restaurant, full of fountains, bas-reliefs, statues and decorations. It all looks very pleasant and harmonious, but be warned: the motto of Sukho Thai is 'spice up your life', and some dishes are heavy on the chilli. Tasty favourites include fresh rice paper roll with vegetables, mango and herbs, and fried noodles with seafood in yellow bean gravy.

乘坐天星小輪下船後，沿著行人天橋一直走，便會找到這家色彩繽紛的泰國餐廳。餐廳有很多噴泉、淺浮雕、雕塑及裝飾，一切看來都很愉快融洽，不過要小心：崇都的格言是「為你的生活加香料」，所以有些菜式裡面放了很多辣椒。最美味的菜式包括芒果香草凍卷，以及崇都海鮮冬陰功喇沙湯河。

■ ADDRESS/地址
TEL.2598 7222
2F, Sun Hung Kai Centre, 30 Harbour Road, Wanchai
灣仔港灣道30號新鴻基中心2樓

■ OPENING HOURS, LAST ORDER
營業時間, 最後點菜時間
Lunch/午膳 12:00-14:30 (L.O.)
Dinner/晚膳 18:00-22:30 (L.O.)

■ PRICE/價錢
Lunch/午膳   carte/點菜 $ 220-320
Dinner/晚膳   carte/點菜 $ 220-320

Summer Palace
夏宮

There's a charming brigade here who provide very attentive, diligent service in this 5th floor room with its crystal chandeliers, traditional Chinese screens and well-placed tables. The Cantonese cooking is to a high standard and uses carefully chosen ingredients prepared without fussiness or overelaboration. To drink, there's a bold selection of wines by the glass, Chinese liquor and exquisite teas.

餐廳位於酒店5樓，裝潢甚見巧思：水晶吊燈、傳統中國屏風，餐桌更是排列得當。侍應服務周到，快捷高效，令人稱心如意。這裡提供一流的粵菜，採用優質食材，並以平實的方式烹調。飲料方面應有盡有，涵蓋各種葡萄酒、中國酒及各式精選茶。

■ ADDRESS/地址
TEL.2820 8553
5F, Island Shangri-La Hotel, Pacific Place, Supreme Court Road, Central
中區法院道太古廣場港島香格里拉大酒店 5樓
www.shangri-la.com

■ OPENING HOURS, LAST ORDER
營業時間, 最後點菜時間
Lunch/午膳 11:30-14:30 (L.O.)
Dinner/晚膳 18:30-22:30 (L.O.)

■ PRICE/價錢
Lunch/午膳 carte/點菜 $ 270-1,100
Dinner/晚膳 carte/點菜 $ 270-1,100

Sushi Kato
加藤壽司

A friendly little eatery that's worth searching out - don't be put off because it's on the first floor of an apartment block. The cosy interior has hand-made wood panelling, and Mr Kato himself is at the sushi bar. Straightforward menus are served at simple tables: sashimi, salads, soups, bento boxes, noodles, and a selection of grilled, fried or steamed favourites. It's good value; all the dishes are fresh, carefully prepared and authentic.

這家親切的小壽司店，位於一幢公寓大樓的一樓，但不要因此而卻步，這店實在值得專程尋找。店裡很舒適，採用了手工製作的木質鑲板，而加藤先生就在壽司吧親自下廚。簡單的餐桌配合簡單的菜單，菜式包括魚生、沙律、湯類、便當、麵食，以及一系列的精選烤物、炸物或蒸物。菜式純正，採用新鮮食材，準備細心，是超值之選。

■ ADDRESS/地址

TEL.2807 3613
Shop 7-9, 1F, 20-36 Wharf Road, North Point
北角和富道20-36號1樓7-9號舖

■ ANNUAL AND WEEKLY CLOSING
　　休息日期
Closed Tuesday
週二休息

■ OPENING HOURS, LAST ORDER
　　營業時間, 最後點菜時間
Lunch/午膳　12:00-14:00 (L.O.)
Dinner/晚膳　18:00-22:00 (L.O.)

■ PRICE/價錢
Lunch/午膳　carte/點菜 $ 350-600
Dinner/晚膳　carte/點菜 $ 350-600

Sushi Kuu
壽司喰

Casual and relaxed, Sushi Kuu is unlike the more formal style Japanese restaurant you might be used to. The bar features an impressive sake list, while the sushi counter's always popular with late-night revellers. You can also eat at quiet tables by the bar, or window booths overlooking busy Wellington Street. There's a good choice of Japanese specialities, including traditional sushi, sashimi, tempura, flavoured miso soup and grilled fish.

Sushi Kuu 洋溢著輕鬆隨意的氣氛，不像那些風格較為正式的日本餐廳。吧檯提供令人驚喜的清酒選擇，而壽司吧則永遠都受夜遊客歡迎。食客亦可以選擇在吧檯附近較靜的餐桌用餐，或是靠窗的雅座，邊吃邊俯瞰繁忙的威靈頓街。這裡有不錯的日本菜選擇，包括傳統壽司、魚生、天婦羅、麵豉湯及烤魚。

■ ADDRESS/地址
TEL.2971 0180
1F, Wellington Place, 2-8 Wellington Street, Central
中環威靈頓街2-8號威靈頓廣場1樓

■ ANNUAL AND WEEKLY CLOSING
　休息日期
Closed Lunar New Year
年初一休息

■ OPENING HOURS, LAST ORDER
　營業時間，最後點菜時間
Lunch/午膳　12:00-15:00 (L.O.)
Dinner/晚膳　18:00-23:00 (L.O.)

■ PRICE/價錢
Lunch/午膳　carte/點菜 $ 200-600
Dinner/晚膳　carte/點菜 $ 200-600

Tai Woo (Causeway Bay)
太湖海鮮城 (銅鑼灣)

In a dense, busy street, this is easy to spot from the series of aquaria displayed on the outside. Inside, the staircase lined with culinary awards leads to some fairly non-descript dining rooms where the freshest of seafood is brought both live and cooked up to a never-ending stream of regulars. The more squeamish amongst you, please take note! Prawns in salted egg yolk and baked lobster with supreme sauce are perennial favourites.

即使在人來人往的繁華街道上，太湖海鮮城亦容易被找到，皆因外面展示著一系列的魚缸。餐廳的樓梯雖然羅列著眾多的美食獎項，但餐室卻略為簡樸。然而這裡的海鮮極其新鮮，大量生猛海鮮以供選購，故此捧場客絡繹不絕，較容易感到煩躁的人，等位時便需特別注意！西施伴霸王及上湯焗龍蝦等菜式長期大受歡迎。

■ ADDRESS/地址
TEL.2893 0822
27 Percival Street, Causeway Bay
銅鑼灣波斯富街27號

■ OPENING HOURS, LAST ORDER
營業時間, 最後點菜時間
10:30-03:00 L.O. 02:15

■ PRICE/價錢
Lunch/午膳   menu/套餐 $ 198-288
              carte/點菜 $ 200-300
Dinner/晚膳 menu/套餐 $ 198-288
              carte/點菜 $ 200-300

Tandoor

A traditional looking Indian restaurant this may be, with its décor resembling a small Indian palace, but the cuisine served casts Tandoor in a special light. Different spices are delicately blended to produce exquisite flavours. Chef's special is lamb chops marinated in ginger and garlic, but his tikka massala and makhani sauces also add a tasty dimension to seafood and chicken. Charming staff and live musicians complete the experience.

這裡也許看似印度小皇宮,擁有傳統印度風格,但餐廳的菜式卻不同凡響。不同的香料巧妙地混合起來,形成細膩的味道。廚師推介包括薑蒜汁羊扒,而 tikka massala 及 makhani 醬亦令海鮮及雞肉的滋味更上一層樓。討人歡喜的服務員和現場的音樂表演,使美食體驗更添姿采。

■ ADDRESS/地址
TEL.2845 2262
1F, Lyndhurst Tower, 1 Lyndhurst Terrace, Central
中環擺花街1號中環大廈1樓
hktandoor.com

■ OPENING HOURS, LAST ORDER
營業時間, 最後點菜時間
Lunch/午膳 12:00-14:30 (L.O.)
Dinner/晚膳 18:00-22:45 (L.O.)

■ PRICE/價錢
Lunch/午膳   menu/套餐 $ 118
             carte/點菜 $ 160-310
Dinner/晚膳 menu/套餐 $ 198
             carte/點菜 $ 160-310

T'ang Court
唐閣

✿ ✿   ✗✗✗✗

♿ ☞ **P** ⬚20 ☎︎🍴

Lavishly furnished on the first floor above the hotel's rather grand lobby, rich silks and contemporary sculptures line the walls; there's also a dramatic staircase leading up to 5 exclusive private dining rooms named after famous Tang Dynasty poets. The cooking demonstrates great finesse with particular emphasis on seafood. This is matched by highly polished and refined service from a very knowledgeable team.

裝潢極盡奢華的唐閣位於酒店一樓，樓下的大堂也不遑多讓，金碧輝煌；牆身鋪滿絲織緞料和當代雕塑，豪華樓梯連接五間私人貴賓房，分別以唐代五位大詩人命名。烹調方式極盡細膩，海鮮尤其出色。此外，管理團隊提供的服務亦非常專業細心。

■ ADDRESS/地址
TEL.2375 1133
1F, The Langham Hotel, 8 Peking Road,
Tsim Sha Tsui, Kowloon
九龍尖沙咀北京道8號朗廷酒店1樓
www.hongkong.langhamhotels.com

■ OPENING HOURS, LAST ORDER
營業時間, 最後點菜時間
Lunch/午膳 12:00-15:00 L.O. 14:30
Dinner/晚膳 18:00-23:00 L.O. 22:30

■ PRICE/價錢
Lunch/午膳   menu/套餐 $ 420
              carte/點菜 $ 300-2,000
Dinner/晚膳   menu/套餐 $ 420
              carte/點菜 $ 500-2,500

Tasty (Happy Valley)
正斗粥麵專家 (跑馬地)

It's worth taking the time to get here, because this is more than the average noodle dining experience. There's a sophisticated air, with polished wood enhancing a feeling of exclusivity. Waitresses wear colourful uniforms, and many customers call them over for the legendary won ton noodles. The range of congee toppings is comprehensive, while chef's special dim sum includes braised goose webs with abalone sauce and pomelo skin with shrimp roe.

這裡值得你花時間走一趟，因為此店有超乎一般的水準。這裡氣氛濃厚，拋光的木飾更添一種獨享感覺。服務員制服色彩繽紛，許多客人被口碑載道的雲吞麵深深吸引。粥的配菜種類很全面，同樣是廚師的點心特別推介包括鮑汁鵝掌及蝦子柚子皮。

■ ADDRESS/地址
TEL.2838 3922
21 King Kwong Street, Happy Valley
跑馬地景光街21號

■ OPENING HOURS, LAST ORDER
營業時間, 最後點菜時間
11:30-24:00 (L.O.)

■ PRICE/價錢
Lunch/午膳 carte/點菜 $ 35-65
Dinner/晚膳 carte/點菜 $ 40-120

Tasty (Hung Hom)
正斗粥麵專家（紅磡）

Shaped like a cruise boat, this outfit is difficult to miss. Inside, everything is kept modest and simple with dark wood walls and Chinese decorations. You can't reserve here and it's often so busy you're forced to queue. But it's worth it for the quality of the noodles, soup, congee and dim sum. Try dishes like salted lean pork and preserved egg congee or stir-fried rice noodle with beef. You won't be disappointed: you won't pay a lot either!

商場外觀像一艘遊船，十分搶眼。正斗內部裝潢簡樸，擁有深色木牆和中式裝飾品。這裡食客眾多，但沒有訂座服務，因此經常需要排隊輪候。不過，這裡的麵、湯、粥和點心都是優質美食，實在值得排隊等候。推介菜式包括皮蛋瘦肉粥或乾炒牛河。此外，這裡的菜式價錢相宜，絕對不會令你失望！

■ ADDRESS/地址
TEL.3152 2328
Shop 111, 1F, Whampoa Plaza, Site 8, Hung Hom, Kowloon
九龍紅磡黃埔花園第8期1樓111號舖

■ OPENING HOURS, LAST ORDER
營業時間，最後點菜時間
11:30-23:30 (L.O.)

■ PRICE/價錢
Lunch/午膳　carte/點菜 $ 75-150
Dinner/晚膳　carte/點菜 $ 75-150

Tasty (IFC)
正斗粥麵專家 (國際金融中心)

Sleek mall surroundings enhance Tasty's strikingly elaborate façade of ornate wood and coloured glass. Inside it's just as vivid: walls covered with 30,000 chopsticks, handmade chairs with intricate floral patterns, and eye-catching metal pots. You'll probably be asked to share a table before tucking into the hallmark shrimp won ton or the much-loved beef and rice noodle stir fry. Also recommended from the vast choice is congee with prawns.

豪華的商場環境突顯了正斗的木飾和彩色玻璃外觀。餐廳裡同樣有生氣：牆壁佈滿一萬五千雙筷子，手工椅子上有複雜精細的花卉圖案，還有引人注目的金屬壺。你可能需與人搭枱，不過能享用美食便值回票價。熱門菜包括招牌鮮蝦雲吞麵，或備受喜愛的干炒牛河。此外，在芸芸選擇中，我們特別推介生猛大蝦粥。

■ ADDRESS/地址

TEL.2295 0101
Shop 3016, Podium 3F, IFC Mall, 1 Harbour View Street, Central
中環港景街1號國際金融中心商場第2期3樓3016號舖

■ OPENING HOURS, LAST ORDER
營業時間, 最後點菜時間
11:30-23:00 (L.O.)

■ PRICE/價錢
Lunch/午膳   carte/點菜 $ 75-150
Dinner/晚膳   carte/點菜 $ 75-150

The Bostonian
美岸海鮮廳

This basement location has been livened up with bright red walls and modern Chinese artwork. It's an omnivore's delight serving up a quintessentially classic Grill menu of American Angus, Australian Grain Fed and Japanese Wagyu beef cuts plus Boston lobster and seafood cocktail. Here, portions are generous, the wine list is sizeable and the service is friendly. On Sundays, there's an extensive buffet lunch.

美岸海鮮廳位於酒店低層大堂，亮紅色的牆身配合現代中國藝術品，帶來無窮生氣。素肉兼食的人士肯定會對這裡的餐單動心：傳統美式安格斯烤肉、澳洲穀飼牛及日本和牛切塊，配上波士頓龍蝦及海鮮大會，且食物份量可觀，並備有多種餐酒可供選擇，服務親切。星期日特設自助午餐。

■ ADDRESS/地址
TEL.2375 1133
GF, The Langham Hotel, 8 Peking Road, Tsim Sha Tsui, Kowloon
九龍尖沙咀北京道8號朗廷酒店地下
www.hongkong.langhamhotels.com

■ OPENING HOURS, LAST ORDER
營業時間, 最後點菜時間
Lunch/午膳 12:00-15:00 L.O. 14:30
Dinner/晚膳 18:30-22:30 L.O. 22:00

■ PRICE/價錢
Lunch/午膳   menu/套餐 $ 268
             carte/點菜 $ 268-1,000
Dinner/晚膳 carte/點菜 $ 600-1,500

The Folks
樂意居

XX X

⊞ 10

This quite compact and discreetly-located dining room offers a comfortable and intimate setting in which to enjoy solidly traditional Cantonese cuisine. Dishes from the long menu such as smoked chicken with tea leaves, crab soup, roast suckling pig and stir-fried pigeon with Chinese ham are diligently prepared by the experienced chef and his brigade. The smiling team of waitresses provide attentive, pleasant service.

餐廳位置不太顯眼，地方小巧，環境舒適親切。這裡提供非常傳統的粵菜，菜式選擇繁多，包括煙燻雞、蟹肉粟米湯、大紅片皮乳豬，以及燒雲腿炒鴿甫。廚師經驗豐富，烹調認真。服務態度親切友善，細心周到。

■ ADDRESS/地址
TEL.2186 6383
22F, Coda Plaza, 51 Garden Road, Central
中環花園街51號科達中心22樓

■ ANNUAL AND WEEKLY CLOSING
　　休息日期
Closed 3 days Lunar New Year
農曆新年休息3天

■ OPENING HOURS, LAST ORDER
　　營業時間, 最後點菜時間
Lunch/午膳 11:30-16:00 (L.O.)
Dinner/晚膳 18:00-22:00 (L.O.)

■ PRICE/價錢
Lunch/午膳　carte/點菜 $ 370-1,300
Dinner/晚膳　carte/點菜 $ 370-1,300

The Golden Leaf
金葉庭

✿   ✕✕✕

👉 🍴12

This extremely popular destination is not best served by its basement location but, once inside, the place is buzzing. The L-shaped room is rather austere and broken up occasionally by some traditional wall panels. It's the food everyone comes for with its emphasis on barbecued meats and live fish. As well as an intricate long list of chef's recommendations, there's also an extensive dim sum lunchtime menu which makes it advisable to book.

這家餐廳雖然位於地庫,不過大受歡迎,總是食客滿座。餐室呈L形,頗為簡樸,有時更會以一些傳統的屏風分隔成不同的用餐區。吸引食客紛紛到訪的是其美食,特別是燒味和游水魚。此外,廚師推介亦涵蓋多款菜式,午市時段的點心更應有盡有,建議預先訂座。

■ ADDRESS/地址
TEL.2521 3838
Lower Level Conrad Hotel, Pacific Place, 88 Queensway, Admiralty
香港金鐘道88號太古廣場港麗酒店大堂低座

■ OPENING HOURS, LAST ORDER
營業時間,最後點菜時間
Lunch/午膳 11:30-15:00 (L.O.)
Dinner/晚膳 18:00-23:00 (L.O.)

■ PRICE/價錢
Lunch/午膳   menu/套餐 $ 368-500
            carte/點菜 $ 400-550
Dinner/晚膳 menu/套餐 $ 368-500
            carte/點菜 $ 400-550

The Mistral
海風餐廳

XX

  ♿ 👉🏻 🅿 🛋20

The menu states that this is a voyage round the flavours and colours of Italy – and it's spot on by featuring many enduring dishes from gnocchi ai funghi trifolati to ossobuco alla Milanese. Apart from American Angus and Wagyu beef, most ingredients arrive directly from Italy and are used to authentic effect. The rustic interior with its open kitchen adds to the atmosphere of this typical Italian trattoria.

意大利各地包羅萬有的色香味全在菜單裡。鎮店之寶包括雜菌意大利貝殼粉 (gnocchi ai funghi trifolati)及米蘭式燴牛仔膝(ossobuco alla Milanese)等等。除了美國安格斯牛及和牛，大部分食材均由意大利直接運抵，原汁原味。樸素的內部裝潢和開放式廚房，營造經典意大利餐館的氣氛。

■ ADDRESS/地址
TEL.2731 2870
B2F Intercontinental Grand Stanford Hotel, 70 Mody Road, Tsim Sha Tsui, Kowloon
九龍尖沙咀麼地道70號海景嘉福酒店地庫2樓
www.hongkong.intercontinental.com

■ OPENING HOURS, LAST ORDER
營業時間，最後點菜時間
Lunch/午膳 11:30-14:30 (L.O.)
Dinner/晚膳 18:30-21:30 (L.O.)

■ PRICE/價錢
Lunch/午膳   menu/套餐 $ 228-628
              carte/點菜 $ 530-810
Dinner/晚膳 menu/套餐 $ 628
              carte/點菜 $ 530-810

The Royal Garden
帝苑軒

Cross a small bridge in the basement to get to this sleek, panelled restaurant, which, on closer inspection, is modelled on a Chinese official's formal water garden of yesteryear. Home-cooked, seasonal Cantonese cuisine and daily fresh seafood are served here, with lunchtime dim sum a big favourite. Specials include pig's lung soup with assorted meat, pak choy and almond juice, or steamed red crab with 'Hua Teow' wine.

在地庫層橫過一道小橋,便可到達這家雅致的中式餐廳。餐廳牆上嵌著飾板,仔細一看,原來餐廳是摹仿昔日中國古色的園林而設計。這裡的四季風味粵菜全是自家烹調,天天採用新鮮的海鮮,而午餐點心更是一大熱門。特色美食包括杏汁白菜膽燉豬肺湯、雞油花雕蒸大紅花蟹等。

■ ADDRESS/地址
TEL.2724 2666
B2F, The Royal Garden Hotel, 69 Mody Road, Tsim Sha Tsui, Kowloon
九龍尖沙咀東部麼地道69號帝苑酒店地庫2樓
www.rghk.com.hk

■ OPENING HOURS, LAST ORDER
營業時間, 最後點菜時間
Lunch/午膳 11:30-14:30 (L.O.)
Dinner/晚膳 18:00-22:30 (L.O.)

■ PRICE/價錢
Lunch/午膳　carte/點菜 $ 170-1,000
Dinner/晚膳　carte/點菜 $ 170-1,000

The Square
翠玉軒

The welcome here from a very professional team is charming. The dining room is extremely elegant with a number of display cabinets dotted around, filled with pieces of porcelain; there are also views out onto a series of Fung Shui trees planted out in the Rotunda. The menu offers a very diligently prepared selection of Cantonese dishes including such specialities as braised white fairy mushrooms and wok-seared beef and onion ring.

翠玉軒的侍應非常專業，服務令人賓至如歸。餐室極盡高貴，四處都設有裝飾櫃，放滿各式各樣的瓷器；圓形大廳種著一列樹木，其風水格局引人入勝。餐廳的粵菜菜式烹調甚見巧思，美食包括蠔汁百靈菇皇扒翡翠及皇室貴族牛柳。

■ ADDRESS/地址

TEL.2525 1163
4F, Exchange Square II, Central
中環交易廣場第2座4樓

■ OPENING HOURS, LAST ORDER
　營業時間, 最後點菜時間
Lunch/午膳 11:00-15:00 (L.O.)
Dinner/晚膳 18:00-23:00 (L.O.)

■ PRICE/價錢
Lunch/午膳　menu/套餐 $ 218-298
　　　　　　carte/點菜 $ 160-750
Dinner/晚膳　menu/套餐 $ 868
　　　　　　carte/點菜 $ 160-750

The Steak House

Possibly one of the most sophisticated grill rooms in town, this area has its own dramatic wine bar with a spectacular wine list – particularly the selection of reds! Service is both professional and friendly and the products used here are top quality. Beef sourced from Australia, the U.S., Japan and Argentina is supplemented by seafood and simple desserts. The cooking is sensibly straightforward.

The Steak House可能是城中功力最到家的扒房之一，更擁有一流的酒吧，提供獨特的葡萄酒，而對紅酒的選擇尤其出色！服務專業友善，美酒佳餚全屬優質。牛肉由澳洲、美國、日本和阿根廷入口，亦有提供海鮮和簡單的甜品。菜式毫不花巧，簡單直接。..

■ ADDRESS/地址
TEL.2313 2323
LF, Intercontinental Hotel, 18 Salisbury Road, Tsim Sha Tsui, Kowloon
九龍尖沙咀梳士巴利道18號洲際酒店地庫1樓

■ OPENING HOURS, LAST ORDER
營業時間, 最後點菜時間
Dinner/晚膳 18:00-23:00 (L.O.)

■ PRICE/價錢
Dinner/晚膳 carte/點菜 $ 540-2,500

Tim's Kitchen
桃花源小廚

✿

✕

☎️🍴

No doubt about it...this is a hidden gem. Don't be put off by the fact it's in a somewhat shabby spot, and has only six tables, plastic seats and no wine. Sweet, endearing service soon wins you round, but it's the exquisite Cantonese cooking that's the real eye-opener – owner Tim has remarkable respect for his ingredients. Confidence in sourcing the best produce is paramount: witness the crystal king prawn, braised crab claw or divine almond soup.

毫無疑問，這是顆隱蔽的寶石。餐廳位於一條頗為簡陋的街，裡面只有六張餐桌，座椅更是塑膠造的，也沒有提供酒類飲料。但不要因此而卻步，親切友善的服務很快便可贏得你的歡心。真正令人大開眼界的是這裡別緻的粵菜。東主黎先生對食材的要求十分嚴謹，採購最佳食材的信心十分重要。嚐嚐這裡的玻璃蝦王、冬瓜蟹鉗或一流的杏仁茶。

■ ADDRESS/地址
TEL.2543 5919
93 Jervois Street, Sheung Wan
上環蘇杭街93號

■ ANNUAL AND WEEKLY CLOSING
　休息日期
Closed Sunday and Public Holdays
週日及公眾假期休息

■ OPENING HOURS, LAST ORDER
　營業時間, 最後點菜時間
Lunch/午膳　12:00-15:00 (L.O.)
Dinner/晚膳　18:30-22:30 (L.O.)

■ PRICE/價錢
Lunch/午膳　carte/點菜 $ 75-180
Dinner/晚膳　carte/點菜 $ 400-600

Toh Lee
桃季

❌❌

◁ 👌🏷️ 📺40 📞🍴

This discreetly located room has charm and views aplenty; there are also a series of private dining rooms that are suitable for both business dinners and family gatherings. Many regular customers return here for the unfalteringly high standard of its carefully prepared Cantonese cooking and enjoy such specialities as braised bamboo topped with crab roe and the drunken shrimp flambé.

桃李位置雖然不太起眼，但坐擁廣闊的景致，魅力十足。餐廳設有一系列的私人餐室，適合商務晚餐和家庭聚會。這裡的粤菜絕對高質，烹調技巧精湛，吸引捧場客再三光顧。特色美食包括蟹皇扒竹笙及火焰基圍蝦。

■ ADDRESS/地址
TEL.2313 4225
1F, Nikko Hotel, 72 Mody Road, Tsim Sha Tsui East, Kowloon
九龍尖沙咀東部麼地道72號日航酒店1樓
www.hotelnikko.com.hk

■ OPENING HOURS, LAST ORDER
營業時間, 最後點菜時間
Lunch/午膳 12:00-15:00 (L.O.)
Dinner/晚膳 18:00-23:00 (L.O.)

■ PRICE/價錢
Lunch/午膳   menu/套餐 $ 175-240
              carte/點菜 $ 250-550
Dinner/晚膳 carte/點菜 $ 250-550

Tokoro

Based around the robatayaki concept of the Japanese barbecue, many raw ingredients are on display here for you to select. Once that's done, you take your seat either at a counter or in one of three bird cages which swivel to face either the kitchen or not. Interaction between guests and chefs makes for a lively atmosphere and there's plenty of sake on hand to lubricate things further. There are also elegant private rooms and a tiny sushi bar.

這家以爐端燒為主題的餐廳，用很多原材料展示出來以供食客挑選。選料後食客可隨意選擇座位，既可以坐在櫃檯用餐，亦可選擇三個鳥籠的其中一個，旋轉致面向廚房或背向廚房位置。食客和廚師之間的交流令這裡充滿生氣。餐廳更有提供多種燒酒，並設有典雅的私人餐室和小型壽司吧。

■ ADDRESS/地址
TEL.3552 3330
3F, Langham Place Hotel, 555 Shanghai Street, Mongkok, Kowloon
九龍旺角上海街555號朗豪酒店3樓
www.tokoro.com.hk

■ OPENING HOURS, LAST ORDER
營業時間, 最後點菜時間
Lunch/午膳 12:00-14:30 (L.O.)
Dinner/晚膳 18:30-22:30 (L.O.)

■ PRICE/價錢
Lunch/午膳   menu/套餐 $ 127-217
             carte/點菜 $ 160
Dinner/晚膳   menu/套餐 $ 400-700
               carte/點菜 $ 450

Tott's Talk of the Town

Tucked up on the 34th floor of the Excelsior Hotel building, this has one of the most commanding views in town – something it makes full use of with tables flanking the enormous windows. The menu is a round-up of some of the most popular classic dishes from around the world – all tried and tested. There's a stylish bar lounge and live music every evening. This must be the perfect romantic feel-good location.

餐廳座落於怡東酒店34樓,餐桌鄰靠巨型窗戶,坐擁城中數一數二的壯麗美景。餐單涵蓋世界各地的著名經典菜式,全部經過試食,食物水準有保證。這裡亦設有時尚的酒廊,每晚更有現場音樂表演,是浪漫餐飲體驗的必然之選。

■ ADDRESS/地址
TEL.2894 8888
34F, The Excelsior Hotel, 281 Gloucester Road, Causeway Bay
銅鑼灣告士打道281號怡東酒店34樓
www.excelsiorhongkong.com

■ ANNUAL AND WEEKLY CLOSING
   休息日期
Closed Lunar New Year
年初一休息

■ OPENING HOURS, LAST ORDER
   營業時間, 最後點菜時間
Lunch/午膳 12:00-14:30 (L.O.)
Dinner/晚膳 18:30-23:00 (L.O.)

■ PRICE/價錢
Lunch/午膳 carte/點菜 $ 500-750
Dinner/晚膳 carte/點菜 $ 500-750

Tru

✕

Don't be put off by the immediate surroundings or the less-than-immaculate lift. Take it to the 2nd floor and you'll find somewhere serving largely Thai cuisine with a waft of Vietnamese influences. Inside, all is charming and friendly with an open kitchen that produces genuine, punchy cooking. They're justifiably proud of their pomelo salad with crispy shallots and Thai herbs and the coconut crêpe with crab meat and green papaya salad.

不要因餐廳附近的環境或不太整潔的升降機而失去興趣。乘升降機到2樓，便能享受到帶有越南風味的泰式美食。餐廳洋溢著友善迷人的氣氛，廚師在開放式廚房裡炮製原汁原味的菜式，令人目不暇給。泰式香脆乾蔥柚子沙律、椰汁蟹肉薄餅和鮮製木瓜沙律，皆是叫令廚師自豪的特色美食。

■ ADDRESS/地址
TEL.2525 6700
2F, 15 Lan Kwai Fong, Central
中環蘭桂坊15號2樓
www.diningconcepts.com.hk

■ ANNUAL AND WEEKLY CLOSING
　　休息日期
Closed Sunday lunch
週日午膳休息

■ OPENING HOURS, LAST ORDER
　　營業時間, 最後點菜時間
Lunch/午膳　12:00-15:00 (L.O.)
Dinner/晚膳　18:00-23:00 (L.O.)

■ PRICE/價錢
Lunch/午膳　menu/套餐 $ 118-138
　　　　　　carte/點菜 $ 390-440
Dinner/晚膳　menu/套餐 $ 398
　　　　　　carte/點菜 $ 390-440

Tsim Chai Kee (Connaught Road)
沾仔記 (干諾道)

This newer brother to the Wellington Street branch may be bigger and adapted for a faster market but it's still operated to the same high standard and its bright, funky décor makes it the ideal refuelling stop. The drill is easy: pay first, grab a tray and your choice is cooked to order in the spotless kitchen. The only tricky decision is whether to choose the king prawn wonton noodle, the water crab fish ball noodle, the beef noodle or all three!

這是威靈頓街沾仔記的兄弟舖，地方較大，上菜速度亦較快，更以一貫的高質素營運；加上明亮型格的裝潢，打造成理想的落腳點。點菜程序簡單；先付款，拿托盤，而食物已在潔淨無瑕的廚房準備妥當。唯一令人頭痛的是選擇招牌雲吞麵、鮮鯪魚球麵、鮮牛肉麵，還是三併麵！

■ ADDRESS/地址
TEL.2581 3369
61 Connaught Road, Central
中環干諾道中61號

■ OPENING HOURS, LAST ORDER
　營業時間, 最後點菜時間
08:00-21:00 (L.O.)

■ PRICE/價錢
Lunch/午膳　carte/點菜 $ 16-21
Dinner/晚膳　carte/點菜 $ 16-24

Tsim Chai Kee (Wellington Street)
沾仔記（威靈頓街）

This highly regarded, simple noodle shop may be ten years old but it's still looking good. The charming staff are as bright as their aprons; the popular side booths are quickly snapped up and the regulars know to eat outside peak times when the pace is less frenetic. The attraction is the hand-made fish balls, the generously filled wontons and the fresh beef served with the noodles. It's easy to spot - just look for the lunchtime queues.

享負盛名的沾仔記營運已有十年，裝修簡單，但依然整潔舒適。侍應制服明亮潔淨，服務亦充滿生氣。卡位非常受歡迎，經常滿座；熟客會在非繁忙時間光顧，氣氛則較為輕鬆。著名菜式包括自製的鮮鯪魚球、餡料豐富的招牌雲吞，以及鮮牛肉麵。餐廳容易尋找，午市時段外面大排長龍的那家就是了！

■ ADDRESS/地址
TEL.2850 6471
98 Wellington Street, Central
中環威靈頓街98號

■ OPENING HOURS, LAST ORDER
營業時間, 最後點菜時間
09:00-22:00 (L.O.)

■ PRICE/價錢
Lunch/午膳　carte/點菜 $ 16-21
Dinner/晚膳　carte/點菜 $ 16-24

Tsui Hang Village
翠亨邨

XX XY

🚌10 ☎️🍴

Not a venue for young couples looking for candle-lit romance. Established over 30 years ago, it takes up all the second floor of the New World Tower, and 400 can be crammed in, making it loud and raucous most of the time. Guests are looked after enthusiastically during their meal. There's a wide choice of Cantonese dishes; signature items include torn boneless chicken and wok seared sea bass in soy sauce, enjoyed in a merry, hectic ambience.

這裡不是年輕情侶尋找燭光浪漫的地方。翠亨邨於30多年前創辦，佔新世界大廈2樓全層，可容納400多人，所以大部分時間都喧鬧不已。客人用餐期間，服務員的照顧十分周到。餐廳提供廣泛的粵菜選擇：招牌菜包括翠亨靚一雞、頭抽白鱸魚球，都可在快樂繁忙的氣氛中享用。

■ ADDRESS/地址
TEL.2524 2012
2F, New World Tower, 16-18 Queen's Road, Central
中環皇后大道中16-18號新世界大廈2樓

■ OPENING HOURS, LAST ORDER
營業時間，最後點菜時間
11:00-23:30 (L.O.)

■ PRICE/價錢
Lunch/午膳　menu/套餐 $328
　　　　　　carte/點菜 $580-760
Dinner/晚膳　menu/套餐 $328
　　　　　　carte/點菜 $580-760

Tycoon Hotpot
聚豪軒

This is a very popular Chinese restaurant hidden in a small street behind Times Square. It's compact, comfy and modern, and its attractions include 'induction cooking tables' which allow you to cook yourself soups ranging from seafood, meats and vegetables to pasta, dumplings and noodles. Daisy, the boss, is on hand to give you advice. Meanwhile, specialities from the kitchen include home-made ravioli, sliced green carp and fresh Wagyu beef.

聚豪軒是一間有名的中菜餐廳位於時代廣場背面一條小街，地方不大，但既舒適又現代化。餐桌設有火鍋，讓食客自行烹調喜愛食材，湯底材料的選擇包括海鮮、肉類、菜類、粉麵、餃子等等，店主王小姐隨時準備助你一臂之力。另一方面，廚房美食包括自製雲吞、魷魚片及新鮮和牛。

■ ADDRESS/地址
TEL.2893 1884
20-22 Tang Lung Street, Causeway Bay
銅鑼灣登龍街20-22號
www.hotpot.com.hk

■ OPENING HOURS, LAST ORDER
營業時間, 最後點菜時間
Lunch/午膳 12:00-17:00 (L.O.)
Dinner/晚膳 18:00-23:00 (L.O.)

■ PRICE/價錢
Lunch/午膳 carte/點菜 $ 220-450
Dinner/晚膳 carte/點菜 $ 220-450

Unkai
雲海

Lots of small rooms emanating from a central bamboo provide a characteristic Japanese minimalist setting for Unkai. There's a tatami room for a taste of real Japan, private rooms for intimacy, or rooms where the chefs will prepare teppanyaki in front of your eyes. Not forgetting the ubiquitous sushi bar. Cuisine from the Osaka region is a speciality here, and sake lovers will raise a smile over the fact there are 62 varieties of it on offer!

由中央的竹，延伸至用來間隔小房間的到頂的木條，構成了雲海的日本極潔抽象風格。餐廳包括一個榻榻米房間、較有私隱的私人餐室，以及廚師即席在人前烹調鐵板燒的房間。此外，壽司吧亦無處不在。這裡的特色美食包括大阪菜式，而這裡有62種清酒之多，愛好清酒者真是口福不淺！

■ ADDRESS/地址
TEL.2369 1111
3F, Sheraton Hotel, 20 Nathan Road, Tsim Sha Tsui, Kowloon
九龍尖沙咀彌敦道20號香港喜來登酒店3樓
www.sheraton.com/hongkong

■ OPENING HOURS, LAST ORDER
營業時間, 最後點菜時間
Lunch/午膳 12:00-14:30 (L.O.)
Dinner/晚膳 18:30-22:30 (L.O.)

■ PRICE/價錢
Lunch/午膳   menu/套餐 $ 250-450
              carte/點菜 $ 300-800
Dinner/晚膳   menu/套餐 $ 350-795
              carte/點菜 $ 300-800

Va Bene

XX

⊡24 ☎☓

This smart Italian establishment offers a little corner of Tuscany when you walk into the endlessly long dining room. But the whole of Italy is featured on the menu where the gastronomic highlight is Casoncelli alla Bergamasca e tartufo nero – their signature dish. What marks this out is the constant presence of the long-standing manager and his highly attentive team. Make room for a little Grappa at the end of the meal.

這家時尚的長形意大利餐廳，提供極具情懷的塔斯卡尼美食體驗。不過，食客可在餐牌上找到意大利全國各地的佳餚，招牌菜是 Casoncelli alla Bergamasca e tartufo nero，堪稱其美食之冠。在此工作多年的經理和服務周到的員工，是餐廳另一特別之處。用膳過後，別忘了品嘗一杯格拉巴酒。

■ ADDRESS/地址
TEL.2845 5577
17-22 Lan Kwai Fong, Central
中環蘭桂坊17-22
www.vabeneristorante.com

■ ANNUAL AND WEEKLY CLOSING
　　休息日期
Closed Sunday lunch and Public Holidays
週日午膳及公眾假期休息

■ OPENING HOURS, LAST ORDER
　　營業時間, 最後點菜時間
Lunch/午膳　12:00-14:30 (L.O.)
Dinner/晚膳　18:30-23:30 (L.O.)

■ PRICE/價錢
Lunch/午膳　menu/套餐 $ 198
　　　　　　 carte/點菜 $ 400-500
Dinner/晚膳　carte/點菜 $ 700-900

Wasabisabi
山葵

This über-chic environment manages to blend together Japanese simplicity with something far more futuristic. As you step onto a subtly lit cat-walk passage, you'll find the brash red of the Lipstick Lounge on one side and the cooler tones of the main dining room on the other. Culinary styles too are thrown up in the air and incorporate everything from mustard beef tenderloin bento boxes to Japanese tiramisu. You have been warned!

餐廳裝潢融合了日本簡約風格和未來主義，走在時尚尖端。踏上燈光黯淡的catwalk大道，可見一邊是豔紅色的Lipstick Lounge，而另一邊的主餐室則以較深沉的色調為主。菜式風格實在是各式各樣，芥辣籽汁燒牛柳便當、綠茶芝士餅等，定會使你驚喜萬分！

■ ADDRESS/地址
TEL.2506 0009
Shop 1301, 13F, Food Forum, Times Square, 1 Matheson Street, Causeway Bay
銅鑼灣勿地臣街1號時代廣場食通天13樓1301號舖
www.aqua.com.hk

■ OPENING HOURS, LAST ORDER
營業時間, 最後點菜時間
Lunch/午膳 12:00-15:00 (L.O.)
Dinner/晚膳 18:00-24:00 (L.O.)

■ PRICE/價錢
Lunch/午膳　menu/套餐 $ 168-268
　　　　　　carte/點菜 $ 400-500
Dinner/晚膳　menu/套餐 $ 588
　　　　　　carte/點菜 $ 400-500

Water Margin
梁山泊

A dedicated lift for the Food Forum will whisk you to the 12th Floor and into another world. Some antique medicine chests set the tone as you walk in. Then old lanterns, furniture and fine silk curtains from Northern China summon up the atmosphere of an early Beijing salon in this delightful series of rooms. The menu offers a very straightforward range of regional dishes with specialities including crispy lamb and Kung Po chicken.

食通天的專用升降機帶你前往12樓，進入另一個美食天地。踏入餐廳，舉目可見一些古董中醫藥箱，散發古式古香的味道；加上舊式燈籠、古代傢具和中國方的優質絲綢窗簾，使一列悅目的餐室更添風格，洋溢著早期北京客廳的氣氛。餐牌上的菜式一目了然，全是中國地方美食，鎮店之寶包括蔥爆羊肉和宮保雞球。

■ ADDRESS/地址
TEL.3102 0088
12F, Food Forum, Times Square, 1 Matheson Street, Causeway Bay
銅鑼灣勿地臣街1號時代廣場食通天12樓 1205號舖
www.aqua.com.hk

■ ANNUAL AND WEEKLY CLOSING
　休息日期
Closed Lunar New Year
年初一休息

■ OPENING HOURS, LAST ORDER
　營業時間, 最後點菜時間
Lunch/午膳 12:00-14:45 (L.O.)
Dinner/晚膳 18:00-23:45 (L.O.)

■ PRICE/價錢
Lunch/午膳　menu/套餐 $ 168
　　　　　　carte/點菜 $ 100-400
Dinner/晚膳　carte/點菜 $ 300-600

West Villa
西苑酒家

✗✗ ✗

🍴300

Housed on the first floor of this fashionable shopping centre, here is a family-run operation gazing out onto a sea of luxury boutiques. Smartly renovated traditional Cantonese décor includes moveable wall panels that allow for personalised private dining areas and special functions. The menu is equally traditional and a definite high point of the cooking is the delicacy and freshness of the Dim Sum.

西苑是一間家族經營的酒家位於時尚的購物中心一樓，遠望一系列時裝名店。融合現代風格的廣東特色裝潢設有活動間牆板，可以改成私人進膳空間，適合特別場合。餐單極具傳統特色，其中最受矚目的可算是精緻新鮮的點心。

■ ADDRESS/地址
TEL.2882 2110
Shop 101-102, 1F, Lee Gardens Two, 28 Yun Ping Road, Causeway Bay
銅鑼灣恩平道28號利園2期1樓101-102號舖
www.westvillahk.com

■ OPENING HOURS, LAST ORDER
營業時間, 最後點菜時間
11:00-21:00 (L.O.)

■ PRICE/價錢

Lunch/午膳	menu/套餐	$ 168-788
	carte/點菜	$ 100-1,500
Dinner/晚膳	menu/套餐	$ 398-1,988
	carte/點菜	$ 250-1,500

Wing Wah
永華雲吞麵家

This simple operation has been maintaining high standards for well over 50 years now. And the secret is that they do everything from scratch upstairs, making their noodles by hand using bamboo. So proud are they of their skills that there's a photographic display on the walls showing what they do. Finest offerings include shrimp wonton and barbecued pork noodle as well as a dessert of coconut milk with honeydew melon and sago.

這家簡單的餐廳營運至今逾50年，依然保持一貫的高水準，成功秘訣在於一手包辦所有工作，在樓上用竹昇手打麵條便可見一斑。他們以自家技術深感自豪，牆上貼著製作過程的照片。招牌美食包括鮮蝦雲吞麵及炸醬麵，甜品方面首推蜜瓜椰汁西米露。

■ ADDRESS/地址
TEL.2527 7476
89 Hennessy Road, Wanchai
灣仔軒尼詩道89號

■ ANNUAL AND WEEKLY CLOSING
　休息日期
Closed Lunar New Year
年初一休息

■ OPENING HOURS, LAST ORDER
　營業時間，最後點菜時間
12:00-04:00 (L.O.)
Sunday/週日 12:00-01:00 (L.O.)

■ PRICE/價錢
Lunch/午膳　carte/點菜 $ 50
Dinner/晚膳　carte/點菜 $ 50

Xinjishi Shanghai
新吉士

✕

🍽15

Space is limited at this unpretentious second floor operation in the heart of a shopping and business centre. It may
take a little while for your dishes to arrive but it's worth the
wait: you can follow their progress as you watch the ingredients of many classic Shanghai dishes being assembled in
the lively open kitchen. Try the unusual preserved crab in
sweet prune.

新吉士位於二樓，座落於購物和商業地帶中心，面積雖稱不上寬闊，但格局實
而不華。菜餚烹飪需時，但絕對值得等待，因為餐廳設有開放式廚房，讓食客
觀看烹調過程，最後便可享用碟碟經典上海美食。記得品嚐獨特的話梅醉羔
蟹。

■ ADDRESS/地址   ■ OPENING HOURS, LAST ORDER
TEL.2890 1122   營業時間, 最後點菜時間
Shop 201-203, 2F, Lee Gardens Two,   Lunch/午膳 12:00-15:00 (L.O.)
28 Yun Ping Road, Causeway Bay   Dinner/晚膳 18:00-22:30 (L.O.)
銅鑼灣恩平道28號利園2期2樓201-203號
舖   ■ PRICE/價錢
                                     Lunch/午膳   carte/點菜 $ 200-350
                                     Dinner/晚膳 carte/點菜 $ 200-350

Yan Toh Heen
欣圖軒

XXX

 ⚅ ← ☞ 🍽20 ✿

This elegant room with its lovely views is smartly detailed by using jade show plates, napkin rings and chopstick rests. The authentic Cantonese menu makes a speciality of shark's fin, abalone and dried seafood and there also several dishes requiring advance ordering such as Hangzhou beggar's fortune chicken which is wrapped in clay. Round things off with a double-boiled imperial bird's nest in whole coconut.

這家高雅的餐廳景致迷人，而墊碟、餐巾圈及筷子架均是玉製品，風格時尚。粵菜菜式原汁原味，特色美食包括魚翅、鮑魚及海味；需預訂的菜式包括杭州富貴雞，甜品則推介椰盅燉官燕。

■ ADDRESS/地址
TEL.2313 2323
LF, Intercontinental Hotel, 18 Salisbury Road, Tsim Sha Tsui, Kowloon
九龍尖沙咀梳士巴利道18號洲際酒店低座

■ OPENING HOURS, LAST ORDER
營業時間, 最後點菜時間
Lunch/午膳 12:00-14:30 (L.O.)
Dinner/晚膳 18:00-23:00 (L.O.)

■ PRICE/價錢
Lunch/午膳   menu/套餐 $ 300-1,780
          carte/點菜 $ 290-8,000
Dinner/晚膳 carte/點菜 $ 310-8,000

Yat Tung Heen
逸東軒

XX

30

Considering its basement setting, this subtly lit restaurant is warm and atmospheric. A highly personable manager heads up a friendly and efficient team. The menu is strictly Cantonese with its emphasis on seafood, refined broths and bird's nests. Dim sum is served both at lunchtime and Sunday breakfast and includes such preparations as steamed mince mud carp fish dumplings and pan-fried turnip cake with conpoy.

逸東軒位於酒店地庫，燈光昏暗，洋溢著溫暖的氣氛。經理親切有禮，而侍應則態度友善，服務高效。餐廳提供純粹粵菜，主打包括海鮮、老火湯及燕窩。午市時段和週日早餐均有點心供應，菜式包括市橋鯪魚賣及瑤柱煎蘿蔔糕。

■ ADDRESS/地址
TEL.2710 1093
B2F, Eaton Hotel, 380 Nathan Road, Kowloon
九龍彌敦道380號逸東酒店地庫2樓
www.eaton-hotels.com

■ OPENING HOURS, LAST ORDER
營業時間, 最後點菜時間
Lunch/午膳 11:00-15:30 L.O.
Dinner/晚膳 18:00-22:30 L.O.

■ PRICE/價錢
Lunch/午膳　carte/點菜 $ 160-1,010
Dinner/晚膳　carte/點菜 $ 200-1,010

Yee Tung Heen
怡東軒

Contemporary Chinese décor and the obligatory aquarium form the backdrop at this friendly 2nd floor operation; there are also sizeable private dining rooms. The Cantonese cooking is assured and uses very fresh ingredients. There's a very good-value dim sum lunch menu and other specialities include sautéed minced pork with pork skin and black beans and steamed winter melon with cabbage rolls and straw mushrooms.

氣氛親切的怡東軒位於2樓，以現代的中式設計，擁有典型的魚缸，亦設有寬敞的私人餐室。這裡的粵菜水準有保證，食材更是十分新鮮。午市點心價錢相宜，其他特色美食包括脆浮皮伴炒豆豉肉碎及仙菇玉蝶。

■ ADDRESS/地址
TEL. 2837 6790
2F, The Excelsior Hotel, 281 Gloucester
Road, Causeway Bay
銅鑼灣告士打道281號怡東酒店2樓
www.excelsiorhongkong.com

■ OPENING HOURS, LAST ORDER
營業時間, 最後點菜時間
Lunch/午膳 11:30-14:30 (L.O.)
Dinner/晚膳 18:00-22:30 (L.O.)

■ PRICE/價錢
Lunch/午膳　menu/套餐 $ 258-458
　　　　　　carte/點菜 $ 230-1,200
Dinner/晚膳　menu/套餐 $ 258-1,298
　　　　　　carte/點菜 $ 230-1,200

Yellow Door Kitchen
黃色門廚房

Go up an elevator to this inconspicuous restaurant where the tightly set tables will have you practically sharing your neighbour's dinner! You'll feel instantly at home with the friendly service, and even more relaxed when you tuck into the tasty Sichuan and Shanghainese cooking...especially if you like spicy dishes. Don't be afraid to tackle the tasting menu of eight starters, six main courses, dim sum and dessert: small, delicious portions.

前往這家不顯眼的餐廳須乘搭電梯。裡面的餐枱緊緊排列在一起，所以你幾乎可以分享鄰座的晚餐！親切的服務令你賓至如歸；嚐到美味的四川和上海菜，特別是喜歡吃辣的人會加倍叫好。放膽試試含八道前菜、六道主菜、點心和甜品的推薦套餐，全部都是份量小而美味的菜式。

■ ADDRESS/地址

TEL. 2858 6555
6F, 37 Cochrane Street, Central
中環閣麟街37號6樓
www.yellowdoorkitchen.com.hk

■ ANNUAL AND WEEKLY CLOSING
    休息日期
Closed Lunar New Year, Sunday and Public Holidays
週日、公眾假期及年初一休息

■ OPENING HOURS, LAST ORDER
    營業時間, 最後點菜時間
Lunch/午膳 12:00-14:30 (L.O.)
Dinner/晚膳 18:30-22:30 (L.O.)

■ PRICE/價錢
Lunch/午膳   carte/點菜 $ 180
Dinner/晚膳   menu/套餐 $ 288

Yè Shanghai (Admiralty)
夜上海 (金鍾)

Surrounded by watch and jewellery shops, and with a bijou chocolate shop at the entrance, this restrained dining room is elegantly divided up by lacquered bamboo screens. Attentive staff are there to guide you through the intricacies of the menu which specialises not only in the cuisine of Shanghai but also its neighbouring provinces of Jiangsu and Zhejiang. Try the sliced pork terrine with Zhejiang black vinegar and the baked stuffed crab shell.

餐廳附近盡是鐘錶和珠寶店，入口處則設有一家小巧的巧克力店。亮漆竹子屏風把高雅的餐室分隔成不同的用餐區，侍應樂於為你介紹餐單上的繁複菜式；特色美食不但包括上海菜，更有江蘇及浙江菜。推介菜式包括鎮江肴肉及蟹粉釀蟹蓋。

■ ADDRESS/地址

TEL.2918 9833
Shop 332, 3F, Pacific Place, 88 Queensway, Admiralty
香港金鐘道88號太古廣場3樓332號舖
www.elite-concepts.com

■ OPENING HOURS, LAST ORDER
營業時間, 最後點菜時間
Lunch/午膳 11:30-14:30 (L.O.)
Dinner/晚膳 18:00-21:30 (L.O.)

■ PRICE/價錢
Lunch/午膳　menu/套餐 $ 380
　　　　　　carte/點菜 $ 220-800
Dinner/晚膳　menu/套餐 $ 380
　　　　　　carte/點菜 $ 220-800

Yè Shanghai (Kowloon)
夜上海 (九龍)

❌❌❌

♿ ☞ 📷18 ☎🍽

Expertly balanced, subtle cooking is provided here, drawing not only on Shanghai but also the neighbouring provinces of Jiangsu and Zhejiang. Specialities include braised Tianjin cabbage with ham and steamed pork belly wrapped in lotus leaves. Contemporary décor recalls echoes of 1930s Shanghai in its use of dark woods, subdued lighting and semi-private alcoves. A lively, sophisticated operation with very attentive service.

這裡的烹調水準專業，技術精湛，不但提供上海菜，更涵蓋江蘇及浙江菜。特色美食包括金華火腿津白及稻草扎肉。餐廳以當代風格設計，燈光昏暗，採用深色木材，設有半掩餐室，散發著三十年代上海的味道。餐廳充滿生氣，營運順暢，服務非常周到。

■ ADDRESS/地址
TEL.2376 3322
6F, Marco Polo Hotel, Harbour City, Canton Road, Tsim Sha Tsui, Kowloon
九龍尖沙咀廣東道3號海運大廈馬哥孛羅酒店6樓

■ OPENING HOURS, LAST ORDER
營業時間, 最後點菜時間
Lunch/午膳 11:30-15:30 L.O. 15:00
Dinner/晚膳 18:00-24:00 L.O. 23:00

■ PRICE/價錢
Lunch/午膳   carte/點菜 $ 200-1,500
Dinner/晚膳   menu/套餐 $ 380
                   carte/點菜 $ 300-2,000

Yeung's Noodle
楊記麵家

Mr Yeung's done it again, this time in Wanchai. There's a fresh and modern red and black interior, and the swift and efficient team keep a beady eye on the proceedings. The recipes are proven, and the prices very reasonable considering the quality. Fish balls, fresh beef and seasonal vegetables flood out of the small kitchen in steaming bowls of soup or upon a choice of noodles. A popular venue for those wanting a modern noodle experience.

楊先生再展拳腳，今次選定灣仔，創立楊記麵家。餐廳內部採用了時尚的紅色和黑色設計，感覺煥然一新。高效的侍應有型有格，反應非常敏捷，隨時為食客提供服務。菜式水準有保證，相對下價錢確是十分合宜。侍應不斷從廚房捧出一碗碗的時菜、魚蛋和鮮牛肉湯或麵；楊記實在是體驗時尚麵食的好去處。

■ ADDRESS/地址

TEL.2511 1336
219 Hennessy Road, Wanchai
灣仔軒尼詩道219號

■ OPENING HOURS, LAST ORDER
　營業時間, 最後點菜時間
11:00-22:00 (L.O.)

■ PRICE/價錢
Lunch/午膳　carte/點菜 $ 19-24
Dinner/晚膳　carte/點菜 $ 19-24

Yun Fu
雲府

XX

🍽22

The presence of Lok Shan Buddha and eerie symbolic music lend a mystical tone to this discreet establishment once you get the other side of its ornate dark wooden front door. Warm lighting leads you past the private rooms to the minimal main dining room. The cooking revolves around Mongolian roasted meats, some of which require ordering in advance. Try the steamed pork cheek wrapped in lotus leaves or the boneless lamb ribs.

甫踏入餐廳的華麗木門，你便會看到樂山大佛，聽到象徵性的詭異音樂，到處洋溢著一片神秘的氣氛。你可在柔和的燈光下，由私人餐室走到簡約的主餐室。菜式包括蒙古烤肉，其中一些需要預訂；特別推介跑三跑或京燒羊肉。

■ ADDRESS/地址
TEL.2116 8855
BF, 43-45 Wyndham Street, Central
中環雲咸街43-55號地庫
www.aqua.com.hk

■ ANNUAL AND WEEKLY CLOSING
　　休息日期
Closed Saturday lunch and Sunday lunch
週六、日午膳休息

■ OPENING HOURS, LAST ORDER
　　營業時間, 最後點菜時間
Lunch/午膳 12:00-15:00 (L.O.)
Dinner/晚膳 18:00-24:00 (L.O.)

■ PRICE/價錢
Lunch/午膳 carte/點菜 $ 450-750
Dinner/晚膳 carte/點菜 $ 450-750

Cantonese/粵菜   MAP/地圖   7/B-2

Yung Kee
鏞記

This can best be described as an institution as it seats over a 1,000 people at every mealtime and the higher the floor the better the food! Outside, the frontage is golden and inside, there's an army of waiters scurrying up and down 4 packed floors delivering a selection of largely Cantonese dishes involving much roasted goose and barbecued pork. If you fancy a fractionally less hectic experience, try to ask for a table on the VIP top floor.

鏞記在午市時段的食客超過一千人，可謂城中最大型的酒家之一，以食物亦一層此一層好！金色的正門內熙熙攘攘，侍應忙得不可開交，在四層樓之間穿插來往，奉上以粵菜為主的美食，包括燒鵝和叉燒。如要享受較為悠閒的美食體驗，建議預訂貴賓房。

■ ADDRESS/地址

TEL.2522 1624
32-40 Wellington Street, Central
中環威靈頓街32-40號
www.yungkee.com.hk

■ ANNUAL AND WEEKLY CLOSING
　休息日期
Closed 3 days Lunar New Year
農曆新年休息3天

■ OPENING HOURS, LAST ORDER
　營業時間, 最後點菜時間
11:00-23:30 (L.O.)

■ PRICE/價錢
Lunch/午膳　menu/套餐 $ 780
　　　　　　carte/點菜 $ 300-800
Dinner/晚膳　menu/套餐 $ 780
　　　　　　carte/點菜 $ 500-800

Yunyan
雲陽閣

P ⌬12

A classic case of 'don't be put off by the appearance', Yun-yan is located in an uninspiring mall, and its bright lights are hardly conducive to a romantic experience. But the quality of the food – and the pricing – sets it apart. Spicy Sichuan dishes are served: it's called 'Red Hot Cuisine', either as an enticement, or a warning! Specialities are pork and shrimp dumplings with chilli oil as dim sum, and sautéed prawns in garlic and chillies.

這是「不要因餐廳外觀而卻步」的典型例子，雲陽閣位於一間不太吸引的商場，餐廳明亮的燈光亦難以營造浪漫的用餐氣氛；不過，菜式的品質和價錢才是致勝之道。這裡供應辛辣的四川菜，又稱為「當紅川菜」，聽上去既像誘惑，又似警告！特色美食點心包括鐘水餃及魚香鮮蝦球。

■ ADDRESS/地址
TEL.2375 0800
4F, Miramar Shopping Centre, 132-134 Nathan Road, Tsim Sha Tsui, Kowloon
九龍尖沙咀彌敦道132-134號美麗華商場4樓

■ OPENING HOURS, LAST ORDER
營業時間，最後點菜時間
Lunch/午膳 11:30-14:45 (L.O.)
Dinner/晚膳 17:30-22:45 (L.O.)

■ PRICE/價錢
Lunch/午膳　carte/點菜 $ 125-840
Dinner/晚膳　carte/點菜 $ 125-840

Zen
采蝶軒

✗✗✗

🍽36

Located in a luxurious shopping centre, this is a new restaurant with a refreshingly contemporary look. It consists of a capacious main room, and two private dining rooms. A generally upmarket clientele knows it's on to a good thing, because the tasty Cantonese cuisine is of excellent quality and the staff are warm and welcoming. Fresh, seasonal ingredients abound in specialities including double boiled sharks fin soup, or stuffed chicken wings.

這家全新的餐廳位於一個豪華的購物中心內，時尚設計煥然一新。餐廳包括一個寬敞的主餐室，以及兩個私人用餐室。這裡的食客一般較高檔，懂得欣賞這家餐廳，因為知道這裡的粵菜品質優良，而且服務員款客熱情。拿手菜式採用的新鮮季節性食材比比皆是，包括燉魚翅和釀雞翼。

■ ADDRESS/地址
TEL.2845 4555
Shop 03, LF, Pacific Place, 88 Queensway, Admiralty
香港金鐘道88號太古廣場第1期地庫1樓

■ OPENING HOURS, LAST ORDER
營業時間, 最後點菜時間
Lunch/午膳 10:45-15:30 (L.O.)
Dinner/晚膳 17:30-22:30 (L.O.)

■ PRICE/價錢
Lunch/午膳　menu/套餐 $ 264
　　　　　　carte/點菜 $ 200-1,000
Dinner/晚膳　menu/套餐 $ 868
　　　　　　carte/點菜 $ 300-1,000

Zuma

♿ 🏠 🛋14 🚃 ⚘

Currently caught in the zeitgeist of fashion and celebrity, this is spread across 2 floors with a cool Sake bar and lounge hovering above the main dining room and both linked by a dramatic spiral staircase. Dishes are prepared in three distinct areas: the open kitchen, the sushi bar and the robata grill allowing a mix of calm precision and dramatic flourish. Over 2,000 wines and 40 different types of sake are available. A DJ plays at weekends.

餐廳風格緊貼名人和時尚潮流，共分為兩層：主餐室樓上設有型格的燒酒吧及酒廊，以螺旋形樓梯連接，設計獨特。廚房包括三個部分：開放式廚房、壽司吧，以及爐端燒，廚藝精巧，味道一流。餐廳提供超過二千種葡萄酒及四十種不同的燒酒，週末更有DJ在場打碟。

■ ADDRESS/地址
TEL.3657 6388
5&6F, The Landmark, 15 Queen's Road, Central
中環皇后大道中15號置地廣場5&6樓
www.zumarestaurant.com

■ OPENING HOURS, LAST ORDER
營業時間, 最後點菜時間
Lunch/午膳 12:00-15:00 (L.O.)
Dinner/晚膳 18:00-23:00 (L.O.)

■ PRICE/價錢
Lunch/午膳   menu/套餐 $ 480-870
                carte/點菜 $ 400-700
Dinner/晚膳   menu/套餐 $ 870-1,280
                carte/點菜 $ 600-800

HOTELS
酒店

HOTELS BY ORDER OF COMFORT
酒店 — 以舒適程度分類

Conrad
港麗

With its enviable location above the Pacific Place shopping and entertainment complex, this skilfully mixes the traditional and the modern. The vast oval lobby superbly showcases Chinese vases and bronze sculptures. Bedrooms are located between the 40th and 61st floors ensuring sweeping views; the suites are particularly spacious and have elegantly marbled bathrooms. An outdoor swimming pool offers an equally dramatic panorama of the city.

RESTAURANTS/ 餐廳

Recommended/推薦			Also/其他
Nicholini's/意寧谷		XXXX	Brasserie on the Eight/懷歐敘
The Golden Leaf/金葉庭	✿	XXX	Garden Café/咖啡園

酒店位處集購物娛樂於一身的太古廣場之上，巧妙地混合了傳統和現代元素。龐大的橢圓形大堂展示著中式花瓶及銅像，優雅而壯麗。寢室全在40至61樓之間，坐擁遼闊美景，而套房則特別寬敞，設有雲石浴室。室外游泳池同樣讓你飽覽香港全景。

■ ADDRESS/地址

TEL.2521 3838

FAX. 2521 3888

Pacific Place, 88 Queensway, Admiralty

金鐘道88號太古廣場

www.conradhotels.com

■ ROOMS AND SUITES/客房及套房

Rooms/客房 =467

Suites/套房 =46

■ PRICE/價錢

🚹	$ 3,400-5,900
🚹🚹	$ 3,400-5,900
Suites/套房	$ 6,500-38,000
☕	$ 280

Cosmopolitan
麗都

This large operation sits on the site of the former Xin Hua News Agency Building, in effect, the old Chinese embassy before Hong Kong's handover. Today, it is the perfect choice for anyone wanting to attend the Happy Valley Racecourse: some rooms even offer a full view of the proceedings. Bedrooms are smart and unpretentious although some may be a little compact. A complimentary shuttle bus links the hotel to a number of local amenities.

RESTAURANTS/ 餐廳

Recommended/推薦

Also/其他

La Maison de L'Orient
大宅門餐廳

這間大型酒店前身為新華社香港分社的所在地，實際上是香港回歸前的中國大使館。今天，對希望觀看跑馬地賽事的人來説，這間酒店是完美選擇，有些客房甚至讓你看到整場賽事的全貌。寢室設計既時尚又不造作，不過部分房間可能有點小巧。設有免費穿梭巴士，往返酒店及一些著名市區設施。

■ ADDRESS/地址
TEL. 3552 1111
FAX. 3552 1122
387-397 Queen's Road East, Wanchai
灣仔皇后大道東 387-397
www.cosmopolitanhotel.com.hk

■ ROOMS AND SUITES/客房及套房
Rooms/客房 ＝434
Suites/套房 ＝19

■ PRICE/價錢

👤	$ 1,800-2,100
👥	$ 1,800-2,100
Suites/套房	$ 4,200-5,200
☕	$ 128

Eaton
逸東

This is located near both the Jade Market and the Tin Hau temple, and in its 4th floor lobby there's a pleasant terrace with fishponds. Nearby, you'll find the colonial Planter's Bar and Metro Buffet & Grill. Bedrooms are compact but neatly kept: a sizeable number have recently been renovated and labelled as "deluxe". This friendly establishment is a firm favourite with marrying couples: they host over 700 wedding receptions each year!

RESTAURANTS/ 餐廳

Recommended/推薦	Also/其他
Yat Tung Heen/逸東軒 ✗✗	Metro Buffet & Grill
	Yagura

這裡鄰近有玉器市場和天后廟，四樓大堂更設有景致宜人的花園和魚池。富殖民地色彩的逸東吧和Metro Buffet & Grill自助烤肉餐廳亦近在咫尺。客房面積不大，但整潔舒適；不少房間最近更翻新為高級客房。這家設備完善的酒店廣受新婚人士歡迎，每年舉行超過七百次婚宴。

■ ADDRESS/地址
TEL.2710 1803
FAX. 2385 5009
380 Nathan Road, Kowloon
九龍彌敦道380號
http://hongkong.eatonhotels.com

■ ROOMS AND SUITES/客房及套房
Rooms/客房 ＝445
Suites/套房 ＝20

■ PRICE/價錢

👤	$ 2,150-2,650
👥	$ 2,150-2,650
Suites/套房	$ 2,850-5,200
☕	$ 170

Four Seasons
四季

Not only does the hotel boast a majestic setting over the harbour but it also offers some of the most spacious and stylish accommodation in Hong Kong. Many rooms have contemporary detailing; others in darker tones are more traditionally oriental. The aptly named Blue Bar offers just that – a wide range of blue-hued cocktails – whilst the vast spa area has two infinity pools overlooking Victoria Harbour that come complete with underwater music.

RESTAURANTS/ 餐廳

Recommended/推薦		Also/其他
Caprice	✿✿ ✕✕✕✕	The Lounge
Lung King Heen/龍景軒	✿✿✿ ✕✕✕	

酒店不僅毗鄰海港，坐擁壯麗景色；而且提供香港最時尚及寬敞的一些客房。很多客房以當代風格裝飾，另一些以較深的色調為主，風格較為傳統東方式。Blue Bar名副其實，提供選擇繁多的藍色雞尾酒。至於龐大的水療區，設有兩個無邊際泳池(infinity pool)，讓你一邊享受水底音樂，一邊俯瞰維港景色。

■ ADDRESS/地址
TEL. 3196 8888
FAX. 3196 8899
8 Finance Street, Central
中環金融街8號
www.fourseasons.com/hongkong

■ ROOMS AND SUITES/客房及套房
Rooms/客房 ＝399
Suites/套房 ＝54

■ PRICE/價錢

👤	$ 4,200-4,700
👥	$ 4,200-4,700
Suites/套房	$ 8,000-10,000
☕	$ 270

Grand Hyatt
君悅

A colourful, bustling foyer makes a fitting introduction to this large business-orientated establishment located very near to the Hong Kong Conventions and Exhibition Centre. All 549 rooms benefit from a palette of calming neutral colours: some are good-sized and some are more compact. Extensive spa facilities include a 50-metre swimming pool shared with the adjacent Renaissance Harbour View Hotel.

RESTAURANTS/ 餐廳

Recommended/推薦		Also/其他
Grissini	※※※	Kaetsu/鹿悅
JJ's	※※	Tiffin/茶園
One Harbour Road/港灣壹號	※※※※	

大堂多采多姿，熙來攘往，這就是以商務為主的君悅酒店。酒店毗鄰香港會議展覽中心，549間客房全都以平靜的中和色組合示人，包括一些空間恰宜的和另一些較為面積小的。水療設施龐大，包括一個與隔鄰萬麗海景酒店共用的50米游泳池。

■ ADDRESS/地址
TEL.2588 1234
FAX. 2802 0677
1 Harbour Road, Wanchai
灣仔港灣道1號
www.hongkong.grandhyatt.com

■ ROOMS AND SUITES/客房及套房
Rooms/客房 ＝535
Suites/套房 ＝14

■ PRICE/價錢
👤	$ 5,000-7,200
👥	$ 5,200-7,600
Suites/套房	$ 8,500-55,000
☕	$ 260

Harbour Plaza Kowloon
海逸

First impressions do not disappoint here. This shimmering glass structure is right on the waterfront, offering superb views across Victoria Harbour, and there's a spectacular lobby with an impressive white marble staircase. The bedrooms are bright, comfortable and well-equipped, if sober by comparison to other areas. Make the most of the dramatic rooftop pool with its glass-sided walls, as well as the top floor fitness centre and steam bath.

RESTAURANTS/餐廳

Recommended/推薦		Also/其他
Harbour Grill	XXX	The Promenade
Hoi Yat Heen	XXX	
Robatayaki/炉端燒	XX	

這裡的第一印象絕對不會令你失望。這座閃閃發亮的玻璃建築毗鄰維港，金碧輝煌的大堂設有白色雲石階梯。房間開揚舒適，設備齊全，相比酒店其他設施或較樸實。住客可盡情享受天台設有玻璃幕牆的游泳池、頂樓健身中心和蒸氣浴。

■ ADDRESS/地址

TEL.2621 3188
FAX. 2621 3311
20 Tak Fung Street, Whampoa Garden, Hunghom, Kowloon
九龍紅磡黃埔花園德豐街20號
www.harbour-plaza.com/hphk

■ ROOMS AND SUITES/客房及套房

Rooms/客房 =506
Suites/套房 =48

■ PRICE/價錢

🚹	$ 2,400-3,500
🚹🚹	$ 2,600-3,800
Suites/套房	$ 4,600-30,000
☕	$ 200

Harbour Plaza Metropolis
都會海逸

This large establishment with its distinctive zigzag frontage is well placed for the Hong Kong Coliseum. Its marble lobby is vast, with great floor-to-ceiling windows and a sweeping staircase. The bedrooms aren't large but are crisply contemporary and many have excellent harbour-front views. Some even have small balcony gardens. An outdoor swimming pool, fitness room and spa offer the chance to get away from it all.

RESTAURANTS/ 餐廳

佔地寬廣，曲線形設計的正門獨具特色，鄰近紅磡香港體育館，佔盡地利。雲石大堂建築宏偉，主樓梯和落地玻璃格外壯觀。客房面積不大，但風格時尚，而且大部分都能飽覽海港醉人景色，部分房間甚至設有小型露台花園。室外游泳池、健身室和水療設備一應俱全，讓你忘卻日常煩憂。

■ ADDRESS/地址
TEL.3160 6888
FAX. 3160 6999
7 Metropolis Drive, Hunghom, Kowloon
九龍紅磡都會道7號
www.harbour-plaza.com/hpme

■ ROOMS AND SUITES/客房及套房
Rooms/客房 =455
Suites/套房 =365

■ PRICE/價錢
👤	$ 2,000-3,050
👥	$ 2,100-3,250
Suites/套房	$ 3,200-29,000
🍽	$ 138

Harbour Plaza North Point
北角海逸

For the moment, this has the longest outdoor swimming pool on Hong Kong Island (at 25 metres) as well as a smartly equipped fitness centre. Spread over 32 floors, everything is very contemporary, right from the moment you enter the lobby with its unusual water feature. Bedrooms here are good sized and quiet - most only have a shower so if you require a bath ask when booking. There are 200 serviced suites designed for long-stay clients.

RESTAURANTS/ 餐廳

Recommended/推薦

Also/其他

Greens/綠怡廳
Hoi Yat Heen/海逸軒

樓高32層的北角海逸酒店擁有目前港島最大型的戶外游泳池（25米），以及設施齊全的健身中心。酒店的裝飾極富時代感，從大堂的水池即可見一斑。客房寬敞而寧靜：大部分房間只有淋浴設備，如需浸浴，緊記在預訂房時事先詢問。酒店另設有200間為長期住客而設的服務式套房。

■ ADDRESS/地址

TEL.2187 8888
FAX. 2187 8899
665 King's Road, North Point
北角英皇道665號
www.harbour-plaza.com

■ ROOMS AND SUITES/客房及套房
Rooms/客房 =400
Suites/套房 =200

■ PRICE/價錢

👤	$ 1,950-2,050
👥	$ 2,150-2,650
Suites/套房	$ 3,650-6,450
☕	$ 135

Intercontinental
洲際

Deceptively unremarkable from the outside, but it is decidedly impressive once you're in the grand lobby with its magnificent harbour views. All bedrooms are spacious and well appointed in quiet neutral tones: they have large marble bathrooms. Relax in either the lovely swimming pool or the infinity spa pool or take a massage in an outside cabana. Options for dining are particularly good (see separate entries) and the service is meticulous.

RESTAURANTS/ 餐廳

Recommended/推薦		Also/其他
Nobu	✗✗	Harbourside
Spoon by Alain Ducasse	✗✗	
The Steak House	✗✗	
Yan Toh Heen/欣圖軒	✗✗✗	

酒店平凡的外表也許會讓人認為不外如是，但踏入富麗堂皇的酒店大堂，望著一流海景，絕對會令你留下深刻印象。所有客房都非常寬敞，淺色調的裝潢亦讓人感覺安靜，更設有寬闊的大理石浴室。你可以在漂亮的游泳池或無邊際水療池鬆弛身心，或在戶外的池邊小室享受一下按摩服務。酒店內的餐飲服務非常出色(請參照其他有關的介紹)，而且服務水準一流。

■ ADDRESS/地址
TEL.2721 1211
FAX. 2739 4546
18 Salisbury Road, Tsim Sha Tsui, Kowloon
九龍尖沙咀梳士巴利道18號
www.intercontinental.com

■ ROOMS AND SUITES/客房及套房
Rooms/客房 = 403
Suites/套房 = 92

■ PRICE/價錢
👤	$ 2,890-3,690
👥	$ 2,890-3,690
Suites/套房	$ 7,500-78,000
🍽	$ 280

Intercontinental Grand Stanford
海景嘉福

Although originally built in 1981, this sizeable 18-storey waterfront property has been drastically upgraded over the last few years but still retains its unusual zigzag frontage. The best bedrooms benefit from excellent views over Victoria Harbour and Hong Kong Island and have charming French "Empire" style furniture. A fitness centre and outdoor heated swimming pool are both perched on the roof of the building.

RESTAURANTS/ 餐廳

Recommended/推薦		Also/其他
The Mistral/海風餐廳	XX	Café Rendezvous/海景咖啡廊
		Hoi King Heen/海景軒

雖然這幢18層的龐大臨海建築物建於1981年，但在過去幾年已大幅升級，並保留了獨特的曲折正門。酒店內最佳的寢室坐擁維港及港島美景，並採用了迷人的法國帝王式傢具。酒店頂層設有健身室及戶外溫水泳池。

■ ADDRESS/地址
TEL. 2721 5161
FAX. 2732 2233
70 Mody Road, Tsim Sha Tsui East, Kowloon
九龍尖沙咀東部麼地道70
www.hongkong.intercontinental.com

■ ROOMS AND SUITES/客房及套房
Rooms/客房 ＝548
Suites/套房 ＝22

■ PRICE/價錢

👤	$ 1,800-3,600
👥	$ 1,800-3,600
Suites/套房	$ 4,700-5,500
☕	$ 185

Island Shangri-La
港島香格里拉

The intricate beauty of possibly the world's largest Chinese silk painting towers over the glamorous atrium and rises up all of 16 storeys. More sparkle is provided by the dazzling array of chandeliers placed round the hotel. Up above, the accommodation is classic and sumptuously appointed, especially those on the executive floors (49th to 55th). The Island Shangri-La feels somewhat like a father-figure of the Hong Kong hotel scene.

RESTAURANTS/ 餐廳

Recommended/推薦			Also/其他
Lobster Bar and Grill/龍蝦吧		✗✗	Cafe TOO
Petrus/珀翠	❀	✗✗✗✗	Nadaman/灘萬
Summer Palace/夏宮	❀❀	✗✗✗	

屹立在迷人的中庭,高高越過酒店的16層:這幅可能是世上最大的中國絲綢畫,散發著複雜精細的美。酒店四處掛著的吊燈燈光,五光十色, 令人眼花撩亂。樓上是奢華典雅的客房,尤其是49至55樓商務樓層的房間,十分豪華。港島香格里拉給人的感覺,就像香港酒店業的前輩一樣。

■ ADDRESS/地址
TEL.2877 3838
FAX. 2521 8742
Pacific Place, Supreme Court Road, Central
中區法院道太古廣場
www.shangri-la.com

■ ROOMS AND SUITES/客房及套房
Rooms/客房 ＝531
Suites/套房 ＝34

■ PRICE/價錢

👤	$ 3,000-4,700
👥	$ 4,300-5,000
Suites/套房	$ 6,000-26,000
☕	$ 240

JW Marriott
萬豪

This business-oriented hotel boasts 602 rooms spread over 35 storeys with, at the pinnacle, a series of executive floors with their own discreet lounge and meeting rooms. The fitness centre remains open 24-hours a day whilst the swimming pool surround is lushly landscaped. Nearby, the Fish Bar serves the freshest seafood and various other outlets include the Canton Tea Company with its exquisite selection of 68 different teas.

RESTAURANTS/ 餐廳

Recommended/推薦		Also/其他
Man Ho/萬豪殿	XX	Fish Bar/魚吧
		JW's California/JW's 加州
		Marriott Cafe/萬豪咖啡室
		Q88 Wine Bar/Q88酒吧

以商務住客為主的萬豪酒店樓高三十五層，客房數量達602間。位於頂樓的一列行政套房，更附有設計素雅的休息室和會議室供住客專用。酒店的健身室二十四小時開放，而游泳池則坐擁著草木繁茂的園林。鄰近的魚吧為住客提供最鮮甜味美的海鮮，此外酒店設有各種其他食肆，包括粵茶莊奉上精挑細選的68種味道茶品。

■ ADDRESS/地址
TEL.2810 8366
FAX. 2845 0737
Pacific Place, 88 Queensway,
Admiralty
金鐘道88號太古廣場
www.jwmarriotthk.com

■ ROOMS AND SUITES/客房及套房
Rooms/客房 =577
Suites/套房 =25

■ PRICE/價錢

👤	$ 4,100-5,500
👥	$ 4,100-5,500
Suites/套房	$ 8,800-40,000
☕	$ 250

Kowloon Shangri-La
九龍香格里拉

Built in the early 1980's, this large business-orientated hotel impresses with the proportions of its breathtaking lobby: the sheer wealth of marble, sparkling chandeliers, even a tiered water fountain. It's the perfect location for a traditional afternoon tea. Heading upstairs, the colour of the carpet in the lifts might seem different: it changes on a daily basis! The Horizon Club floors offer the best bedrooms and their own exclusive lounge.

RESTAURANTS/ 餐廳

Recommended/推薦		Also/其他
Angelini	✕✕✕	Cafe Kool
Nadaman (Kowloon)/灘萬（九龍）	✕✕	
Shang Palace/香宮	✿✿ ✕✕✕	

這間以商務為主的大型酒店建於80年代初，大堂很多部分都十分壯麗：多不勝數的大理石，波光粼粼的吊燈，甚至有個分層的噴水池！這裡是享用傳統下午茶的完美地點。你在上樓時可能發覺電梯的地毯很特別，那是因為每天都會更換顏色！豪華閣的樓層提供最佳寢室及其專用休息室。

■ ADDRESS/地址
TEL.2721 2111
FAX. 2723 8686
64 Mody Road, Kowloon
九龍麼地道64號
www.shangri-la.com

■ ROOMS AND SUITES/客房及套房
Rooms/客房 ＝670
Suites/套房 ＝30

■ PRICE/價錢
♦ $ 2,850-4,400
♦♦ $ 3,150-4,700
Suites/套房 $ 4,800-17,800

Langham Place
郎豪

♿ 〈 👤 🚗 🚭 🏊 🛀 Spa 🚴

Not only is this 42-storey glass tower filled with every gadget a technophile could want, it also functions as a wonderfully airy showcase for Chinese Modern Art. Over 1,500 paintings, sculptures and installations are dotted impressively round the building. Bedrooms are crisply contemporary and there are several restaurants including the innovative Portal - Work & Play. Equally clever are walking tours of the neighbourhood markets daily at 6pm.

RESTAURANTS/ 餐廳

Recommended/推薦			Also/其他
Ming Court/明閣	✿	✗✗✗	Portal - Work and Play
Tokoro		✗✗	The Place

玻璃塔般的大樓樓高42層，不僅有每個科技發燒友夢寐以求的電子產品，亦是個空間廣闊的中國現代美術展覽場。超過1,500 幅畫作、雕塑與裝置藝術品分佈於整棟大樓之內。客房的設計極富現代感，酒店內亦有不少高級餐廳，包括概念創新的Portal - Work & Play。每天下午6時更設有本地市場導賞團，服務值得一讚。

■ ADDRESS/地址

TEL.3552 3388
FAX. 3552 3322
555 Shanghai Street, Mongkok
九龍旺角上海街555號
www.hongkong.langhamplacehotels.com

■ ROOMS AND SUITES/客房及套房
Rooms/客房 ＝615
Suites/套房 ＝50

■ PRICE/價錢
🛉	$ 2,600-3,550
🛉🛉	$ 2,600-3,550
Suites/套房	$ 4,300-15,000
➴	$ 120

Lan Kwai Fong
蘭桂坊

Set well back from the harbour but conveniently located near to Government House, this charming hotel offers compact accommodation. A stylish mix of neutral tones and dark wood veneers has been used to create a calming environment. Try to secure one of the corner bedrooms if you need a little more space. Breezes coffee shop is perfect for breakfast: sit either inside or on the decked terrace.

RESTAURANTS/ 餐廳

Recommended/推薦

Also/其他

Celebrity Cuisine/名人坊

這裡未必能欣賞維港景觀，但附近大樓的璀璨燈光也絕不遜色，友善高效率的員工使酒店更添魅力。所有客房均以迷人的東方風格設計，即使有不足的部分亦被巧妙地掩飾，甚見心思。浴室雖然地方不大，但非常整潔。在晴朗的早上你亦可以去Breezes咖啡店的有蓋露天雅座享用早餐。

■ ADDRESS/地址

TEL.3650 0000
FAX. 3650 0088
3 Kau U Fong, Central
中環九如坊3號
www.lankwaifonghotel.com.hk

■ ROOMS AND SUITES/客房及套房

Rooms/客房 =157
Suites/套房 =5

■ PRICE/價錢

🚹	$ 1,500-4,300
🚹🚹	$ 1,500-4,300
Suites/套房	$ 4,100-7,700
☕	$ 130

Lanson Place

An elegant European style façade marks Lanson Place out as a stylish boutique hotel, dovetailing effortlessly with its chic location. Classical and contemporary designs interweave to create a calm exclusivity. There's a serene patio, and the interior artwork creates a feel of warmth and tranquillity. The spacious rooms include a small kitchen for long-stay guests, and many look out to HK Stadium. A cool, calm lounge fits the bill perfectly.

RESTAURANTS/ 餐廳

Recommended/推薦　　　　　　　　Also/其他

Lanson Place擁有歐洲風格的優雅外觀,是時尚的精品酒店,與時尚的地理位置一脈相承。古典和當代設計交織成這裡的專屬氣派。寧靜的露台配合室內的藝術作品,營造溫暖寧靜的感覺。寬敞客房內的小廚房,專為長期逗留的客人而設。另一方面,很多人都會觀望外面的香港大球場。寧靜安逸的酒廊可說是完全值回票價。

■ ADDRESS/地址
TEL.3477 6888
FAX. 3477 6999
133 Leighton Road, Causeway Bay
銅鑼灣禮頓道133號
www.lansonplace.com

■ ROOMS AND SUITES/客房及套房
Rooms/客房 ＝144
Suites/套房 ＝50

■ PRICE/價錢
🧍 　　　　$ 2,300-3,600
🧍🧍 　　　$ 2,300-3,600
Suites/套房 $ 4,500-10,500

Le Méridien Cyberport
數碼港艾美

This design-led, über-stylish corporate hotel is an ultra-chic place to stay with a spectacular sea-front setting. The slinky lobby, with its eye-catching fabric cylinders that stretch to the ceiling, makes its own statement. Up-to-the-minute business facilities, attractive outside pool, and hip bedrooms with rain shower bathrooms, all enhance the wow factor. Choose from three restaurants, with Japanese, Cantonese or international menus.

RESTAURANTS/ 餐廳

這間設計新穎的公司酒店極度時尚，同時更坐擁壯麗的海景，是高尚的住宿地點。閃爍的大堂內，布質圓柱伸延至天花板，十分矚目。酒店提供分秒更新的商業設施、吸引的室外泳池，以及設有陣雨浴室的時尚寢室，全都令人驚嘆不已。酒店內有三間餐廳選擇，分別是日式、粵式和國際菜式。

■ ADDRESS/地址
TEL.2980 7806
FAX. 2980 7850
100 Cyberport Road
數碼港道100號
www.lemeridien.com/hongkong

■ ROOMS AND SUITES/客房及套房
Rooms/客房 ＝167
Suites/套房 ＝3

■ PRICE/價錢

👤	$ 2,900-3,500
👥	$ 2,900-3,500
Suites/套房	$ 7,800
☕	$ 230

LKF
蘭桂坊

Smaller than most hotels in Central, LKF naturally styles it-self in the 'boutique' class. Its hub centres round the higher floors. Slash, on the 29th, is a modern and intimate lounge bar. Up the staircase on floor 30 Azure is a cool restaurant serving fusion or grill dishes and offering eye-popping city views. Spacious bedrooms have espresso machines to give you a high, and pristine beds with sumptuous goose down pillows to bring you back down.

RESTAURANTS/ 餐廳

Recommended/推薦

Also/其他

Azure

LKF 比中環大部分酒店細，自然歸入「精品」級酒店。其樞紐中心位處較高樓層：29樓的Slash是舒適的現代酒廊；30樓的Azure是一家風格不凡的餐廳，提供融合菜式或燒烤菜餚，客人更可將迷人的景觀盡收眼底。寬敞的客房設有特濃咖啡機讓你提神，而純樸的床放置了豪華的鵝絨枕頭，讓你好好休息。

■ ADDRESS/地址
TEL. 3518 9688
FAX. 3518 9699
33 Wyndham Street, Lan Kwai Fong, Central
中環蘭桂坊雲咸街33號
www.hotel-LKF.com.hk

■ ROOMS AND SUITES/客房及套房
Rooms/客房 ＝85
Suites/套房 ＝6

■ PRICE/價錢

🧍	$ 3,500-4,800
🧍🧍	$ 3,700-5,000
Suites/套房	$ 6,000-7,000
☕	$ 140

Mandarin Oriental
文華東方

A luxury hotel that defines the term; recent renovation has made it even more special. Superb bedrooms now include a secret valet box, and former verandas are integrated into the room space. The Spa is a spiritual haven, rated the best in Asia. The Mandarin Suite has to be seen to be believed: your own private treatment room. Quality of service is iconic. Dining options are many and varied; raise a glass to it all in the legendary Captain's Bar!

RESTAURANTS/ 餐廳

Recommended/推薦		Also/其他
Mandarin Grill	✗✗✗	Chinnery/千日里
Man Wah/文華廳	✗✗	Clipper Lounge/快船廊
Pierre	✿ ✗✗✗✗	

文華東方完全可以闡釋「豪華酒店」的含意，近期的裝修也令酒店變得更特別。華麗的寢室現時增加了一個私人服務箱(洗燙及擦鞋服務)，而從前的露台亦重整到客房內。被評為亞洲最佳的水療設施，是心靈的避難所。而Mandarin Suite(總統套房)更是眼見為實：有自己的私人治療室。服務質素一向稱著，餐飲選擇林林總總；讓我們向享負盛名的Captain's Bar敬一杯！

■ ADDRESS/地址

TEL.2522 0111
FAX. 2810 6190
5 Connaught Road, Central
中環干諾道中5號
www.mandarinoriental.com

■ ROOMS AND SUITES/客房及套房
Rooms/客房 ＝434
Suites/套房 ＝68

■ PRICE/價錢

👤	$ 3,800-5,400
👥	$ 3,800-5,400
Suites/套房	$ 9,000-12,000
☕	$ 238

Marco Polo
馬哥孛羅

First opened in 1969, this waterfront operation is well placed for transport links plus plentiful shopping opportunities. The modern stylish Lobby Lounge is well laid out, whilst Café Marco offers a broad range of international dishes. Bedrooms are less contemporary in feel but the best accommodation is on the 17th and 18th Club Continental floors with a dedicated private lounge. A fitness centre is located in the shopping mall next door.

RESTAURANTS/ 餐廳

Recommended/推薦		Also/其他
Cucina	XX	Café Marco/馬哥孛羅咖啡廳
Yè Shanghai (Kowloon)/夜上海 (九龍)	XXX	Nishimura/西村

馬可孛羅酒店於1969年創辦，毗鄰維港，座落於海港城，交通和購物都極為便利。餐廳方面，「大堂雅座」設計時尚現代，佈局精巧；「馬可孛羅咖啡廳」則提供形形色色的國際美食。客房的設計風格較為普通，而最佳的客房位於17及18樓的貴賓樓層，可尊享私人休息室；至於健身中心則位於海港城內。

■ ADDRESS/地址
TEL.2113 0088
FAX. 2113 0011
Harbour City, Tsim Sha Tsui, Kowloon
九龍尖沙咀海港城
www.marcopolohotels.com

■ ROOMS AND SUITES/客房及套房
Rooms/客房 ＝615
Suites/套房 ＝49

■ PRICE/價錢

👤	$ 2,450-4,420
👥	$ 2,550-4,520
Suites/套房	$ 4,900-11,700
🍽	$ 160

Metropark
銅鑼灣維景

Near to Victoria Park, this 31-storey tower offers very good comforts and facilities for business travellers. Most bedrooms have excellent harbour views and all have bathrooms lined with marble. The roof-top swimming pool is extremely well laid out with its glass walls and underwater music. The Café du Parc offers all-day buffet dining and blends French and Japanese cooking plus other international favourites.

RESTAURANTS/ 餐廳

Recommended/推薦	Also/其他
	Café Du Parc/繽紛維苑餐廳

酒店大樓樓高三十一層，鄰近維多利亞公園，為商務旅客提供舒適環境及設施。大部分客房都坐擁無敵海景及設有大理石浴室。天台游泳池經過精心設計，玻璃幕牆和水底音樂別出心裁。繽紛維苑餐廳(Café Du Parc)提供全日自助餐，搜羅法國、日本及其他國際美食。

■ ADDRESS/地址
TEL. 2600 1000
FAX. 2600 1111
148 Tung Lo Wan Road, Causeway Bay
銅鑼灣道148號
www.metroparkhotel.com

■ ROOMS AND SUITES/客房及套房
Rooms/客房 ＝243
Suites/套房 ＝23

■ PRICE/價錢
👤	$ 900-3,000
👥	$ 1,700-3,000
Suites/套房	$ 5,500
☕	$ 120

Nikko
日航

Just over 20 years old, this hotel is well placed for shopping and business links and provides a free shuttle-bus service for its guests. Large, comfortable rooms are stylishly decorated using a palette of earthy tones; the top 4 floors house executive rooms with their own private lounge. The rooftop swimming pool offers an away-from-it-all atmosphere. It has unparalleled views during the day, and so does the Sky Lounge at night.

RESTAURANTS/ 餐廳

Recommended/推薦		Also/其他
Les Célébrités/名仕餐廳	❌❌	
Sagano/嵯峨野	❌❌	
Toh Lee/桃季	❌❌	

簇新的日航酒店營運僅20年，鄰近購物和商務中心，更為住客提供免費穿梭巴士服務。客房寬敞舒適，以土系色調為主，設計時尚；位於最高四層的商務樓層客房更設有私人休憩中心。天台泳池氣氛悠然，仿如世外桃源，日間更坐擁無敵景致。晚上則可於星月廊欣賞醉人夜景。

■ ADDRESS/地址

TEL. 2739 1111
FAX. 2311 3122
72 Mody Road, Tsim Sha Tsui East, Kowloon
九龍尖沙咀麼地道72號
www.hotelnikko.com.hk

■ ROOMS AND SUITES/客房及套房
Rooms/客房 ＝445
Suites/套房 ＝18

■ PRICE/價錢

👤	$ 2,400-3,400
👥	$ 2,400-3,400
Suites/套房	$ 6,000-14,000
☕	$ 190

Panorama
麗景

This relative newcomer offers the latest in contemporary design with its 324 rooms slotting into 3 different bedroom types: silver, gold and platinum. The higher you go, the better the view but the best rooms are on corner sites where you can even enjoy the stunning harbour vista relaxing in the bath tub. On the 38th floor is the Santa Lucia restaurant that offers a broad range of international dishes in an exhilarating modern setting.

RESTAURANTS/ 餐廳

Recommended/推薦

Also/其他

Santa Lucia/樂醉西餐廳

這家酒店簇新落成，324間客房均以當代最新穎的款式，設計出三種不同的房間類別，包括銀賓、黃金和白金。要從更佳位置俯瞰景色，便要更上一層樓；而酒店的最佳客房則位於角位，客人更可以一邊享受浸浴，一邊欣賞迷人的維港景致。位於38樓的樂醉西餐廳佈置時尚，教人心動，各式各樣的各國佳餚正待君細嚐。

■ ADDRESS/地址
TEL.3550 0388
FAX. 3550 0288
8A Hart Avenue, Tsim Sha Tsui, Kowloon
九龍尖沙咀赫德道8A
www.hotelpanorama.com.hk

■ ROOMS AND SUITES/客房及套房
Rooms/客房 ＝312
Suites/套房 ＝12

■ PRICE/價錢

🧍	$ 2,400-3,900
🧍🧍	$ 2,400-3,900
Suites/套房	$ 5,800

273

Renaissance Kowloon
九龍萬麗

Built in 1978 but now possibly lacking the gloss of some of its more cutting-edge neighbours and competitors, this is nonetheless a well-placed, comfortable hotel - next to the New World Centre and the harbour-front promenade. Whilst the compact bedrooms don't always benefit from expansive views, they are well maintained. The 4th floor Panorama restaurant is a popular focal point for its buffet Sunday brunch.

RESTAURANTS/ 餐廳

Recommended/推薦		Also/其他
Dynasty/滿福樓	✕✕	Panorama/港畔

於1978年落成的九龍萬麗酒店，在鄰近的新興競爭對手比較下，至今可能略為失色；不過，酒店毗鄰新世界中心和星光大道，依然坐擁位置之便利，亦不失為一家舒適的酒店。客房並非全都坐擁廣闊景致，空間亦不算大，但是設備齊全。港畔餐廳位於酒店四樓，這裡的周日海景早午自助餐十分受歡迎。

■ ADDRESS/地址
TEL. 2369 4111
FAX. 2369 9387
22 Salisbury Road, Tsim Sha Tsui, Kowloon
九龍尖沙咀梳士巴利道22號
www.renaissancehotels.com/HKGNW

■ ROOMS AND SUITES/客房及套房
Rooms/客房 ＝492
Suites/套房 ＝53

■ PRICE/價錢
🧍	$ 2,300-4,600
🧍🧍	$ 2,300-4,600
Suites/套房	$ 5,600-8,600
☕	$ 175

Royal Plaza
帝京

The Royal Plaza's impressive marble lobby creates a rather grand ambience for arriving guests. Bedrooms are designed in a range of styles: from sober, classic elegance, via early 19th century French Empire, to the contemporary 'Executive Club' on the top two floors. Whatever the choice, all have great views. There's an outdoor pool with an unexpected Roman décor complete with columns; the solarium area boasts a particularly relaxing atmosphere.

RESTAURANTS/ 餐廳

Recommended/推薦

Also/其他

La Scala/花月庭
Royal Plaza/帝京軒

帝京酒店的雲石大堂格調相當華麗，造成一種堂皇的格調迎接來賓。客房的風格琳琳總總，包括十九世紀法國帝國的沉實古雅設計、最高兩層「行政樓層」的當代設計等，各適其式，所有客房更坐擁醉人美景。酒店的露天羅馬式泳池以圓柱作裝飾，設計風格令人驚喜；而日光浴地區的氣氛則特別輕鬆惬意。

■ ADDRESS/地址

TEL. 2928 8822
FAX. 2606 0088
193 Prince Edward Road West,
Kowloon
九龍太子道西193號
www.royalplaza.com.hk

■ ROOMS AND SUITES/客房及套房
Rooms/客房 ＝658
Suites/套房 ＝35

■ PRICE/價錢

👤	$ 1,800-3,200
👥	$ 2,000-3,400
Suites/套房	$ 4,900-23,800
☕	$ 140

Sheraton
喜來登

One of Hong Kong's biggest hotels, it's located on the mainland but is a short walk from the Star Ferry Pier. All of which adds up to great views of Victoria Harbour. These can be best appreciated from the Health Club's roof-top pool, over a plate of oysters in the wine bar, or from a swish sea-facing executive room on the 16th and 17th floors. More down-to-earth but thoroughly pleasant are a cigar room, a wine shop and an international café.

RESTAURANTS/ 餐廳

Recommended/推薦		Also/其他
Celestial Court/天寶閣	ХХ	Oyster & Wine Bar/蠔酒吧
Morton's of Chicago	ХХ	The Café
Unkai/雲海	ХХ	

這是香港最大的酒店之一，位於九龍半島，只需短短的步行距離便到天星碼頭。客人可盡覽維多利亞港的壯麗景色，最佳位置包括Health Club的天台游泳池、16樓及17樓的高級面海行政室，在蠔酒吧吃蠔時亦可享受美景。較為沉實但完全舒適的有雪茄廊、酒舖和國際咖啡廳。

■ ADDRESS/地址
TEL. 2369 1111
FAX. 2739 8707
20 Nathan Road, Kowloon
九龍彌敦道20號
www.sheraton.com/hongkong

■ ROOMS AND SUITES/客房及套房
Rooms/客房 =750
Suites/套房 =32

■ PRICE/價錢

👤	$ 2,800-4,800
👥	$ 3,000-5,000
Suites/套房	$ 6,900-12,600

The Landmark Mandarin Oriental
置地文華東方

No less exclusive than its larger sibling, this luxury boutique-styled hotel is the destination of choice for visiting glitterati. Spa opportunities are endless and include the signature Time Ritual treatment. Rooms are large on luxury and large in size – the city's most spacious. Centrepiece is the bathroom: luxuriate while enjoying surround-sound TV or your iPod system. MO bar's offerings include various Wagu burgers, or a comfort seafood meal.

RESTAURANTS/ 餐廳

Recommended/推薦		Also/其他
Amber	✿✿ ☓☓☓	MO Bar

一點都不比文華東方遜色的置地文華東方是一間精品風格的豪華酒店，更是訪港社會名流的最佳落腳點。在這裡你可盡享水療設施，包括招牌服務Time Ritual。客房盡極奢華，並十分寬敞，是香港最大的酒店房。浴室位於客房中心，可一邊享受沐浴，一邊聽著立體聲電視或自己的iPod選曲系統。MO Bar提供各種和牛漢堡、海鮮餐等等。

■ ADDRESS/地址
TEL. 2132 0188
FAX. 2132 0199
15 Queen's Road, Central
中環皇后大道中15號
www.mandarinoriental.com

■ ROOMS AND SUITES/客房及套房
Rooms/客房 ＝101
Suites/套房 ＝12

■ PRICE/價錢
🛏	$ 4,500-6,900
🛏🛏	$ 4,500-6,900
Suites/套房	$ 8,800-9,800
☕	$ 180

The Langham
朗廷

♿ 📖 🅿 ⚥ 🏋 🏊 🚴

Perfectly located for numerous transport links including the Star Ferry, all the hubbub and noise drops away as you enter the hushed confines of this elegant establishment. The spacious lobby is dominated by a stunning Dale Chihuly glass sculpture and the bedrooms, particularly the Grand Rooms, benefit from luxurious Chinese silks and gold leaf artwork. Here, timeless old world charm is underpinned by modern facilities and attentive service.

RESTAURANTS/ 餐廳

Recommended/推薦		Also/其他
T'ang Court/唐閣	❀❀ ҳ̆ҳ̆ҳ̆	L'Eclipse Main St. Deli
The Bostonian/美岸海鮮廳	ҳ̆ҳ̆	

朗廷酒店地點優越，交通便利，毗鄰天星小輪等多個交通點。踏入這家優雅恬靜的酒店，外面的嘈雜聲便一揮而散。著名藝術家Dale Chihuly的一座玻璃雕塑，屹立於寬敞大堂的中央，教人目不暇給。酒店的客房以名貴的中國絲織品和金箔藝術品裝飾，當中以總統套房最為華麗。酒店的現化設施，加上稱心周全的服務，交織成一種不老的古式情懷。

■ ADDRESS/地址
TEL. 2375 1133
FAX. 2375 6611
8 Peking Road, Tsim Sha Tsui, Kowloon
九龍尖沙咀北京道8號
www.hongkong.langhamhotels.com

■ ROOMS AND SUITES/客房及套房
Rooms/客房 =469
Suites/套房 =26

■ PRICE/價錢

🧍	$ 3,000-4,000
🧍🧍	$ 3,000-4,000
Suites/套房	$ 6,000-12,000
☕	$ 250

The Luxe Manor
帝樂文娜公館

Leaving the outside world behind, you enter a stylish jewel-box that somehow manages to jumble up oriental influences with Surrealist furnishings creating plenty of quirky charm. The dramatically lit red and black lobby flings together gilt-edged thrones, scallop-shaped banquettes and Baroque armchairs upholstered in cartoon characters. Most bedrooms are small, apart from the studio rooms and six individually themed suites on the 12th floor.

RESTAURANTS/ 餐廳

Recommended/推薦	Also/其他

Aspasia	✕✕

踏入珠寶盒般的時尚酒店，仿如置身世外桃源。帝樂文娜揉合了東方元素和超現實設計，營造迷人的虛幻氣氛。紅黑色的大堂燈光璀璨，照亮鍍金邊的寶座、印有扇貝圖案的走廊，以及裝上卡通人物坐墊的巴洛克風格扶手椅。除了12樓的尊尚客房及六間獨立主題套房外，大部分客房的空間不算大。

■ ADDRESS/地址
TEL. 3763 8888
FAX. 3763 8899
39 Kimberley Road, Tsim Sha Tsui, Kowloon
九龍尖沙咀金巴利道39號
www.theluxemanor.com

■ ROOMS AND SUITES/客房及套房
Rooms/客房 ＝153
Suites/套房 ＝6

■ PRICE/價錢

👤	$ 2,200-2,800
👥	$ 2,200-2,800
Suites/套房	$ 5,800-6,800
☕	$ 140

The Park Lane
柏寧

Within easy walking distance of Times Square, this tall block directly faces Victoria Park with its jogging routes and tennis courts. Many of the rooms offer superb views of the park's lush greenery. Accommodation is stylish and understated with the Premier Club rooms proving especially spacious and well equipped. Of all the food outlets, Riva (on the top floor) enjoys a decent reputation for its French cooking.

RESTAURANTS/ 餐廳

Recommended/推薦	Also/其他
	Riva

柏寧酒店高聳而立，座落於銅鑼灣區，距離時代廣場僅咫尺之遙，面向維多利亞公園的緩跑徑和網球場。酒店大部分客房均坐擁綠樹林蔭的維園美景。客房設計時尚，與商務樓層(Premier Club)的房間實為完美配搭，地方特別寬敞，設備亦更齊全。位於頂層的Riva法國餐廳冠絕全酒店的食肆，憑著精湛的法國佳餚享負盛名。

■ ADDRESS/地址
TEL.2293 8888
FAX. 2576 7853
310 Gloucester Road, Causeway Bay
銅鑼灣告士打道310號
www.parklane.com.hk

■ ROOMS AND SUITES/客房及套房
Rooms/客房 =771
Suites/套房 =39

■ PRICE/價錢
  � $ 2,500-5,500
     $ 2,500-5,500
Suites/套房 $ 6,500-18,000

The Peninsula
半島

Celebrating 80 years of operation, this is the grandee of Hong Kong hotels. Testimony to its niche position is the fleet of Rolls-Royces and unique helipad. The iconic lobby is the place for afternoon tea, though its proximity to exclusive shops on both sides makes it something of a thoroughfare. Superb spa boasts Roman styled pool and swish terrace. Rooms blend Victorian English and delicate Asian touch; corner suites make most of harbour vista.

RESTAURANTS/餐廳

Recommended/推薦		Also/其他
Chesa/瑞樵閣	⚒	Felix Imasa/今佐
Gaddi's/吉地士	⚒⚒⚒⚒⚒	Verandah/露台餐廳
Spring Moon/嘉麟樓	⚒⚒⚒	

營運了80年，半島是香港酒店的一哥。一列列的勞斯萊斯和獨有的直昇機坪，印證了這裡的特殊地位。具代表性的大堂雖有如大街船，可由兩邊的名店舖進入，但在大堂茶座嘆下午茶可是必然的節目。一流的水療設施包括羅馬式游泳池和時尚的陽台。客房揉合了維多利亞英式及雅緻的亞洲風格，角位套房可將狹長的海景盡收眼底。

■ ADDRESS/地址
TEL.2920 2888
FAX. 2722 4170
Salisbury Road, Kowloon
九龍尖沙咀梳士巴利道
www.peninsula.com

■ ROOMS AND SUITES/客房及套房
Rooms/客房 ＝248
Suites/套房 ＝52
■ PRICE/價錢

👤	$ 4,200-5,600
👥	$ 4,200-5,600
Suites/套房	$ 6,600-68,000
🛏	$ 250

The Royal Garden
帝苑

In a prized position close to Victoria Harbour, the Royal Garden exudes cool class. Its prized possession is a 110 foot atrium that brims with daylight. Its foliage-strewn presence is ubiquitous, as guestrooms are accessible through corridors overlooking it. Some of the rooms boast an enviable harbour view, all of them have relaxing tones: they're more functional than trendy. On the roof is a welcoming surprise: a very pleasant swimming pool.

RESTAURANTS/ 餐廳

Recommended/推薦			Also/其他
Dong Lai Shun/東來順		✗✗	
Inagiku (Kowloon)/稻菊 (九龍)		✗✗	
Le Soleil	☺	✗✗	
Sabatini		✗✗✗	
The Royal Garden/帝苑軒		✗✗	

帝苑酒店毗鄰維多利亞港，地理位置優越，別樹一格。110呎高的中庭陽光普照，氣派不同凡響；又以葉飾作為點綴，從通往客房的走廊望去舉目皆是。部份客房更坐擁怡人海景，所有客房均採用了休閒放鬆的格調，重實用多於潮流。此外，頂層設有一個非常舒適的露天泳池，為住客帶來意想不到的驚喜。

■ ADDRESS/地址
TEL.2721 5215
FAX. 2369 9976
69 Mody Road, Tsim Sha Tsui East,
Kowloon
九龍尖沙咀東部麼地道69號
www.rghk.com.hk

■ ROOMS AND SUITES/客房及套房
Rooms/客房 ＝371
Suites/套房 ＝48

■ PRICE/價錢

🧍	$ 2,900-3,900
🧍🧍	$ 3,100-4,100
Suites/套房	$ 4,800-15,800
🛏	$ 160

The Royal Pacific
皇家太平洋

Situated very near the China and Macao Ferry terminal, this sizeable operation is made up of two buildings: the Hotel wing and the Tower wing. Most bedrooms in the Hotel have been recently renovated and offer sharp modern comforts with minimalist styling. In the Tower, things are more traditional but equally well-maintained. The business traveller is well catered for with a good communications centre and meeting facilities.

RESTAURANTS/ 餐廳

Recommended/推薦

Also/其他

Café on the Park/柏景餐廳
Pierside/堤岸
Satay Inn/沙嗲軒

酒店位置優越，港澳碼頭近在咫尺，共分為兩部分：園景翼和海景翼。園景翼的大部分客房最近經過裝修，風格簡單時尚，十分舒適。至於海景翼，裝潢則較為傳統，但同樣舒適。商務客人更可享用先進的視聽通訊設備和會議設施。

■ ADDRESS/地址
TEL.2736 1188
FAX. 2736 1212
33 Canton Road, China Hong Kong
City, Tsim Sha Tsui, Kowloon
九龍尖沙咀中港城廣東道33號
www.royalpacific.com.hk

■ ROOMS AND SUITES/客房及套房
Rooms/客房 ＝629
Suites/套房 ＝34

■ PRICE/價錢
👤	$ 1,400-2,300
👥	$ 1,400-2,300
Suites/套房	$ 4,800-13,800
☕	$ 130

MACAU
澳門

RESTAURANTS
餐廳

STARRED RESTAURANTS

Within this selection, we have highlighted a number of restaurants for their particularly good cooking. When awarding one, two or three Michelin Stars there are a number of factors we consider: the quality and compatibility of the ingredients, the technical skill and flair that goes into their preparation, the clarity and combination of flavours, the value for money and above all, the taste. Equally important is the ability to produce excellent cooking not once but time and time again. Our inspectors make as many visits as necessary, so that you can be sure of the quality and consistency.

A two or three star restaurant has to offer something very special that separates it from the rest. Three stars – our highest award – are given to the very best.

Cuisines in any style of restaurant and of any nationality are eligible for a star. The decoration, service and comfort levels have no bearing on the award.

星級餐廳

在這系列的選擇裡,我們特意指出菜式上佳的餐廳。
給予一、二或三粒米芝蓮星時,我們考慮到以下因
素:材料的質素和相容性、烹調技巧和特色、氣味
濃度和組合、價錢是否相宜,以及味道。 同樣重要
的是能夠持續提供美食。 我們的評審員會因應需要
而多次到訪,所以讀者可肯定食物品質和一致性。
二或三星餐廳必有獨特之處,比其他餐廳更出眾。
最高評級-三星-只會給予最好的餐廳。
不論餐廳的風格如何,供應哪個國家的菜式,都可獲
星級。 餐廳陳設、服務及舒適程度亦不會影響評級 。

Exceptional cuisine, worth a special journey.
出類拔萃的菜餚，值得專程到訪。

One always eats here extremely well, sometimes superbly. Distinctive dishes are precisely executed, using superlative ingredients.

食客可在這裡享用美味的菜餚，有時令人更讚不絕口。獨特的菜式以最高級的材料精密地烹調。

Robuchon a Galera 法國餐廳	XxXX	330	MAP/地圖 3/B-3

Excellent cuisine, worth a detour.
傑出美食，值得繞道前往。

Skilfully and carefully crafted dishes of outstanding quality.

有技巧地精心烹調菜餚，品質優秀。

Tim's Kitchen 桃花源小廚	XxX	337	MAP/地圖 3/B-3

A very good restaurant in its category.
同類別中出眾的餐廳。

A place offering cuisine prepared to a consistently high standard.

持續高水準菜式的地方。

Imperial Court 金殿堂	XxX	316	MAP/地圖 4/C-1
The Eight 8餐廳	XxX	335	MAP/地圖 3/B-3
Tung Yee Heen 東怡軒	XxX	338	MAP/地圖 4/D-2
Ying 帝影樓	XxX	340	MAP/地圖 5/B-1

BIB GOURMAND

This symbol indicates our inspector's favourites for good value. Restaurants offering good quality cooking for $ 300 or less (price of a 3 course meal excluding drinks).

這標誌表示評審員認為價錢合理而美味的餐廳。300 元或以下便可享用優質美食（三道菜式的價錢，不包括飲料）。

Noodle & Congee Corner 粥麵莊	🍜	326	MAP/地圖 3/B-3
Square Eight 食 · 八方	✗	333	MAP/地圖 4/C-1

RESTAURANTS BY AREA
餐廳 — 以地區分類

Coloane/路環

Kwun Hoi Heen 觀海軒		XxX	319	MAP/地圖 8/C-2

Macau/澳門

Aux Beaux Arts 寶雅座		XX	311	MAP/地圖 4/C-1
Clube Militar de Macau 澳門陸軍俱樂部		XX	313	MAP/地圖 3/B-2
Don Alfonso 當奧豐素		XxxX	314	MAP/地圖 3/B-3
Il Teatro 帝雅廷		XxX	315	MAP/地圖 3/B-3
Imperial Court 金殿堂	✿	XxX	316	MAP/地圖 4/C-1
Inagiku 稻菊		XX	317	MAP/地圖 4/C-3
La Paloma 芭朗瑪		XX	320	MAP/地圖 3/A-2
Litoral 海灣		X	322	MAP/地圖 3/A-1
Naam 藍		XX	324	MAP/地圖 4/D-2
New Furusato 新故鄉		XX	325	MAP/地圖 3/B-3
Noodle & Congee Corner 粥麵莊	⊕	劉	326	MAP/地圖 3/B-3
Okada 岡田		XX	327	MAP/地圖 3/B-3
Portas do Sol 葡京日麗		XX	328	MAP/地圖 3/B-3
Red 8 紅8		X	329	MAP/地圖 3/B-3
Robuchon a Galera 法國餐廳	✿✿✿	XxxX	330	MAP/地圖 3/B-3
Rossio 盛事		XX	332	MAP/地圖 4/C-1
Square Eight 食・八方	⊕	X	333	MAP/地圖 4/C-1
The Eight 8餐廳	✿	XxX	335	MAP/地圖 3/B-3
The Kitchen 大廚		XX	336	MAP/地圖 3/B-3
Tim's Kitchen 桃花源小廚	✿✿	XxX	337	MAP/地圖 3/B-3
Tung Yee Heen 東怡軒	✿	XxX	338	MAP/地圖 4/D-2
Wing Lei 永利軒		XxX	339	MAP/地圖 3/B-3

Taipa/氹仔

Antonio 安東尼奧		ⅩⅩ	308	MAP/地圖 5/B-2
A Petisqueira 葡國美食天地		Ⅹ	309	MAP/地圖 5/B-2
Aurora 奧羅拉		ⅩⅹⅩ	310	MAP/地圖 5/B-1
Canton 喜粵		ⅩⅹⅩ	312	MAP/地圖 6/C-3
Kira 吉良		ⅩⅹⅩ	318	MAP/地圖 5/B-1
Lei Garden 利苑酒家		ⅩⅩ	321	MAP/地圖 6/C-3
Morton's of Chicago		ⅩⅹⅩ	323	MAP/地圖 6/C-3
Roka		ⅩⅩ	331	MAP/地圖 6/C-3
Tenmasa 天政		ⅩⅩ	334	MAP/地圖 5/B-1
Ying 帝影樓	❀	ⅩⅹⅩ	340	MAP/地圖 5/B-1

RESTAURANTS BY CUISINE TYPE
餐廳 — 以菜式分類

Asian / 亞洲菜

Red 8 紅8		✗	329	MAP/地圖 3/B-3
Square Eight 食・八方	🔊	✗	333	MAP/地圖 4/C-1

Cantonese / 粵菜

Canton 喜粵		✗✗✗	312	MAP/地圖 6/C-3
Imperial Court 金殿堂	✿	✗✗✗	316	MAP/地圖 4/C-1
Kwun Hoi Heen 觀海軒		✗✗✗	319	MAP/地圖 8/C-2
Lei Garden 利苑酒家		✗✗	321	MAP/地圖 6/C-3
Portas do Sol 葡京日麗		✗✗	330	MAP/地圖 3/B-3
The Eight 8餐廳	✿	✗✗✗	335	MAP/地圖 3/B-3
Tim's Kitchen 桃花源小廚	✿✿	✗✗✗	337	MAP/地圖 3/B-3
Tung Yee Heen 東怡軒	✿	✗✗✗	338	MAP/地圖 4/D-2
Wing Lei 永利軒		✗✗✗	339	MAP/地圖 3/B-3
Ying 帝影樓	✿	✗✗✗	340	MAP/地圖 5/B-1

French / 法式

Aux Beaux Arts 寶雅座		✗✗	311	MAP/地圖 4/C-1

French contemporary / 時尚法式

Aurora 奧羅拉		✗✗✗	310	MAP/地圖 5/B-1
Robuchon a Galera 法國餐廳	✿✿✿	✗✗✗✗	330	MAP/地圖 3/B-3

Italian / 意式

Don Alfonso 當奧豐素		✗✗✗✗	314	MAP/地圖 3/B-3
Il Teatro 帝雅廷		✗✗✗	315	MAP/地圖 3/B-3

Japanese / 日式

Inagiku 稻菊		✗✗	317	MAP/地圖 4/C-3
Kira 吉良		✗✗✗	318	MAP/地圖 5/B-1
New Furusato 新故鄉		✗✗	325	MAP/地圖 3/B-3
Okada 岡田		✗✗	327	MAP/地圖 3/B-3
Roka		✗✗	331	MAP/地圖 6/C-3

Japanese tempura / 日式天婦羅

Tenmasa 天政		✗✗	334	MAP/地圖 5/B-1

Macanese / 澳門菜

Litoral 海灣		✗	322	MAP/地圖 3/A-1

Mediterranean / 地中海菜

Rossio 盛事		✗✗	332	MAP/地圖 4/C-1

Noodle & congee / 粥麵

Noodle & Congee Corner 粥麵莊	✆	🍜	326	MAP/地圖 3/B-3

Portuguese / 葡式

Antonio 安東尼奧		✗✗	308	MAP/地圖 5/B-2
A Petisqueira 葡國美食天地		✗	309	MAP/地圖 5/B-2
Clube Militar de Macau 澳門陸軍俱樂部		✗✗	313	MAP/地圖 3/B-2

Spanish / 西班牙菜

La Paloma 芭朗瑪		✗✗	320	MAP/地圖 3/A-2

Steakhouse / 扒房

Morton's of Chicago		✗✗✗	323	MAP/地圖 6/C-3
The Kitchen 大廚		✗✗	336	MAP/地圖 3/B-3

Thai / 泰式

Naam 藍		✗✗	324	MAP/地圖 4/D-2

RESTAURANTS PARTICULARLY PLEASANT
上佳的餐廳

RESTAURANTS WITH A VIEW
有景觀的餐廳

RESTAURANTS
WITH PRIVATE ROOMS
具備私人房間的餐廳

Aurora 奧羅拉		XxX	310	MAP/地圖 5/B-1
Aux Beaux Arts 寶雅座		XX	311	MAP/地圖 4/C-1
Canton 喜粵		XxX	312	MAP/地圖 6/C-3
Clube Militar de Macau 澳門陸軍俱樂部		XX	313	MAP/地圖 3/B-2
Don Alfonso 當奧豐素		XxxX	314	MAP/地圖 3/B-3
Il Teatro 帝雅廷		XxX	315	MAP/地圖 3/B-3
Imperial Court 金殿堂	✿	XxX	316	MAP/地圖 4/C-1
Inagiku 稻菊		XX	317	MAP/地圖 4/C-3
Kira 吉良		XxX	318	MAP/地圖 5/B-1
Kwun Hoi Heen 觀海軒		XxX	319	MAP/地圖 8/C-2
La Paloma 芭朗瑪		XX	320	MAP/地圖 3/A-2
Lei Garden 利苑酒家		XX	321	MAP/地圖 6/C-3
Litoral 海灣		X	322	MAP/地圖 3/A-1
Morton's of Chicago		XxX	323	MAP/地圖 6/C-3
New Furusato 新故鄉		XX	325	MAP/地圖 3/B-3
Robuchon a Galera 法國餐廳	✿✿✿	XxxX	330	MAP/地圖 3/B-3
Roka		XX	331	MAP/地圖 6/C-3
Rossio 盛事		XX	332	MAP/地圖 4/C-1
Tenmasa 天政		XX	334	MAP/地圖 5/B-1
The Eight 8餐廳	✿	XxX	335	MAP/地圖 3/B-3
The Kitchen 大廚		XX	336	MAP/地圖 3/B-3
Tim's Kitchen 桃花源小廚	✿✿	XxX	337	MAP/地圖 3/B-3
Tung Yee Heen 東怡軒	✿	XxX	338	MAP/地圖 4/D-2
Wing Lei 永利軒		XxX	339	MAP/地圖 3/B-3
Ying 帝影樓	✿	XxX	340	MAP/地圖 5/B-1

Antonio
安東尼奧

You really feel you're in Portugal when you're in cosy little Antonio's, with its dark wood floor, Portuguese inspired
paintings and crisp blue and white tiles. Ask Antonio for his
menu recommendations: not only will he tell you his specials, which include gratinated goat cheese with honey and
olive oil as a starter, and monkfish, rice and prawns as a
main course; he'll also happily give you the lowdown on how
he got from Portugal to Macau.

置身於舒適的安東尼奧餐廳，感覺就像身處葡萄牙一樣：深色木地板、葡式油
畫，以及典型的藍白色瓷磚，裝潢甚具風味。安東尼奧的推介相當不錯，他不
但會向你推薦他的拿手菜式，包括蜜糖橄欖油烤山羊芝士作前菜，以及鮟鱇魚
鮮蝦飯作主菜；同時亦很樂於細說他從葡萄牙來到澳門的故事。

■ ADDRESS/地址   ■ OPENING HOURS, LAST ORDER
TEL.2899 9998   營業時間, 最後點菜時間
Rua dos Negociantes 3, Taipa   Lunch/午膳 12:00-15:00 (L.O.)
氹仔客商街3號   Dinner/晚膳 18:00-23:00 (L.O.)
www.antoniomacau.com
                                    ■ PRICE/價錢
                                    Lunch/午膳 carte/點菜 MOP200-500
                                    Dinner/晚膳 carte/點菜 MOP200-500

A Petisqueira
葡國美食天地

Don't be put off by the unattractive façade. Step through the door here and you could be in a cosy little restaurant in the Portuguese countryside. A tiny bar at the entrance leads you into a simple, rustic dining room with nothing fancy on the menu, just decent Portuguese cuisine served in a friendly, unpretentious atmosphere. Authentic dishes include bacalhau prepared in five different ways, fried clams, and six to seven specials of the day.

不要因餐廳外觀不吸引而卻步，踏入大門你便會感受到這裡舒適的葡國風情。餐廳入口設有小酒吧，而餐室本身設計簡樸，菜式亦毫不花巧，以親切友善的服務奉上不俗的葡國美食。正宗的菜式包括以五種不同方法烹調的馬介休、炒蜆，以及六至七款是日精選。

■ ADDRESS/地址
TEL.2882 5354
Rua S. Joao 15, Taipa
氹仔生央街15號

■ ANNUAL AND WEEKLY CLOSING
　　休息日期
Closed 10 days April, 10 days
September and Monday
週一、四月及九月各休息十天

■ OPENING HOURS, LAST ORDER
　　營業時間, 最後點菜時間
Lunch/午膳 12:00-14:30 (L.O.)
Dinner/晚膳 18:30-22:15 (L.O.)

■ PRICE/價錢
Lunch/午膳　carte/點菜 MOP160-260
Dinner/晚膳　carte/點菜 MOP160-260

Aurora
奧羅拉

Diners are spoilt for choice at Aurora: there's the option of
easy-going Gallic brasserie fare or a more upmarket gastronomic menu based on contemporary French cuisine. You
have a choice of where to eat, too: the casual brasserie, the
elegant dining room with its silver cutlery, the outside terrace with its great view over Macau, or an exclusive dining
room in a small terrace tower. Another choice: select from a
remarkable 500-strong wine list.

這裡菜式選擇之多令食客三心兩意，涵蓋高盧式簡樸餐館的菜式，以及以時尚
法國美食為主的較高價菜式。食客亦可自選用餐的地方，包括無拘束的簡樸餐
室範圍、採用銀器食具的高雅餐室、坐擁澳門美景的露台，以及座落於小塔上
的私人餐室。可供選擇的還有五百種烈酒，琳瑯滿目。

■ ADDRESS/地址
TEL.8803 6622
10F, Crown Towers Hotel, Avenida de
Kwong Tung, Taipa
氹仔廣東大馬路皇冠酒店10樓
www.crown-macau.com

■ OPENING HOURS, LAST ORDER
營業時間, 最後點菜時間
Dinner/晚膳 18:00-24:00 (L.O.)

■ PRICE/價錢
Dinner/晚膳 menu/套餐 MOP250-1,180
carte/點菜 MOP280-650

Aux Beaux Arts
寶雅座

This elegant Parisian-style brasserie has a true Belle Epoque feel with classic 1930s bubble-glass chandeliers, and original French paintings from that period, loaned from a Shanghai museum. There's a pleasant terrace for the romantically inclined, as well as a beautiful glass-enclosed cellar for private parties, the Russian room for caviar, and the Ice bar for champagne. Authentic French classics include 'les cocottes': casserole specialities.

這家巴黎風格的餐廳配置著三十年代的經典氣泡玻璃吊燈，與從上海博物館借回來的法國原畫，交織成美麗時期(Belle Epoque)的優雅品味和純正氣質。追求浪漫的食客可選擇在舒適的陽台用餐，而漂亮的玻璃牆地窖則適合舉辦私人派對。魚子屋 供應魚子醬，香檳庫 則提供香檳，美饌佳釀各適其適。經典法國菜式原汁原味，包括公認為砂鍋美食的各種烤肉(les cocottes)。

■ ADDRESS/地址

TEL.8802 3888
GF, MGM Grand Hotel, Avenida Dr Sun Yat Sen , Nape
外港新填海區孫逸仙大馬路美高梅金殿地下
www.mgmgrandmacau.com

■ OPENING HOURS, LAST ORDER
營業時間, 最後點菜時間
Dinner/晚膳 18:30-22:30 (L.O.)

■ PRICE/價錢
Dinner/晚膳 carte/點菜 MOP360-660

Canton
喜粵

Located in a corner of the world's biggest indoor gaming floor, Canton is a smart restaurant with a chic smoked glass façade and elegant walkway that has a glass floor and classic English Georgian-style plaster ceiling! The dining room of just eight tables is a deep sensual red in colour, and very modern in design. A Kouan-Chiau (gastronomic) version of Cantonese cooking prevails, though Shanghai steamed dumplings have their own section.

座落於世上最大室內娛樂場的一角，喜粵擁有時尚的煙灰玻璃外觀，配備玻璃地板的高貴走廊，以及英國喬治風格的經典灰泥天花板，設計別出心裁！只有八張餐桌的餐室呈誘人的深紅色，設計甚具現代感。喜粵的菜單以廣州粵菜為主，亦有提供一系列的餃子。

■ ADDRESS/地址

TEL.8118 9930

Shop 1018, Casino level, The Venetian Resort, Estrada da Baia de N. Senhora de Esperanca, s/n, The Cotai Strip, Taipa

冰仔路冰金光大道-望德聖母灣大馬路威尼斯人酒店地下1018號舖

■ OPENING HOURS, LAST ORDER
營業時間, 最後點菜時間

Lunch/午膳 11:00-15:00 (L.O.)
Dinner/晚膳 18:00-23:00 (L.O.)

■ PRICE/價錢

Lunch/午膳 carte/點菜 MOP160-590
Dinner/晚膳 carte/點菜 MOP160-590

Clube Militar de Macau
澳門陸軍俱樂部

🍽20 📞🍴

This classic piece of 19th century Portuguese architecture used to be an army mess hall – unfortunately its lovely bar and lounge is only available to club members. Dining – for the public – takes place in a big, rather empty, room with echoing wood floors, potted palms at netted windows, and Colonial ambience. The Portuguese cooking is straightforward, hearty and tasty. Typical dishes are bacalhau (dried cod) and 'Bairrada' style suckling pig.

陸軍俱樂部始建於十九世紀，氣派典雅，原興建以供葡軍的食堂。雖然酒吧及休息室都是會員專用，不過餐廳對外開放，讓食客可盡情大快朵頤。餐廳地方寬敞，採用木地板，窗前擺放棕櫚盆栽，襯托著整幢建築的殖民地色彩。這裡的葡國菜既簡單又充滿心思，味道濃郁，香味十足。經典菜式包括馬介休(鹽醃製深海鱈魚)及葡式烤乳豬。

■ ADDRESS/地址

TEL.2871 4000
Avenida da Praia Grande 975
南灣大馬路975號

■ OPENING HOURS, LAST ORDER
 營業時間, 最後點菜時間
Lunch/午膳 12:00-15:00 L.O. 14:45
Dinner/晚膳 19:00-23:00 L.O. 22:30

■ PRICE/價錢
Lunch/午膳 carte/點菜 MOP189-264
Dinner/晚膳 carte/點菜 MOP189-264

Don Alfonso
當奧豐素

X X X X

& ☞ **P** 🍴10 ☎🍴 🎴

Don Alfonso is a Chinese 'take' on an Italian restaurant. There's an opulent dining room featuring dozens of red Murano chandeliers and a huge fresco of the Italian coast divided into five parts. A pity then that the local waitresses can't speak Italian. The dated feel and bright lights can also detract from the experience, but the cuisine uses well selected ingredients, and flavours are clean and sharp. Service can be almost overly attentive.

Don Alfonso可説是「意大利在澳門」，豪華的餐室設有許多紅色的穆拉諾穆玻璃吊燈，以及一幅把意大利海岸分為五部分的巨型壁畫，盡顯其獨特之處；只可惜本地侍應不懂説意大利語。古老的風格和明亮的燈光可能令人分心，不過這裡的菜式選材不俗，清新味美，服務更幾乎是太過周到。

■ ADDRESS/地址

TEL.8803 7722

3F, Grand Lisboa Hotel, Avenida de Lisboa
葡京路新葡京酒店3樓
www.grandlisboa.com

■ OPENING HOURS, LAST ORDER
營業時間, 最後點菜時間
Lunch/午膳　12:00-14:30 (L.O.)
Dinner/晚膳　18:30-22:30 (L.O.)

■ PRICE/價錢
Lunch/午膳　menu/套餐MOP1,390
　　　　　　carte/點菜 MOP510-1,230
Dinner/晚膳　menu/套餐MOP1,390
　　　　　　carte/點菜 MOP510-1,230

Il Teatro
帝雅廷

To recommend a restaurant for something other than its food may seem odd, but at Il Teatro it appears most diners turn up primarily to watch the stunning fountains; these are in a lake and are musically choreographed to change colour and appearance every few minutes. Book a table with a good view! And don't wear sneakers, or you won't get in. The cuisine? Straightforward Italian fare, such as seafood risotto or pasta, served with style and élan.

推薦一家餐廳的菜餚以外的物品聽上來有點奇怪，不過大部分到帝雅廷的食客似乎主要是為了觀賞噴泉美景。餐廳七成以上的座位是面向表演湖噴池，每數分鐘音樂水柱交替、激光穿梭的震撼，在帝雅廷可盡收眼簾。記得預訂面向噴泉的座位！不過要記住穿著波鞋是不准進入的。至於菜餚方面，餐廳提供簡單的意大利菜，例如海鮮意大利飯或意大利粉，菜式風格獨特，服務殷勤周到。

■ ADDRESS/地址

TEL.8986 3663
GF, Wynn Hotel, Rua Cidade de Sintra, Nape
外港填海區仙德麗街永利酒店地下
www.wynnmacau.com

■ OPENING HOURS, LAST ORDER
營業時間, 最後點菜時間
Dinner/晚膳 17:30-24:30 (L.O.)

■ PRICE/價錢
Dinner/晚膳 carte/點菜 MOP380-650

Imperial Court
金殿堂

❄

🦽 👆 **P** 🍽30 🍽 🎴

An elegant and contemporary restaurant on the same floor as the hotel lobby. Chinese status seekers select from six private dining rooms; most visitors are content with the main room, where they can stare at the main point of interest: a massive marble pillar with carved dragon. Celebrity chef Chow Chong supervises Cantonese cuisine that seeks to make the most of refined preparations based on the finest ingredients, served by attentive staff.

這家現代風格的高雅餐廳位於酒店大堂同層。餐廳設有六間私人餐室，名人貴冑樂在其中；而大部分其他食客都喜歡在主餐室用餐，因為可觀賞大型的大理石雕龍圓柱，氣派富麗堂皇。由名廚周中主理的高級粵菜，是以頂級材料烹調的出色菜式。服務周全，態度一流。

■ ADDRESS/地址

TEL.8802 3888
GF, MGM Grand Hotel, Avenida Dr. Sun Yat Sen, Nape
外港新填海區孫逸仙大馬路美高梅金殿堂店地下
www.mgmgrandmacau.com

■ OPENING HOURS, LAST ORDER
營業時間，最後點菜時間
Lunch/午膳 12:00-14:30 L.O. 14:00
Dinner/晚膳 18:00-23:00 L.O. 22:30

■ PRICE/價錢
Lunch/午膳   carte/點菜 MOP300-1,000
Dinner/晚膳   carte/點菜 MOP500-1,000

Inagiku
稻菊

XX

☞ 🚋20 🚃

Gamblers, fashionistas and foodies make this a destination of choice in Macau. A serious and well-run Japanese restaurant, Inagiku stands out from the others in Starworld because of its laid-back, relaxing aura, which balances contemporary style, Japanese culture and clubby vibes. You can select a table, or sit at the sushi bar, tempura area or teppanyaki counter. Excellent ingredients are fresh from the market, and prepared with skill and flair.

稻菊是一家成功的日本餐廳，營運認真，娛樂場玩家、追捧潮流者和食家紛紛到此朝聖。稻菊與酒店其他食肆的不同之處在於其輕鬆悠閒的氣氛，與現代風格、日本文化及夜店感覺相映成趣。食客可以選擇在餐桌、壽司吧、天婦羅區或鐵板燒檯用餐。一流食材由市場新鮮運抵，並經精心炮製，廚藝出眾。

■ ADDRESS/地址
TEL.2878 1111
5F, StarWorld Hotel, Avenida da Amizade
友誼大馬路星際酒店5樓
www.starworldmacau.com

■ OPENING HOURS, LAST ORDER
營業時間, 最後點菜時間
Lunch/午膳 12:00-14:30 (L.O.)
Dinner/晚膳 18:00-23:30 (L.O.)

■ PRICE/價錢
Lunch/午膳　carte/點菜 MOP200-600
Dinner/晚膳　carte/點菜 MOP200-600

Kira
吉良

Kira's dramatically designed private rooms contrast with the stylishly subdued lighting of the main restaurant as customers choose ingredients from behind a glass counter, and see them prepared at two teppanyaki bars. Best of all is to dine in one of the four small Japanese-style houses on a nearby terrace with Macau views. Dishes are cooked with skill, flair and precision to a high quality: a quiet ambience reveals diners focused on the food.

這裡的貴賓房設計大膽，與照明時髦的主廳相映成趣。在主廳的顧客可以在玻璃櫃檯前選擇喜愛的食材，然後在看著大廚在兩個鐵板燒吧後炮製美食。在露台上的四個日式小室裡一邊觀賞澳門美景，一邊品嘗精美菜色，簡直是最佳享受。大廚不僅廚藝出色，極具天賦，而且對品質非常堅持；在幽靜的餐廳裏，你絕對能感受到客人對美食的專注！

■ ADDRESS/地址
TEL.8803 6633
10F, Crown Towers Hotel, Avenida de Kwong Tung, Taipa
氹仔廣東大馬路皇冠酒店10樓
www.crown-macau.com

■ OPENING HOURS, LAST ORDER
營業時間, 最後點菜時間
Dinner/晚膳 18:00-24:00 (L.O.)

■ PRICE/價錢
Dinner/晚膳 menu/套餐 MOP480-1,800
carte/點菜 MOP300-1,200

Kwun Hoi Heen
觀海軒

The restaurant name translates as 'with a nice sea view', and it can't be contradicted on that score, as its large picture windows overlook Hac Sa Bay. It's a popular weekend spot for locals escaping Macau city, though the vibe is more corporate on weekdays. Appealing menus feature a great lunchtime selection of fresh and tasty dim sum; in the evenings there's a good seasonally changing Cantonese choice of dumpling, rice, noodles and dessert.

觀海軒名副其實,坐擁怡人的黑沙灣海景。澳門人喜愛在週末到訪,遠離城市的煩囂,而週日則較多商務客人光顧。餐廳的菜餚令人食指大動,包括午膳時間供應的點心,既新鮮又味美;而傍晚時分供應的粵菜,四季風味不同,更有多種選擇,涵蓋各種餃子、飯類、麵食及甜品。

■ ADDRESS/地址
TEL. 8899 1320
3F, The Westin Resort, 1918 Estrata de Hac Sa, Coloane
路環黑沙馬路1918號威斯汀度假酒店3號
www.westin.com/macau

■ OPENING HOURS, LAST ORDER
營業時間,最後點菜時間
Lunch/午膳 12:00-15:00 L.O. 14:30
Dinner/晚膳 18:30-23:00 L.O. 22:30

■ PRICE/價錢
Lunch/午膳   carte/點菜 MOP200-1,000
Dinner/晚膳   carte/點菜 MOP250-1,000

La Paloma
芭朗瑪

Secluded like hidden treasure from the rest of the city, La Paloma is a very appealing restaurant and bar, enhanced by a charming terrace, floor-to-ceiling glass, and stone walls, which are part of the original 17th century fortress foundations. A bold nouveau riche style of furniture lends it a casual chic; it's wonderfully intimate and romantic at nights. The refined Spanish cuisine offers a great assortment of tapas and exquisite paellas.

芭朗瑪餐廳及酒吧，位於一座十七世紀舊城堡改建而成的酒店，遠離城市的煩囂。迷人的露台、落地玻璃和古堡原來的石牆，構成芭朗瑪的獨特風采。傢具陳設高尚優雅，氣派舒適時尚，晚上更是浪漫醉人。餐廳的西班牙菜精緻優雅，涵蓋多種西班牙前菜(tapas)及精美的西班牙海鮮飯(paella)。

■ ADDRESS/地址
TEL.2837 8111
2F, Pousada de São Tiago Hotel, Avenida da República, Fortaleza de São Tiago da Barra
西灣民國大馬路聖地牙哥古堡酒店2樓
www.saotiago.com.mo

■ OPENING HOURS, LAST ORDER
營業時間, 最後點菜時間
Lunch/午膳 12:00-14:30 (L.O.)
Dinner/晚膳 18:30-22:30 (L.O.)

■ PRICE/價錢
Lunch/午膳   menu/套餐MOP1,600
                     carte/點菜 MOP400-700
Dinner/晚膳 menu/套餐MOP1,600
                     carte/點菜 MOP400-700

Lei Garden
利苑酒家

⚒

☞♀ ⌂16

Smart restaurant set amongst the canals of this vast hotel's third floor! Arrive on a gondola if you wish...Venetian guests predominate here; gamblers mostly give it a miss as it's too far from the gaming tables. Walls of marble provide the backdrop to a comprehensive range of traditional Cantonese dishes served at breakneck speed by an efficient team of waiters. The best place to be seated is in one of the cosy booths just inside the front door.

餐廳設於三樓，佔據此巨型酒店的運河旁位置，雄據地利。有興趣不妨乘坐貢朵拉前往餐廳。這裡的顧客以酒店住客為主；因為離博彩桌太遠，娛樂場玩家通常會選擇其他餐廳。大理石的牆壁與清一色的傳統廣東菜配合得天衣無縫。侍應生服務速度簡直快如閃電，極有效率！這裡最好的座位是靠近前門的舒適卡位。

■ ADDRESS/地址

TEL.2882 8689
Shop 2130, 3F Grand Canal Shoppes, The Venetian Resort, Estrada da Baia de N. Senhora de Esperança, Taipa
氹仔路望德聖母灣大馬路威尼斯人酒店大運河購物中心3樓2130號舖

■ OPENING HOURS, LAST ORDER
   營業時間, 最後點菜時間
Lunch/午膳 11:30-14:30 L.O. 14:00
Dinner/晚膳 18:00-23:00 L.O. 22:00

■ PRICE/價錢
Lunch/午膳   carte/點菜 MOP136-240
Dinner/晚膳 carte/點菜 MOP136-240

Litoral
海灣餐廳

✂

🍽120

The neat and tidy façade of Litoral compensates for the charmless street in which it's located. The small exterior is deceiving: the interior goes over two floors and 250 diners can be accommodated – though this can prove a bit of a challenge to the waiting staff! The rustic atmosphere is courtesy of Portuguese nuance, which also influences the menus, along with local Macanese dishes. Specialities include baked crab meat and grilled dried cod.

雖然餐廳所處的街道稍欠魅力，但整潔的正門令人留下好印象。看似狹窄的外觀頗有誤導成份：內裡共分為兩層，可以容納約250位顧客—不過這對餐廳員工來説可能是個挑戰！樸素的氣氛極具葡萄牙特色，這亦反映在餐廳菜式及本地菜式中。特別推介焗蟹蓋及燒馬介休。

■ ADDRESS/地址
TEL.2896 7878
Rua do Almirante Sérgio, 261A
河邊新街261A舖

■ OPENING HOURS, LAST ORDER
　營業時間, 最後點菜時間
Lunch/午膳 12:00-15:00 L.O. 14:45
Dinner/晚膳 18:00-22:30 L.O. 22:00

■ PRICE/價錢
Lunch/午膳　carte/點菜 MOP200-450
Dinner/晚膳　carte/點菜 MOP200-450

Morton's of Chicago

Big, butch and boasting a masculine-friendly ambience of dark wood, tuxedo-attired Maitre D' and swinging Rat Pack music, Morton's dishes up the 1950s big city US experience. There's even a bar serving all kinds of Martinis! The prices are certainly higher than they would have been fifty years ago, but casually elegant clientele create a lively atmosphere as they attack the hash browns, cream spinach and, of course, platefuls of prime cut beef.

地方寬敞、深色木材裝潢、身穿禮服的侍應總管，加上Rat Pack背景音樂，揉合成Morton's餐廳的男士格調，營造五十年代的美國大城市體驗。這家扒房餐廳的酒吧更提供各式各樣的Martini！餐飲價格當然比五十年前高，不過客人無拘無束，自然令餐廳氣氛輕鬆。經典美式佳餚包括馬鈴薯煎餅、忌廉菠菜，更少不了的當然是豐富的頂級牛扒。

■ ADDRESS/地址

TEL.8117 5000

Shop 1016, Grand Canal Shoppes, The Venetian Resort, Estrada da Baia de N. Senhora de Esperanca, s/n, The Cotai Strip, Taipa

氹仔路氹金光大道-望德聖母灣大馬路威尼斯人酒店大運河購物中心1016號舖

www.mortons.com

■ OPENING HOURS, LAST ORDER
營業時間, 最後點菜時間
Dinner/晚膳 18:00-24:00 L.O. 23:30

■ PRICE/價錢
Dinner/晚膳 carte/點菜 MOP400-700

Naam
藍

An elegant and serene restaurant that's spot-on for décor and location: there's the tranquil presence of a fountain in the middle of the room and views on to a pool and luxurious tropical garden outside. The restaurant, bathed in natural light, focuses entirely on Thai cuisine, with recipes from all regions of the country. Best way to start is to sample the range of appetisers. Then follow symbols for vegetarian, spicy or chef's signature dishes.

藍泰國餐廳優雅寧靜，地點和裝潢均恰到好處。餐廳中心設有寧靜的噴泉，外面是泳池和茂密的熱帶花園，景致優美，天然陽光更滲透餐廳裡頭。菜餚全都是泰國菜，包含不同地區的特色美食。建議先從前菜入手，然後從素食、辛辣或廚師推介的云云菜式中挑選。

■ ADDRESS/地址
TEL.8793 4818
Mandarin Oriental , 956-1110 Avenida da Amizade
友誼大馬路文華東方酒店956-1110號
www.mandarinoriental.com/macau

■ OPENING HOURS, LAST ORDER
營業時間, 最後點菜時間
Lunch/午膳 12:00-14:30 (L.O.)
Dinner/晚膳 18:30-22:30 (L.O.)

■ PRICE/價錢
Lunch/午膳　carte/點菜 MOP220-550
Dinner/晚膳　carte/點菜 MOP220-550

New Furusato
新故鄉

✗✗

🖐️ 🅿️ 🍽️10 🚇 🍇

Called 'New' Furusato because of a recent total refurbishment, this chic restaurant boasts quite tasteful décor which combines Japanese style with modern art and swish fabrics...though the walk-in wine cellar at the entrance, with a choice of 60 sake, may grab your attention first! There's the customary sushi bar, teppanyaki and tempura counters, the latter two having views onto the shimmering Wynns Hotel. Professional service is a bonus.

由於餐廳最近進行全面裝修，顧名思義，這裡便命名為 'New'Furusato。餐廳風格時尚，設計品味獨特，揉合日本風格和現代藝術，並採用型格布料。不過，入口處擁有60種燒酒的酒櫃，可能已搶先吸引了你的注意力！餐廳設有壽司吧、鐵板燒和天婦羅檯，於後兩者就座都可觀賞永利酒店的景色。此外，專業的服務態度更令人賓至如歸。

■ ADDRESS/地址

TEL.2888 3888
2F, Lisboa Hotel, East Wing, 2-4
Avenida de Lisboa
葡京路2-4號葡京酒店東翼2樓
www.hotelisboa.com

■ OPENING HOURS, LAST ORDER
營業時間, 最後點菜時間
Lunch/午膳 12:00-14:30 (L.O.)
Dinner/晚膳 18:30-22:30 (L.O.)

■ PRICE/價錢
Lunch/午膳　menu/套餐 MOP400-780
　　　　　　carte/點菜 MOP160-820
Dinner/晚膳　menu/套餐 MOP400-780
　　　　　　carte/點菜 MOP160-820

Noodle & Congee Corner
粥麵莊

This simple, good value eatery is located – incongruously – on a gallery that opens onto the casino. It's really a cafeteria, or even 'tea-eria', as one wall is full of teapots. What's special for diners is the view they have of chefs from different parts of the country preparing a noodle speciality from their home region using fresh, tasty produce. These can be combined with various soups and ingredients: the menus, handily, include photos.

這家簡樸的餐廳提供價錢合宜的美食，位於娛樂場上層樓上，彼此風格迥然不同。粥麵莊的確是一家餐館，而其中一道牆更放滿茶壺，洋溢著「茶 檔」的感覺。特別的是食客更可在晚餐時觀賞來自五湖四海的廚師，採用新鮮味美的食材，分別炮製出家鄉的特色麵食的烹飪過程！餐廳亦提供不同款式的湯類和其他菜式；菜單附有圖片，便於瀏覽。

■ ADDRESS/地址
TEL.2828 3838
1F, Grand Lisboa Hotel, Avenida de Lisboa
葡京路新葡京酒店1樓
www.grandlisboa.com

■ OPENING HOURS, LAST ORDER
營業時間, 最後點菜時間
Open 24 hours
24小時營業

■ PRICE/價錢
Lunch/午膳　carte/點菜 MOP90-380
Dinner/晚膳　carte/點菜 MOP90-380

Okada
岡田

Situated alongside the casino, there are no prizes for guessing the clientele of this attractive restaurant whose pale, dry-stone walls are its most appealing feature, its garden views obscured by a wall of bamboo. Apart from the main room, there's a sushi counter and grill bar. The menu delivers a large Japanese menu – sushi, sashimi, tempura, teppanyaki, grilled fish – but authenticity can be sacrificed in the desire to 'refuel' gamblers.

毗鄰娛樂場的日式料理不用猜想都知食客固然也是娛樂場的顧客。餐廳的淺色石牆魅力獨特，十分迷人；而竹林的排列則使園林景致若隱若現。餐廳設有主餐室、壽司吧和燒烤吧。菜單涵蓋大量日本菜式，包括壽司、天婦羅、鐵板燒、烤魚等等。味道可能不夠正宗，不過可以為食客「充 電」，然後繼續到娛樂場大展身手。

■ ADDRESS/地址
TEL.8986 3663
Wynn Hotel, Rua Cidade de Sintra, Nape
外港新填海區仙德麗街永利酒店
www.wynnmacau.com

■ OPENING HOURS, LAST ORDER
營業時間, 最後點菜時間
Dinner/晚膳 17:30-24:30 (L.O.)

■ PRICE/價錢
Dinner/晚膳 carte/點菜 MOP240-560

Portas do Sol
葡京日麗

✗✗

Never mind the food – Portas do Sol is as popular for its dancing as its menus. Macau's most kitsch restaurant is a 1960s ballroom with a stage and regular live music catering to all tastes. Large round tables and mirrored pillars surround the dance floor; when customers get round to eating, it's well-executed Cantonese cuisine that's on offer, served attentively by waitresses in bright pink dresses. On weekends, dim sum is served from 9:30am.

別只談菜餚，在Portas do Sol跳舞和用餐同是一大享受。巨型圓桌和鑲鏡柱子環繞著舞池，六十年代的舞池除設有舞台外，定期更會有不同類型的即場音樂表演，不愧為澳門最懷舊的餐廳。這裡的粵菜味道出眾；侍應穿著鮮粉紅色裙子，服務更是周到。每逢週末，午市由早上9時30分開始供應點心。

■ ADDRESS/地址
TEL.2888 3888
2F, Lisboa Hotel, 2-4 Avenida de Lisboa
葡京路2-4號葡京酒店2樓

■ OPENING HOURS, LAST ORDER
    營業時間, 最後點菜時間
Lunch/午膳 11:30-14:30 (L.O.)
Dinner/晚膳 18:30-23:30 (L.O.)

■ PRICE/價錢
Lunch/午膳   carte/點菜 MOP100-2,800
Dinner/晚膳   carte/點菜 MOP130-2,800

Red 8
紅8

If you enjoy a buzzing atmosphere full of gamblers, then this is the place to eat. Mind you, if you like to gaze at the world outside, then give Red 8 a wide berth, as it's located in the hotel's casino room and there are no windows. You either face the chefs preparing food behind large glass windows, or stare at the players. Cheap, unpretentious cuisine features the signature Beijing duck, and an array of noodle dishes from across Asia.

假如你喜愛在滿佈娛樂場玩家的熱鬧的環境下用餐,這裡不失為一家好餐廳。假如你喜歡觀賞戶外景色,紅8在這方面則略嫌不足-餐廳位處酒店的娛樂場裡,沒有窗戶;你可面向玻璃窗後的廚師,或轉向娛樂場內的玩家。菜式簡單正宗,價錢便宜。招牌菜包括北京填鴨,以及多款亞洲各地風味的麵食。

■ ADDRESS/地址

TEL.2888 9966

GF, Wynn Hotel, Rua Cidade de Sintra, Nape

外港新填海區仙德麗街永利酒店地下

www.wynnmacau.com

■ OPENING HOURS, LAST ORDER
營業時間, 最後點菜時間

Open 24 hours

24小時營業

■ PRICE/價錢

Lunch/午膳 carte/點菜 MOP150-300

Dinner/晚膳 carte/點菜 MOP150-300

Robuchon a Galera
法國餐廳

World famous Joël Robuchon's chic offering in Macau offers a suitably stylish location to dine. The restaurant's early 19th century ambience has a warm, soft, and cosy feel, accentuated by elegant and expensive fabrics. Excellent fresh ingredients underpin contemporary Gallic cuisine; the bread trolley, with its large choice of wonderful home-made breads, is of note. The wine list, too, is superb, with over 3,400 wines from around the world.

蜚聲國際的名廚Joël Robuchon於澳門營運時尚的Robuchon a Galera，餐廳洋溢著十九世紀初的氣氛，採用昂貴而高雅的布料，感覺溫暖舒適。當代風格的高廬菜式沿用新鮮的優質食材，而自製麵包更是選擇繁多，味道一流。此外，餐廳亦供應超過3,400種來自世界各地的上等美酒。

■ ADDRESS/地址
TEL.2888 3888
3F, Lisboa Hotel, 2-4 Avenida de Lisboa
葡京路2-4號葡京酒店3樓
www.hotelisboa.com

■ OPENING HOURS, LAST ORDER
營業時間, 最後點菜時間
Lunch/午膳 12:00-14:30 (L.O.)
Dinner/晚膳 18:30-22:30 (L.O.)

■ PRICE/價錢
Lunch/午膳   menu/套餐MOP328-538
     carte/點菜 MOP720-1,970
Dinner/晚膳 menu/套餐MOP1,850
     carte/點菜 MOP720-1,970

Roka

XX

♿ ☝ **P** ⏤30 🚉

A clean and minimalist décor ensures a refreshing respite from the Venetian's slot machines. Epicentre of Roka is the Robata grill and its surrounding counter: signature dish is rib-eye steak. Also recommended is excellent sashimi and artfully presented maki rolls, with premium quality fish flown from the Tokyo market. Also of note is the wide range of tempura. Friendly service and a convivial shochu bar add lustre to an agreeable experience.

Roka地方整潔，裝潢設計風格抽象簡約。從威尼斯人的老虎機踱過來，感覺煥然一新。餐廳中心是爐端燒和周邊櫃檯，招牌菜式包括肉眼扒。其他推介菜色包括頂級的刺身和手工精細的壽司卷，所採用的魚類品質一流，由東京市場新鮮運到。此外，天婦羅更是選擇繁多。服務賓至如歸，Roka設有燒酎吧，使佳餚美酒的體驗更添姿采。

■ ADDRESS/地址

TEL.2882 5666

Shop 1015, GF, Grand Canal Shoppes, The Venetian Resort, Estrada da Baia de N. Senhora de Esperanca, s/n, The Cotai Strip, Taipa

氹仔路氹金光大道 - 望德聖母灣大馬路威尼斯人酒店地下大運河購物中心1015號鋪

www.rokarestaurant.com

■ OPENING HOURS, LAST ORDER
營業時間, 最後點菜時間

Lunch/午膳 12:00-15:00 L.O. 14:30
Dinner/晚膳 18:00-23:00 L.O. 22:30

■ PRICE/價錢

Lunch/午膳   menu/套餐 MOP230-290
              carte/點菜 MOP400-1,400
Dinner/晚膳   menu/套餐 MOP888-1,588
              carte/點菜 MOP400-1,400

Rossio
盛事

There's a minimalist Zen calm here: natural elements such as waterfalls and Japanese granite stones merge seamlessly into an elegant terrace. Chefs in the open kitchen conjure up a vibrant contrast as they produce a plethora of delicious international dishes on grill, steamer and wok. Pre-eminence is Mediterranean cuisine, particularly Portuguese, although sushi and steak are well represented, too. Ingredients and preparations are top-notch.

高雅的陽台採用了天然元素，包括瀑布和日本花崗石，交織成極簡抽象派藝術氣息及禪的寧靜感。開放式廚房呈獻豐富的美饌，菜式風味林林總總，包括來自不同國家的烤、蒸、炒菜式，令人目不暇給。著名菜色包括地中海菜，特別是葡國菜，而壽司及牛排亦非常出眾。食材及烹調方式堪稱一流。

■ ADDRESS/地址
TEL.8802 3888
GF, MGM Grand Hotel, Avenida Dr. Sun Yat Sen, Nape
外港新填海區孫逸仙大馬路美高梅金殿酒店地下
www.mgmgrandmacau.com

■ ANNUAL AND WEEKLY CLOSING
　休息日期
Closed Sunday lunch
週日午膳休息

■ OPENING HOURS, LAST ORDER
　營業時間，最後點菜時間
Lunch/午膳 11:30-14:30 L.O. 14:00
Dinner/晚膳 18:00-23:00 L.O. 22:30

■ PRICE/價錢
Lunch/午膳　carte/點菜 MOP200-650
Dinner/晚膳　carte/點菜 MOP200-650

Square Eight
食·八方

Square Eight is a large, informal, western-styled eatery that never closes its doors. It's vibrant and busy, and its cuisine covers large swathes of Asia, from China to Thailand to Korea. You're given a large sheet of paper with all the dishes, and you just tick the ones you'd like. Service is fast and furious, but staff are engaging and attentive. A long, open-plan kitchen adds to the hustle and bustle of the place. Cheap and very cheerful food

食·八方二十四小時開放，地方寬敞，環境輕鬆時尚。餐廳人氣旺盛，生氣勃勃，美食超越中西界限，涵蓋中菜、泰國菜、韓國菜等。點菜單上羅列出全部菜式，食客可以自行打剔點選。環境時而喧鬧，不過服務快捷周到。長形的開放式廚房為餐廳更添一份忙碌氣氛。菜餚討人歡喜，價錢亦相當便宜。

■ ADDRESS/地址
TEL.8802 3888
GF, MGM Grand Hotel, Avenida Dr. Sun Yat Sen, Nape
外港新填海區孫逸仙大馬路美高梅金殿地下
www.mgmgrandmacau.com

■ OPENING HOURS, LAST ORDER
營業時間, 最後點菜時間
Open 24 hours
24小時營業

■ PRICE/價錢
Lunch/午膳　carte/點菜 MOP150-250
Dinner/晚膳　carte/點菜 MOP150-250

Tenmasa
天政

An utterly charming restaurant named after the original Tenmasa, which opened in Tokyo in 1937 and is still going strong. Taipa's version boasts sushi bar, tatami floor, decked walkways leading across golden pebble ponds to private rooms, and a tempura counter. Here you can sit and watch the chef at work, admiring his precise light frying of superb ingredients and wonderfully well-balanced dishes. Attentive waitresses wear smart kimonos.

譽滿東京的天政早於1937年開業，至今仍廣受歡迎，更把料理帶到澳門皇冠。澳門的天政設有壽司吧、榻榻米地板、鋪板走廊、金石水池、私人餐室，以及天婦羅檯。食客可安坐在天婦羅檯，觀看廚師大顯身手，將優質食材炮製成美味菜式。服務員穿著整潔的和服，服務周到。

■ ADDRESS/地址
TEL.8803 6611
11F, Crown Towers Hotel, Avenida de Kwong Tung, Taipa
氹仔廣東大馬路皇冠酒店11樓

■ OPENING HOURS, LAST ORDER
營業時間, 最後點菜時間
Lunch/午膳 12:00-14:30 (L.O.)
Dinner/晚膳 18:00-22:30 (L.O.)

■ PRICE/價錢
Lunch/午膳   menu/套餐 MOP270-900
           carte/點菜 MOP400-1,200
Dinner/晚膳   menu/套餐 MOP380-1,600
           carte/點菜 MOP400-1,200

The Eight
8

The Eight's stylish appearance can't fail to impress: water cascades down walls, images of goldfish are projected onto the floor...and that's just the entrance corridor! The restaurant, too, is fabulous, with spheres of glass beads and tabletops of abalone shell. The service and Cantonese cuisine, however, cannot quite match these standards. Dishes, from a large menu, are average in flavour, and the waitresses seem to be in awe of their surroundings.

8餐廳的時尚設計令人印象深刻：流水沿著牆壁潺潺而下，地板上更投射著很多金魚的影像…這只是入口走廊而已！餐廳裡面同樣精彩：一粒粒玻璃小珠、一顆顆放在桌上的鮑魚殼等，果然心思不減。至於這裡的服務及粵菜則稍為遜色。菜式選擇很多，然而菜式味道一般，而侍應似乎有點心不在焉。

■ ADDRESS/地址
TEL.2828 3838
2F, Grand Lisboa Hotel, Avenida de Lisboa
葡京路新葡京酒店2樓
www.grandlisboa.com

■ OPENING HOURS, LAST ORDER
營業時間, 最後點菜時間
Lunch/午膳 12:00-14:30 (L.O.)
Dinner/晚膳 18:30-22:30 (L.O.)

■ PRICE/價錢
Lunch/午膳　carte/點菜 MOP160-800
Dinner/晚膳　carte/點菜 MOP160-800

The Kitchen
大厨

You can tell this is somewhere slightly different when you enter via a beautiful wooden screen and gain access to a bar in the shape of a golden cow. The restaurant itself is intimate and stylish, with shiny metal rods suspended from the ceiling and a wall of water behind the sushi counter. Cuisine is a curious, but well executed, mix of Western steakhouse and Japanese dishes. There's also live fish from the tank and a superb wine list.

踏進餐廳，經過美麗的木製屏風，看到金牛形的酒吧，你便會意識到這裡的非凡之處。餐廳時尚愜意，天花板懸掛著閃閃生輝的金屬棒，壽司吧後方更設有一道水牆。菜式獨特，揉合西式扒房風格和日本菜餚而成，廚藝出色。餐廳亦設有游水魚魚缸，並提供優質美酒。

■ ADDRESS/地址
TEL.8803 7777
3F, Grand Lisboa Hotel, Avenida de Lisboa
葡京路新葡京酒店3樓
www.grandlisboa.com

■ OPENING HOURS, LAST ORDER
營業時間, 最後點菜時間
Lunch/午膳　12:00-14:30 (L.O.)
Dinner/晚膳　18:30-22:30 (L.O.)
■ PRICE/價錢
Lunch/午膳　carte/點菜 MOP600-1,400
Dinner/晚膳　carte/點菜 MOP600-1,400

Tim's Kitchen
桃花源小廚

One for the connoisseurs – Hong Kong foodies make special pilgrimages here. It's only a small restaurant, with very large tables and brutal lighting, but the opera photos and costumes go some way to alleviate this. The Cantonese dishes may look simple, but they are perfectly prepared. The cooking technique is very precise, employing an impressive ability to bring out the flavours of the excellent ingredients. A joy for the taste buds!

香港食家紛紛到此朝聖，桃花源必然是行家之選。餐廳地方不大，而餐桌巨大，燈光猛烈，不過裝飾的歌劇照片和戲服，卻起了某程度的中和作用。餐廳的粵菜看似簡單，其實經過精心炮製。廚師的烹調技巧精湛，巧妙地帶出優質食材的味道，實在能「感動味蕾」！

■ ADDRESS/地址

TEL.8803 3682
Shop F25, GF, Lisboa Hotel, East Wing, 2-4 Avenida de Lisboa
葡京路2-4號葡京酒店東翼地下F25號舖

■ OPENING HOURS, LAST ORDER
營業時間, 最後點菜時間
Lunch/午膳 12:00-15:00 L.O. 14:30
Dinner/晚膳 18:30-23:00 L.O. 22:00

■ PRICE/價錢
Lunch/午膳 carte/點菜 MOP350-1,200
Dinner/晚膳 carte/點菜 MOP350-1,200

Tung Yee Heen
東怡軒

Seriously run Cantonese restaurant that exudes comfort, its decor finding a nice balance between Chinese influences and contemporary flair. This is somewhere for a special occasion. There's a big choice of traditional dishes; specialities are shark's fin soup, deep-fried prawns with garlic in chilli sauce, or abalone - with options for all appetites. The well-regarded cuisine is prepared with unerringly fresh ingredients and cooked with talent.

這家舒適的粵菜餐廳營運認真，裝潢設計方面，中式和現代元素混合得宜，適合舉辦特別飲宴。餐廳提供多款傳統菜式，招牌菜包括魚翅、香辣蒜蝦或鮑魚，以及各種各樣的選擇，適合任何食客的胃口。這裡的菜餚享負盛名，採用了新鮮食材，貫徹始終，廚藝亦十分精湛。

■ ADDRESS/地址
TEL.8793 3821
2F, Mandarin Oriental Hotel, 956-1110 Avenida da Amizade
友誼大馬路956-1110號2樓
www.mandarinoriental.com.macau

■ OPENING HOURS, LAST ORDER
營業時間, 最後點菜時間
Lunch/午膳 11:00-14:30 (L.O.)
Dinner/晚膳 18:00-23:00 (L.O.)

■ PRICE/價錢
Lunch/午膳   menu/套餐 MOP388-1,788
              carte/點菜 MOP200-1,000
Dinner/晚膳   menu/套餐 MOP388-1,788
              carte/點菜 MOP200-1,000

Wing Lei
永利軒

XXX

☞ ▯ 14

An opulent restaurant in vibrant red, characterised by vast lanterns at the entrance, and a superb three-dimensional dragon made of ninety thousand pieces of crystal. The comfy red dining chairs add to a feeling of well-being. The décor may be excellent, but the service can occasionally be somewhat lacklustre. Gamblers and a large number of families create a noisy ambience as they tuck in to a big menu of classical Cantonese dishes.

紅當當的餐廳入口掛著一些大型燈籠，襯托一條以九千片水晶製成的立體龍，盡展豪華氣派；而舒適的紅色座椅讓人更添好感。餐廳的裝潢實屬一流，不過相比之下，服務態度有時略嫌失色。食客多是一家大小或娛樂場玩家，環境熱鬧非常。餐廳供應傳統粵菜，菜式選擇良多。

■ ADDRESS/地址
TEL.8986 3663
GF, Wynn Hotel, Rua Cidade de Sintra, Nape
外港新填海區仙德麗街永利酒店地下
www.wynnmacau.com

■ OPENING HOURS, LAST ORDER
營業時間, 最後點菜時間
Lunch/午膳 11:30-15:00 (L.O.)
Dinner/晚膳 18:00-23:00 (L.O.)
■ PRICE/價錢
Lunch/午膳   carte/點菜 MOP110-230
Dinner/晚膳 carte/點菜 MOP150-920

Ying
帝影樓

XXX

♿ ← ☞ 🖥14 🍇

This is a terrific restaurant with breathtaking views looking north to Macau. The beautifully styled interior has been designed with real taste and quality; even the beaded curtains – featuring gold cranes and crystal trees – are fantastic. The Cantonese dishes on offer are prepared with contemporary twists and great flair, and are served by charmingly professional staff. The place to come for some of the best Cantonese cooking in the region.

帝影樓坐擁澳門北部的壯麗景致，扣人心弦。餐廳內部設計品味獨特，風格絢麗；甚至珠簾亦配有金鶴和水晶樹，使裝潢更添神采。餐廳的粵菜融入了當代元素，烹調技藝精湛。服務專業，態度令人賓至如歸。這裡的一些粵菜菜式可謂冠絕全城。

■ ADDRESS/地址
TEL.8803 6600
11F, Crown Towers Hotel, Avenida de Kwong Tung, Taipa
氹仔廣東大馬路皇冠酒店11樓
www.crown-macau.com

■ OPENING HOURS, LAST ORDER
營業時間, 最後點菜時間
Lunch/午膳　11:30-16:30 (L.O.)
Dinner/晚膳　18:00-22:30 (L.O.)

■ PRICE/價錢
Lunch/午膳　　menu/套餐 MOP420-700
　　　　　　　carte/點菜 MOP150-800
Dinner/晚膳　menu/套餐 MOP550-1,280
　　　　　　　carte/點菜 MOP150-800

HOTELS
酒店

HOTELS BY ORDER OF COMFORT
酒店 — 以舒適程度分類

Pousada de São Tiago 聖地牙哥古堡   358   MAP/地圖 3/A-2

Rocks 萊斯   362   MAP/地圖 4/D-1

Lisboa 葡京   350   MAP/地圖 3/B-3

Rio 利澳   360   MAP/地圖 4/C-2

Pousada de Mong-Há 望廈賓館   356   MAP/地圖 2/C-2

Crown Towers
皇冠

High quality design, a serene atmosphere and wondrous peninsula views produce something jaw-droppingly spectacular here. Guests arrive at the stylish lobby on the 38th floor; the luxury penthouse feel is enhanced by a superb lounge and terrace on the same level. Rooms, all on a lower floor, face the sea and merge tranquil tones with sheer contemporary style. As if this weren't enough, there's also a sumptuous spa boasting a pool-with-a-view.

RESTAURANTS/ 餐廳

Recommended/推薦		Also/其他
Aurora/奧羅拉	✗✗	
Kira/吉良	✗✗✗	
Tenmasa/天政	✗✗	
Ying/帝影樓	✿ ✗✗✗	

皇冠酒店設計獨特，舒適典雅，位處優越地段，讓澳門半島的環迴美景盡入眼簾，令人讚嘆不已。時尚尊貴的大堂位於38樓，同層的「天 宮」酒廊備有室內酒廊及露天陽台高雅舒適，散發著豪華瑰麗的味道。客房位於其他較低樓層，海景一望無際，寧靜感覺和現代設計相互交織，氣派超凡。此外，酒店設有豪華的水療設施，享用服務的同時更可飽覽美景。

■ ADDRESS/地址
TEL.2886 8888
FAX. 2886 8666
Avenida de Kwong Tung, Taipa
氹仔廣東大馬路
www.crown-macau.com

■ ROOMS AND SUITES/客房及套房
Rooms/客房 ＝184
Suites/套房 ＝32

■ PRICE/價錢
👤	MOP5,380
👥	MOP5,380
Suites/套房	MOP8,880
☕	MOP250

Grand Lisboa
新葡京

Impossible to miss, the Grand Lisboa, opened in 2008, can be seen from miles away with its eye-popping, brightly-lit lotus design atop a shining diamond! Opulent soundproofed bedrooms typically feature brown walls, red armchairs and Asian paintings, and offer grand sea or city vistas. If you have a corner room or a suite, you'll get the added bonus of a sauna. If you have neither corner room nor suite, you can make use of a sumptuous spa.

RESTAURANTS/ 餐廳

Recommended/推薦		Also/其他

Don Alfonso/當奧豐素   ✗✗✗✗

Noodle & Congee Corner

粥麵莊   ☺   🍴

The Eight/8   ❀   ✗✗✗

The Kitchen/大廚   ✗✗

2008年開幕的新葡京外形像一片耀目的黃蓮葉，座落於一顆閃爍的鑽石之上，遠處可見，實在不容錯過！客房非常隔音，擁有典型的棕色牆壁、紅色扶手椅和亞洲油畫，並坐擁豪華海景或澳門的秀麗風光。角位客房及套房更設有桑拿設施，其他客房亦可享用豪華的水療設施。

■ ADDRESS/地址
TEL.2828 3838
FAX. 8803 3310
Avenida de Lisboa
葡京路
www.grandlisboa.com

■ ROOMS AND SUITES/客房及套房
Rooms/客房 ＝381
Suites/套房 ＝50

■ PRICE/價錢
🧍   MOP3,800-5,700
🧍🧍   MOP3,800-5,700
Suites/套房 MOP5,800-48,000
☕   MOP150

Lisboa
葡京酒店

Featuring the biggest round-the-clock casino in Macau, the Lisboa is one of the city's more 'traditional' hotels with its 1970s style façade providing a stark contrast to the brand new Grand Lisboa. There are two types of guestroom: ask for a Tower room, as these are more luxurious and larger in size than rooms in the east wing. You won't find a swimming pool, but, rather handily, you can nip over to the Grand Lisboa and use theirs.

RESTAURANTS/ 餐廳

Recommended/推薦			Also/其他
New Furusato/新故鄉	✗✗		
Portas do Sol/葡京日麗	✗✗		
Robuchon a Galera			
法國餐廳	✿✿✿	✗✗✗	
Tim's Kitchen/桃花源小廚	✿✿	✗✗✗	

葡京酒店是澳門的「傳統」酒店之一，設有二十四小時開放的娛樂場。酒店保留著七十年代的外觀，與新落成的新葡京相映成趣。酒店共有兩種客房，尊尚客房比東翼的客房更大更豪華，物有所值。雖然葡京沒有泳池，不過走到新葡京那邊使用泳池，亦十分方便快捷。

■ ADDRESS/地址
TEL.2888 3888
FAX. 2888 3838
2-4 Avenida de Lisboa
葡京路2-4樓
www.hotelisboa.com

■ ROOMS AND SUITES/客房及套房
Rooms/客房 ＝906
Suites/套房 ＝20

■ PRICE/價錢

👤	MOP1,850-3,400
👥	MOP1,850-3,400
Suites/套房	MOP4,400-18,000
☕	MOP78

Mandarin Oriental
文華東方

One of the high points of this 25 year-old hotel is its staff, full of smiles and attentive to your every whim. Check in, and after a couple of hours the peaceful atmosphere induces a distinctly relaxing effect on even the most jaded guest. Rooms, of a good size and with a Portuguese slant, offer either a city or seaside and garden view, while the adjacent private resort is a hidden treasure, with a pool, Jacuzzi, tropical gardens and spa area.

RESTAURANTS/ 餐廳

Recommended/推薦			Also/其他
Naam/藍		※※	Café Bela Vista
Tung Yee Heen/東怡軒	✿	※※※	

文華東方酒店投入服務已有25年，過人之處首推其員工，不但笑容可掬，而且服務周到。寧靜舒適的氣氛四處洋溢，辦理登記手續後，客人很快便會感到輕鬆閒適，就算最疲倦的客人亦會頓時疲勞盡消。客房地方寬敞，設計偏重葡式，可遠眺城市美景，或欣賞園林景致及海景。至於毗鄰的私人度假中心，實在是隱秘的寶藏，設施包括泳池、水力按摩浴池、熱帶園林及水療區。

■ ADDRESS/地址
TEL. 2856 7888
FAX. 2859 4589
956-1110 Avenida da Amizade
友誼大馬路956-1110號
www.mandarinoriental.com/macau

■ ROOMS AND SUITES/客房及套房
Rooms/客房 = 388
Suites/套房 = 28

■ PRICE/價錢

🧍	MOP2,000-3,900
🧍🧍	MOP2,000-3,900
Suites/套房	MOP5,300-28,000
☕	MOP188

MGM Grand
美高梅金殿

This is one of the jewels of Macau. It's a stunning glass sky-scraper with Taipa views. The 35 floors have three distinct horizontal layers designed in chic curves – bronze, silver and gold – gold signifying the best rooms, although all are luxurious, built in a well-judged modern style with very fine materials, the huge windows proffering wow-factor views. A Chihuly glass display dominates the vast lobby; the superb spa boasts infinity pool.

RESTAURANTS/ 餐廳

Recommended/推薦			Also/其他
Aux Beaux Arts/寶雅座		✕✕	
Imperial Court/金殿堂	❀	✕✕✕	
Rossio/盛事		✕✕	
Square Eight/食 · 八方	😊	✕	

美高梅金殿是澳門的一顆璀璨明珠。這幢摩天大樓擁有玻璃外牆，坐擁氹仔景色。樓高35層的酒店設計獨特，以波浪曲線由三種不同顏色(黃金色、白金色及玫瑰金色)的玻璃舖設外牆。黃金色部分標示著最佳的客房，但事實上所有客房都極盡奢華，以精細的物料塑造悅目的時尚風格。透過寬闊的窗戶，更將動人美景盡收眼底，令人讚嘆不已。宏偉的大堂展示著國際玻璃藝術大師Dale Chihuly的作品，星級的水療設施包括無邊際泳池。

■ ADDRESS/地址
TEL.8802 8888
FAX. 8802 1333
Avenida Dr. Sun Yat Sen, Nape
外港新填海區孫逸仙大馬路
www.mgmgrandmacau.com

■ ROOMS AND SUITES/客房及套房
Rooms/客房 ＝477
Suites/套房 ＝123

■ PRICE/價錢
👤	MOP2,300-2,900
👥	MOP2,300-2,900
Suites/套房	MOP4,200-6,200
🍽	MOP150

Pousada de Mong-Há
望廈賓館

A very good value hotel with a distinct difference...it's run by the Institute for Tourism Studies, with a guaranteed peaceful environment away from the casinos. It's surrounded by a lovely garden, while inside, students learning their trade welcome you at the reception desk. Bedrooms are not big (especially singles), but they're quiet and feature some nice Asian touches. There's a restaurant offering a good opportunity to enjoy Macanese cuisine.

RESTAURANTS/ 餐廳

Recommended/推薦

Also/其他

IFT Educational Restaurant
旅遊學院教學餐廳

這家超值的賓館由旅遊學院營運，位處寧靜的望廈山半山腰，遠離娛樂場的煩囂，確是與眾不同。賓館被一個可愛的花園環繞著，而接待處的學院學生則隨時為你服務。客房地方不大，尤其是單人房，不過環境寧靜，並擁有亞洲設計風格。賓館的餐廳是體驗澳門菜的好去處。

■ ADDRESS/地址
TEL.2851 5222
FAX. 2855 6925
Colina de Mong-Há, Rampe do Forte de Mong-Há
望廈山
www.ift.edu.mo

■ ROOMS AND SUITES/客房及套房
Rooms/客房 = 16
Suites/套房 = 4

■ PRICE/價錢

👤	MOP500-600
👥	MOP600-800

Suites/套房 MOP1,000-1,200

Pousada de São Tiago
聖地牙哥古堡

Exquisite boutique hotel, built into the hillside on the foundations of a 17th century fort alongside traditional Portuguese villas. Atmospheric old steps lead from the entrance up to reception. By contrast, the interior is modern, chic and very stylish, with subdued taste the key. Guestrooms boast cool marble floors and rich colours and fabrics; all look onto the Straits of Macau. Discover the pool amongst charming little hillside terraces.

RESTAURANTS/ 餐廳

Recommended/推薦	Also/其他

La Paloma/芭朗瑪　　　　　　　　 ⚒

座落於山腰的精品酒店，精緻優雅，由一座十七世紀的舊城堡改建而成，毗鄰傳統的葡式住宅。古樸的石階別具風情，拾級而上便可由入口到達接待處。酒店內部與外觀形成鮮明的對比，設計十分現代時尚，獨樹一格，卻不浮誇造作。客房採用大理石地板、鮮明的顏色和布質材料，品味非凡；所有客房都坐擁澳門內港的醉人景色。迷人的山腰陽台設有一個戶外泳池。

■ ADDRESS/地址
TEL.2837 8111
FAX. 2855 2170
Avenida da República, Fortaleza de
São Tiago da Barra
西灣民國大馬路聖地牙哥大炮台
www.saotiago.com

■ ROOMS AND SUITES/客房及套房
Suites/套房 ＝12

■ PRICE/價錢
Suites/套房 MOP3,200-3,500
🖵　　　　MOP120

Rio
利澳

Handy for visiting gamblers, the Rio is located between Macau Ferry Terminal and the casino area. The capacious lobby bases its inspiration on the European Renaissance, though twenty first century escalators whisk gamblers to the casino floors. Functional guestrooms are large, well-kept and clean: choose a room on the upper floors to enjoy the benefit of a better view. Women need read no further...the rather inviting Spa is for male guests only!

RESTAURANTS/餐廳

Recommended/推薦	Also/其他
	Fu Ho Ah Yung/富豪阿翁
	Iida/飯田

地點優越，交通便捷的利澳酒店是位於港澳碼頭旁的娛樂場區。寬廣的大堂以歐洲文藝復興風格設計，而廿一世紀式電梯則引領玩家到娛樂場。客戶地方寬敞，設備完善，整潔乾淨。高層的客房讓你飽覽更廣闊的美景。水療設施頗為吸引，不過女士們，不好意思⋯該設施只供男士使用！

■ ADDRESS/地址
TEL. 2871 8718
FAX. 2871 8728
Rua Luis Gonzaga Gomes 33
新口岸高美士街33樓
www.riomacau.com

■ ROOMS AND SUITES/客房及套房
Rooms/客房 ＝385
Suites/套房 ＝64

■ PRICE/價錢
👤 　　　MOP1,680-2,880
👥 　　　MOP1,680-2,880
Suites/套房 MOP4,080-28,880

Rocks
萊斯

Interesting seaside hotel modelled on the "elaborate charms of 18th Century Victoriana"...though the Victorian era was not until the 19th century! The lobby is full of Victorian-style décor and furnishings including fireplace, paintings, and large white marble staircase. Staff look smart in appropriate attire. A cosy terrace overlooks the marina, while relaxing bedrooms have a balcony and sea view. Of particular note...there's no casino here.

RESTAURANTS/ 餐廳

Recommended/推薦	Also/其他
	Vic's Café

雖說維多利亞時代到十九世紀才展開，這家坐落於海邊的萊斯酒店，其風格卻散發著「十八世紀在維多利亞時代發揮的魅力」！酒店大堂充滿維多利亞式的裝潢和傢具，包括壁爐、油畫，以及宏偉的白色大理石樓梯。員工穿著合宜，時尚醒目。露台舒適愜意，可飽覽碼頭景色；而舒適的客房則坐擁怡人海景，並設有露台。特別一提，酒店不設娛樂場。

■ ADDRESS/地址
TEL. 2878 2782
FAX. 2872 8800
Macau Fisherman's Wharf
澳門漁人碼頭
www.rockshotel.com.mo

■ ROOMS AND SUITES/客房及套房
Rooms/客房 ＝66
Suites/套房 ＝6

■ PRICE/價錢

🧍	MOP1,880-2,880
🧍🧍	MOP1,880-2,880
Suites/套房	MOP4,080-6,660
☕	MOP123

Sands
金沙

This huge, bright gold building has a vast 'Sands' logo – prime Las Vegas real estate relocated in Asia. The hotel, with its own entrance and areas, is separate from the casino, though dining on the mezzanine, overlooking three vast gaming areas, resembles peering down onto a stock exchange trading floor! The spacious lobby is of western style, as are the bedrooms, which are all large and luxurious suites; each has a sea or city view.

RESTAURANTS/ 餐廳

Recommended/推薦	Also/其他
	Copa/高雅
	Perola/金帆船

這家龐大的金沙酒店，金色外牆閃閃發亮，並擁有巨型的「金 沙」霓虹燈招牌，是拉斯維加斯博彩業鉅頭於亞洲營運的娛樂場酒店。酒店與娛樂場分開，設有獨立的入口和範圍，不過在夾樓用餐時，卻可俯瞰三個大型博彩廳，恰似觀看股交所會場一般！寬敞的大堂和客房均以西式設計，所有客房都是寬闊的豪華套房，更坐擁海景或城市美景。

■ ADDRESS/地址
TEL.2888 3388
FAX. 2888 3377
Largo de Monte Carlo 203
蒙地卡羅前地203號
www.sands.com.mo

■ ROOMS AND SUITES/客房及套房
Rooms/客房 ＝204
Suites/套房 ＝34

■ PRICE/價錢

👤	MOP2,088-2,788
👥	MOP2,088-2,788
Suites/套房	MOP3,588-4,588
☕	MOP200

Sofitel at Ponte 16
十六浦索菲特

Swish new boutique hotel in an enviable location on the harbour front, with views reflecting the fine setting. Sofitel has a gracious feel, the rooms well appointed with a blend of brown and beige creating an atmosphere of restful chic. The good taste unites French style with soft Portuguese nuance. And for those with the ability to really splash out, there are 19 super luxury suites in a beautiful mansion next door to the main building.

RESTAURANTS/ 餐廳

Recommended/推薦   Also/其他

新開幕的索菲特大酒店，是時尚的精品酒店。酒店地理位置優越，海景與酒店
外形相映成趣。索菲特氣派優雅，棕色和杏色的融合，為客房營造時尚悠閑
之感。酒店結合了法國和葡萄牙風格，演繹高雅品味。主建築旁的漂亮大樓，
設有19間貴賓豪華套房，適合高消費的客人。

■ ADDRESS/地址
TEL.8861 0016
FAX. 8861 0018
Rua do Visconde Paço de Arcos
內港巴素打爾古街
www.sofitel.com.cn

■ ROOMS AND SUITES/客房及套房
Rooms/客房 ＝364
Suites/套房 ＝44
■ PRICE/價錢
  ♦   MOP1,420-2,920
  ♦♦   MOP1,420-2,920
Suites/套房 MOP4,100-5,650
  ☕   MOP150

StarWorld
星際

The attractive glass façade, and its impressive night lighting, might serve to lure guests, but the huge and busy lobby - access to the different casinos - might equally put them off. Those who stick with Starworld will find supremely luxurious rooms, full of every mod con. They're named after the view – City, Sea or Lake – with Lake rooms offering the best vista. Go past the gaming floors and check out the 17th level's spacious outdoor pool.

RESTAURANTS/ 餐廳

Recommended/推薦

Inagiku/稻菊 ✗✗

Also/其他

Jade Garden/蘇浙滙

Laurel/丹桂軒

星際酒店擁有吸引的玻璃外觀，晚上燈光璀璨奪目，客似雲來亦不足為奇；不過龐大的大堂十分繁忙，娛樂場玩家熙來攘往，亦足以令人卻步。決定入住的客人可享用極盡奢華的客房，以及各式各樣的現代化設備。客房根據景觀而命名 - 城市、海、湖 - 湖景客房擁有冠絕全場的景色。略過娛樂場的樓層，於17樓便可享用寬敞的露天泳池。

■ ADDRESS/地址

TEL.2838 3838

FAX. 2838 3888

Avenida da Amizade

友誼大馬路

www.starworldmacau.com

■ ROOMS AND SUITES/客房及套房

Rooms/客房 =473

Suites/套房 =36

■ PRICE/價錢

🚹	MOP1,900-2,700
🚹🚹	MOP1,900-2,700
Suites/套房	MOP3,500-38,000

The Landmark
置地廣場酒店

The sober façade hides a classically-styled lobby full of black marble and helpful staff, such as bellboys and guest-relation employees. Guestrooms are European in style, without the ubiquitous Macau 'fancy décor': a deluxe room offers more space and comfort. Pharaoh's casino is over-the-top Vegas: gamblers with a mind to test their muscles rather than their luck can choose between an indoor pool, a fitness centre or a tiny golf practice room.

RESTAURANTS/ 餐廳

Recommended/推薦

Also/其他

Kawato/川戶
Petrus Royal Orchid/秀蘭小館

酒店外觀樸實，令人意想不到裡面的設計竟隱藏了：用黑色大理石建設風格古典的大堂，和服務殷切的；員工，大堂服務生和客戶服務員便是高效率的表表者。客房以歐洲風格設計，沒有澳門普遍的「花巧裝潢」，因此豪華客房可以提供更多空間和更舒適的環境。法老王宮殿娛樂場比起拉斯維加斯，實在是小巫見大巫；喜愛享受運動多於博彩的娛樂場玩家，可選擇使用酒店的室內泳池、健身室或小型的高爾夫球練習室。

■ ADDRESS/地址
TEL.2878 1781
FAX. 2878 6611
Avenida da Amizade 555
友誼大馬路555號
www.landmarkhotel.com.mo

■ ROOMS AND SUITES/客房及套房
Rooms/客房 ＝403
Suites/套房 ＝48

■ PRICE/價錢
♦　　　MOP1,780-2,880
♦♦　　MOP1,780-2,880
Suites/套房 MOP3,080-35,000

The Venetian
威尼斯人

This is the largest hotel in Asia and you need a map to get around it! It's a vast resort, based on Venice: third floor canals feature singing gondoliers! Identikit luxury is assured in a towering bedroom skyscraper that has 3,000 capacious rooms. Opulent fakes are everywhere: frescoes, colonnades, sculptures. It's impossible to stay here without being swept along by hoards of gamblers: ten million came to Cotai gaming strip in its first year!

RESTAURANTS/ 餐廳

Recommended/推薦		Also/其他
Canton/喜粵	✕✕✕	Cecconi's
Morton's of Chicago	✕✕✕	
Roka	✕✕	

威尼斯人是亞洲最大型的酒店，在裡面四處逛甚至要動用地圖！威尼斯人是一家龐大的度假村酒店，以威尼斯為主題，三樓運河上的貢多拉船夫更會一邊掌船一邊唱歌！高聳而立的摩天大樓擁有三千間寬敞客房，同樣極盡奢華。壁畫、列柱、雕塑等均仿照原物而製，展露豪華氣派。置身於威尼斯人難免會到娛樂場一展身手，單是營運首年，路氹金光大道的娛樂場便招徠了一千萬人！

■ ADDRESS/地址

TEL.2882 8888

FAX. 2882 8889
Estrada da Baia de N. Senhora de
Esperanca, s/n, The Cotai Strip, Taipa
氹仔路氹金光大道-望德聖母灣大馬路
www.venetianmacao.com

■ ROOMS AND SUITES/客房及套房
Rooms/客房 ＝3000

■ PRICE/價錢

👤	MOP2,000-5,500
👥	MOP2,000-5,500
🛏	MOP200

The Westin Resort
威斯汀度假酒店

A rather stark cream pyramid in a hilly oasis a long way from the nearest casino! Its best feature is the superb vista it offers over the beach and sea to outlying islands. It also boasts a beautiful garden with attractive roofed terrace, pool and bar. A decent leisure facility and indoor pool livens up the spacious, somewhat unremarkable interior. Each bedroom has a large terrace with views, fitting compensation for the rather ordinary décor.

RESTAURANTS/ 餐廳

Recommended/推薦		Also/其他
Kwun Hoi Heen/觀海軒	✗✗✗	Café Panorama

威斯汀度假村座落於路環島，米色金字塔形的外觀頗為突出。酒店離最近的娛樂場也有一段距離，實在是城市中的綠洲！威斯汀坐擁黑沙海灘及離島的怡人海景，景致堪稱一絕。酒店亦設有漂亮的花園、迷人的有蓋露台、游泳池及酒吧。酒店內部寬敞但較不起眼，不過優良的消閒設施及室內泳池使其生色不少。所有客房均設有寬廣的美景露台，補足較為普通的裝潢設計。

■ ADDRESS/地址
TEL.2887 1111
FAX. 2887 1122
1918 Estrada de Hac Sa, Coloane
路環黑沙馬路1918號
www.westin.com.macau

■ ROOMS AND SUITES/客房及套房
Rooms/客房 =202
Suites/套房 =6

■ PRICE/價錢

👤	MOP2,200-2,400
👥	MOP2,300-2,700
☕	MOP180

Wynn
永利

The Wynn's easy-on-the-eye curving glass façade is enhanced with a lake and dancing fountains, while the classically luxurious interior includes Murano glass chandeliers, plush carpets and ubiquitous marble. An attractively landscaped oasis pool forms the centrepiece to corridors lined with the top retail names. Bedrooms – classical but contemporary - display a considerable degree of taste. The Prosperity tree, meanwhile, is not easily forgotten...

RESTAURANTS/ 餐廳

Recommended/推薦		Also/其他
Il Teatro/帝雅廷	🍴🍴🍴	
Okada/岡田	🍴🍴	
Red 8/紅8	🍴	
Wing Lei/永利軒	🍴🍴🍴	

永利的弧形玻璃外觀十分奪目，更設有表演湖及噴池。至於酒店內部則散發著
經典的豪華氣息：穆拉諾穆玻璃吊燈、豪華的地毯，且觸目所及皆是大理石。
走廊中心設有一個造形迷人的綠洲池，而兩旁則置滿名店。客房融合了經典和
當代的風格設計，盡顯優越品味。此外，永利的吉祥樹更會令你印象深刻。

■ ADDRESS/地址
TEL.2888 9966
FAX. 2832 9966
Rua Cidade de Sintra, Nape
外港新填海區仙德麗街
www.wynnmacau.com

■ ROOMS AND SUITES/客房及套房
Rooms/客房 ＝480
Suites/套房 ＝120
■ PRICE/價錢

🧍	MOP3,000
🧍🧍	MOP3,700
Suites/套房	MOP7,800-35,000
☕	MOP168

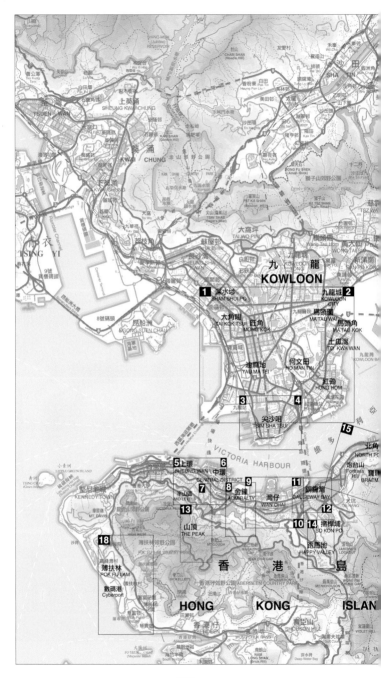

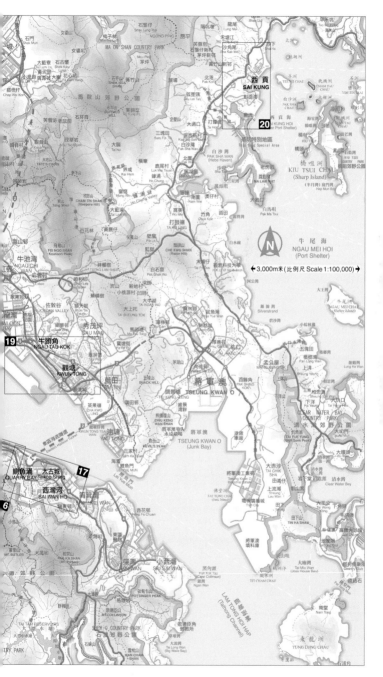

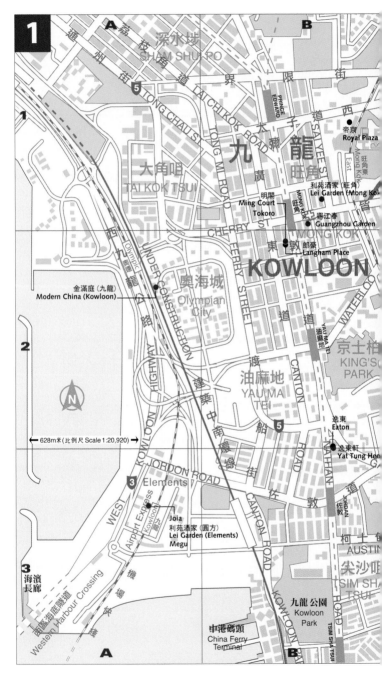

BOUNDARY STREET

PRINCE EDWARD ROAD WEST

窩　九龍醫院

打

ARGYLE STREET

馬頭圍
MA TAU WAI

馬頭角
MA TAU KOK

MA TAU WAI RD

土瓜灣
TO KWA WAN

EAST KOWLOON CORRIDOR

TO KWA WAN RD

柯

佛

光

道

PRINCESS

MARGARET

5

東九龍走廊

2

柯文田
HO MAN TIN

FAT KWONG STREET

伊利沙伯
醫院
Hosp.

瓜

灣

道

OIGNE ROAD

紅磡
HUNG HOM

正斗粥麵專家 (紅磡)
Tasty (Hung Hom)

ROAD

道

理工大學
Hong Kong
Polytechnic
University

黃埔花園
Whampoa
Garden

海逸

Harbour Plaza Kowloon

香港科學館
Hong Kong
Science Museum

Hung Hom

千鶴
Senzuru

都會海逸
Harbour Plaza Metropolis

Harbour Grill

海逸軒
Hoi Yat Heen

炉端燒
Robatayaki

香港體育館
Hong Kong Coliseum

3

SBURY ROAD

C   1

維多利亞港
VICTORIA HARBOUR

D

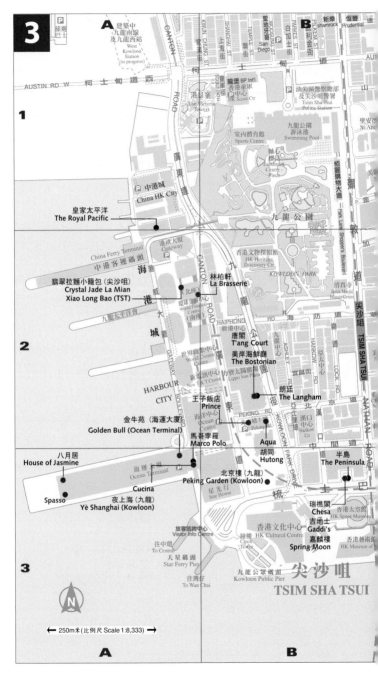

P 旅遊巴士

A 建築中
九龍南線
及九龍西站
West
Kowloon
Station
(in progress)

CANTON ROAD

KWUN CHUNG ST
SHANGHAI ST
TEMPLE ST

B 新樂 shamrock 恒豐 Prudential

聖堡壘 San Diego

PILKEM ST
PARKES ST
白加士街
佐敦道
甘肅街

油尖區警察總部
及尖沙咀警署
Tsim Sha Tsui
Police Station

AUSTIN RD W 柯士甸道西

港京峯
The Victoria
Towers

P 港京峯

龍堡 BP Int'l
香港童軍
中心
HK Scout Ctr

P 油尖區警察總部

聖安
St. An

1

室內體育館
Sports Centre

九龍公園
游泳池
Swimming Pool

栢麗購物大道
Park Lane Shopper's Boulevard

九龍公園

柏麗購物大道
Landmark
Centre-
Piece

廣東道

中港城
China HK City

P 中港城

皇家太平洋
The Royal Pacific ●

港威大廈
Gateway

China Ferry Terminal
中港客運碼頭

香港文物探知館
HK Heritage
Discovery Ctr

KOWLOON PARK

九龍公園

清真寺
Jamia Masjid
Islamic Centre

海
港

翡翠拉麵小籠包 (尖沙咀)
**Crystal Jade La Mian
Xiao Long Bao (TST)** ●

港
城
道

CANTON ROAD

北京
環球貿易
World Finance
Centre
(南座)

林柏軒
La Brasserie ●

TSIM SHA TSUI 尖沙咀

九龍太平洋百貨

2

HARBOUR
CITY

GATEWAY BOULEVARD

世界商業中心
World Commerce
Centre

新港中心
New T & T Centre

HAIPHONG RD
海防道

九龍公園
Kowloon
Park

唐閣
T'ang Court ●

美岸海鮮廳
The Bostonian ●

力寶太陽廣場
Lippo Sun Plaza

宜昌街

ASHLEY RD

HANKOW RD

亞細亞中心

漢口中心
Hankow
Ctr

LOCK RD

朗廷
The Langham ●

東

王子飯店
Prince ●

海港城
Ocean
Centre

P 北京道

PEKING RD

金巴利
中心

河口
中心
Hankow
Ctr

KOWLOON PARK DRIVE

NATHAN ROAD

金牛苑 (海運大廈)
Golden Bull (Ocean Terminal) ●

馬哥孛羅
Marco Polo ●

胡同
**Aqua
Hutong** ●

中間道

半島
The Peninsula ●

八月居
House of Jasmine ●

Cucina ●

Spasso ●

海運大廈
Ocean Terminal

P

夜上海 (九龍)
Yè Shanghai (Kowloon)

星光行
Star House

北京樓 (九龍)
Peking Garden (Kowloon) ●

梳士巴利道

瑞樵閣
Chesa ●

香港太空館
HK Space Museum

吉地士
Gaddi's ●

嘉麟樓
Spring Moon ●

香港藝術館
HK Museum of

旅客諮詢中心
Visitor Info Centre

香港文化中心
HK Cultural Centre

鐘樓
Clock
Tower

往中環
To Central

天星碼頭
Star Ferry Pier

往灣仔
To Wan Chai

九龍公眾碼頭
Kowloon Public Pier

尖沙咀
TSIM SHA TSUI

3

← 250m米 (比例尺 Scale 1:8,333) →

N

C

Kowloon Cricket Club
先龍草地滾球會
Kowloon Bowling
Green Club

ROAD 柯士甸道

松山道 HILLWOOD RD

香港天文台
HK Observatory

AUSTIN AVE

CHATHAM C 加連威老道

帝樂文娜公館
The Luxe Manor

豐陽閣
Funyan

諾士佛臺
Aspasia

KNUTSFORD TCE

KIMBERLEY RD
KOBE RD
天文臺道

KIMBERLEY STREET

金巴利道
CARNARVON RD

GRANVILLE

ROAD

梳士巴利道

威

南

茘苑街 HALFCOURT

CAMERON

ROAD

馬倫道

格蘭中心
HUMPHREYS AVE

寶勒巷 PRAT AVE

HART AVE

D

4

香港理工大學
The Hong Kong
Polytechnic University

漆咸道

SCIENCE 科學館道 SCIENCE MUSEUM RD

GRANVILLE RD

HONG CHONG

CHEONG WAN ROAD

1

香港歷史博物館
HK Museum of
History

香港科學館
Hong Kong
Science Museum

福臨門（九龍）
Fook Lam Moon (Kowloon)

新港中心
新文華廣場

尖沙咀中心
帝國中心

柯士甸道

加連威老道

帝國中心

MODY

ROAD

日航
Nikko

名仕餐廳
Les Célébrités

嵯峨野
Sagano

桃季
Toh Lee

快船來往中環
Ferry to Central

Intercontinental Grand Stanford

海景嘉福

海鳳餐廳
The Mistral

帝苑
The Royal Garden

茘苑酒家（尖沙咀）
Lei Garden (Tsim Sha Tsui)

麗景
Panorama

九龍香格里拉大
Kowloon Shangri-La

CHATHAM ROAD

SALISBURY

尖沙咀東海濱平台花園 Tsim Sha Tsui Promenade

維多利亞港
VICTORIA HARBOUR

2

3

Morton's of Chicago

天寶閣
Celestial Court

雲海
Unkai

喜來登
Sheraton

利東 EAST TSIM SHA TSUI

信號山花園
Signal Hill Garden

Angelini

灘萬（九龍）
Nadaman (Kowloon)

香宮
Shang Palace

九龍萬麗
Renaissance Kowloon

銀座
Ginza

滿福樓
Dynasty

新世界中心
New World Centre

淵際
Intercontinental

Avenue of Stars

Nobu
Spoon by Alain Ducasse
The Steak House

欣圖軒
Yan Toh Heen

東來順
Dong Lai Shun

稻菊（九龍）
Inagiku (Kowloon)

Le Soleil

Sabatini

帝苑軒
The Royal Garden

C

D

385

A

B

SERVICES STREET

消防處港島總區
及島島海務總部
HK Fire & Marine
Fire Command HQ

巴士
停車場

中港道
CHUNG KONG ROAD

消防分隊警署

Hong Kong
Heliport
香港直升機場

HK-Macau
HK-Macau FERRY TERMINAL
港澳碼頭

1

CONNAUGHT RD C 干諾道西

西消街

CONNAUGHT RD W

永樂街

NEW MARKET ST 新街市街

干諾道中

信德中心
Shun Tak Ctr

招商局大廈
China Merchants
Tower

林士街
多層停車場

Queen's
Terrace
帝后
華庭

BONHAM STRAND W

WING LOK ST 永樂街

西港城
Western Market

客西
TUNG LOI

干諾道中

永安中心
Wing On
Centre

孫逸仙紀念
Plaza

QUEEN'S RD W

上　環

文咸東街

永樂街

LING WING

LOK ST

SHEUNG WAN 上環

DES

荷李活道公園
Hollywood Road Park

SHEUNG WAN
中環麗柏

MORRISON ST

BONHAM

STRAND

永樂街

桃花源小廚
Tim's Kitchen

中遠大廈
Cosco Tower

新紀元
廣場
Grand
Millennium
Plaza

卜公花園
Blake Garden

皇后
同文街

荷李活道

QUEEN'S

LOK KU RO

BURD ST

JERVOIS ST

CENTRAL

Gaia

2

文武廟
Man Mo
Temple

荷李活華庭
Hollywood
Terrace

聖公會
基恩

LADDER

撰賢居
Centre Stage

Lan Kwai Fong
蘭桂坊

PU YU TONG 九如坊

GOUGH ST

香港醫學博物館
HK Museum of
Medical Sciences

CAINE LANE

食一寮

LADDER ST

王后街

永利街 WING LEE ST

BRIDGES ST

Chez Patrick (Soho)

HOLLYWOOD

SHING WONG ST

英華女學校
Ying Wah
Girls' Sch

SEYMOUR

香港公園
HK Garden

CAINE

ROAD

麻辣燙
Chilli Fagara

擺花街

美麗閣
Merry Court

莫翠台
Merry Terr

CASTLE RD

劉大廟
Ohel Leah
Synagogue

雞籠台
Robinson
Place

高雲台
Golden Valley

(些利街)

STAUNTON ST

3

富景花園
Scenic Heights

列堤頓
Excelsior Ct

ROBINSON

寶珊道

(忌連拿利)

GLENEALY

水滸居
Shui Hu Ju

中
Cen
Static

城多利
(已停
Victoria (
Closed)

慧明苑
Elegant Terr

清真寺
Jamia Mosque

PEEL ST

Buxey Lodge

承德山莊
Scenecliff

嘉諾撒聖心
商學書院
Sacred Heart Canossian
College of Commerce

ROBINSON

康威閣
Conway
Mansion

康苑
Cliffview
Mansions

嘉光築
The Grand
Panorama

天主
Ro
Cathe

全景大廈
Panorama

CONDUIT

ROAD

ROBINSON

ROAD

羅便臣
Robinson
Heights

A

B

386

GRAHAM ST

Man Yee Building

MAN YEE ST

POTTINGER ST

沾仔記 (威靈頓街)
Tsim Chai Kee (Wellington St)

Pedestrian Escalator

COCHRANE ST

麥×雲吞麵世家
Mak's Noodle

LI YUEN ST W

LI YUEN ST E

DOUGLAS ST

Tandoor

GUTZLAFF
GAGE ST

黃色門廚房
Yellow Door Kitchen

攦花街

LYNDHURST TERR

STANLEY ST

QUEEN'S RD C

羅富記
Law Fu Kee

Café Siam

WELLINGTON

陸羽茶室
Luk Yu Tea House

伊沙里

Jashan

HOLLYWOOD RD

Au Belge

OLD BAILEY ST

中區警署
(已停用)
Central Police
Station (Closed)

Goccia

なお膳
Naozen

鏞記
Yung Kee

客家爺爺
Hakka Ye Yé

WO ON L

世紀廣場

Entertainment
Building

2

域多利監獄
(已停用)
Victoria Prison
(Closed)

CHANCERY L

WYNDHAM

N

中央廣場
The Centrium

金家美食
Gunga Din's

桂桂坊
LAN KWAI FONG

D'AGUILAR ST

Tru
Va Bene

壽司喰
Sushi Kuu

蘭桂坊
LKF

雲府
Yun Fu

M at the Fringe

Fringe Club

會督府

ARBUTHNOT

環貿
Universal Trade

Beo

聖公會

聖保羅堂

港中
醫院
HKC
Hospital

3

天主教
總堂
Rome
Catholic
Cathedral

CAINE RD

GLENEALY

聖母無
原罪堂

Church
Guest Hse

宏基
國際
賓館

明愛大廈
CaritasHouse

UPPER ALBANY RD

ALBANY RD

LOWER ALBERT RD

ICE HOUSE

UPPER ALBERT RD

← 98m 米 (比例尺 Scale 1:3,250) →

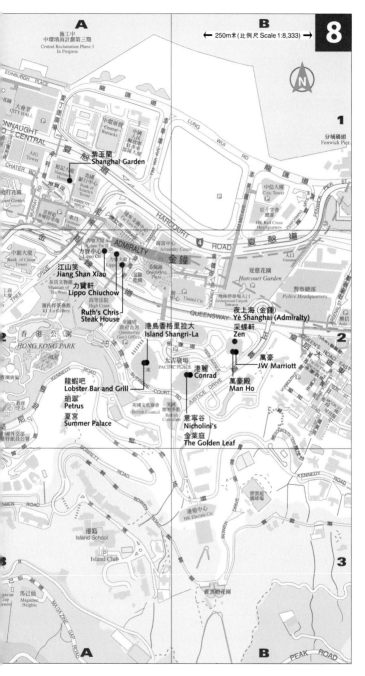

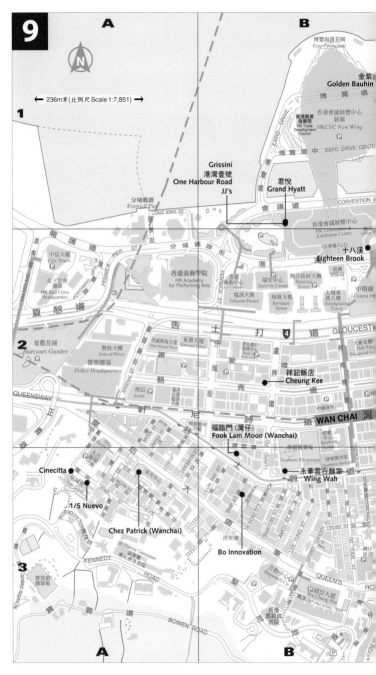

灣仔海濱長廊
Wan Chai Waterfront Promenade

灣仔渡輪碼頭
Wan Chai Ferry Pier

灣仔運動場
WAN CHAI
SPORTS GROUND

崇都
Sukho Thai
新鴻基中心
Sun Hung Kai Centre

鷹君中心
Great Eagle Centre

海港中心
Harbour Centre

香港會議中心
HK Exhibition Centre

華潤大廈
China Resources Building

富聲
Fu Sing

灣仔警署
Wan Chai Police Station

楊記麵家
Yeung's Noodle

HENNESSY ROAD

灣仔
WAN CHAI

灣仔公園
Wan Chai Park

律敦治醫院
Ruttonjee Hospital

聖若瑟墓
St Joseph's

摩理臣山游泳池
Morrison Hill Swimming Pool

摩理臣山
MORRISON HILL

畢公會鄧蔭棠紀念中學
SKH Tang Shiu Kin

伊利沙伯酒館
QE Stadium

馬會總部
HKJC Headquarters

賽馬博物館
Racing Museum

香港足球會球場
HKFC Soccer/Rugby Field

Methodist Church

WAN CHAI EAST

香港華仁書院
Wah Yan Coll. HK

AIA友邦大廈

麗都
Cosmopolitan

聖瑪加利書院
St Margaret's Coll.

回教墳場
MUSLIM CEMETERY

KENNEDY RD

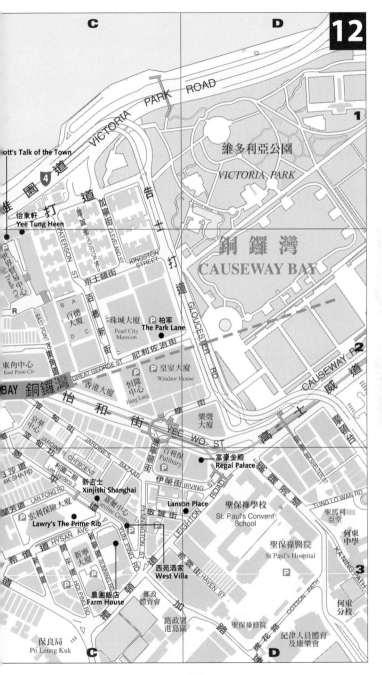

ott's Talk of the Town

怡東軒
Yee Tung Heen

世界貿易中心
ld Trade Ctr

東角中心
East Point Ctr

珠城大廈
Pearl City Mansion

柏寧
The Park Lane

皇室大廈
Windsor House

恆隆中心
Hang Lung

維多利亞公園
VICTORIA PARK

銅鑼灣
CAUSEWAY BAY

樂聲大廈

百利保
Palibury

富豪金殿
Regal Palace

新吉士
Xinjishi Shanghai

Lanson Place

聖保祿學校
St. Paul's Convent School

Lawry's The Prime Rib

西苑酒家
West Villa

聖保祿醫院
St Paul's Hospital

農圃飯店
Farm House

郵政體育會

何東中學

何東分校

路政署
港島區

聖保祿修院

保良局
Po Leung Kuk

紀律人員體育
及康樂會

VICTORIA PARK ROAD

PATERSON ST

HOUSTON ST

CLEVELAND ST

KINGSTON STREET

京士頓街

告士打道

GLOUCESTER RD

CAUSEWAY

威道

EAST POINT RD 東角道

GREAT GEORGE ST

怡和街

YEE WO ST

高士威道

JARDINE'S CRESCENT

JARDINE'S BAZAAR

利園二期
Lee Gardens 2

新寧大廈

宏利保險大廈

LAN FONG RD 蘭芳道

HYSAN AVE 希慎道

SUNNING RD

開平道

何平道 HO PING RD

PENNINGTON ST

勿地臣街

IRVING ST 伊榮街

敬誠街

LEIGHTON ROAD

HAVEN ST

加路連山道

COTTON PATH

TUNG LO WAN RD

KA NING PATH

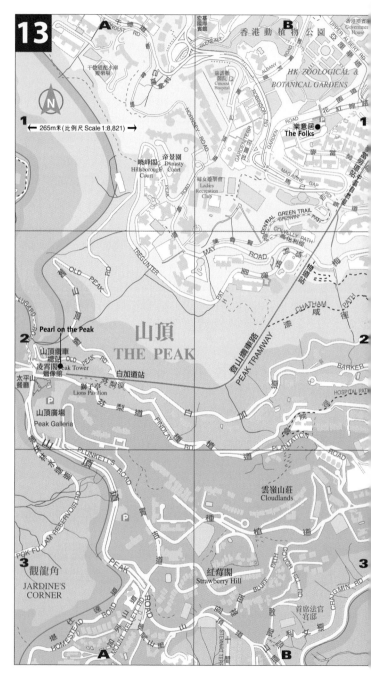

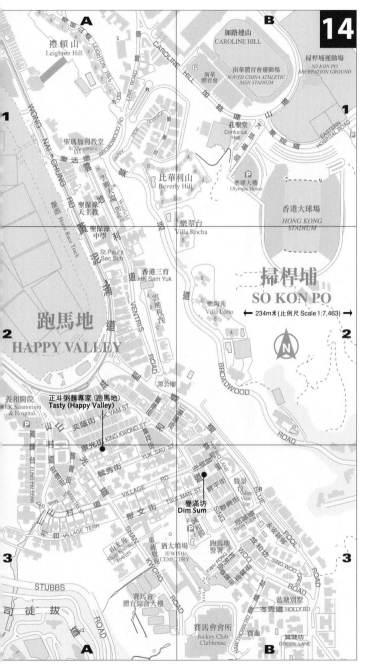

礼頓山
Leighton Hill

加路連山
CAROLINE HILL

掃桿埔運動場
SO KON PO
RECREATION GROUND

南華體育會運動場
SOUTH CHINA ATHLETIC
ASSN STADIUM

聖瑪加利教堂
St Margaret's

孔聖堂
Confucius
Hall

比華利山
Beverly Hill

奧運大樓
Olympic House

聖保祿
天主教

聖保祿
中學
St.Paul's
Sec Sch

樂翠台
Villa Rocha

香港大球場
HONG KONG
STADIUM

香港三育
HK Sam Yuk

掃桿埔
SO KON PO

樂陶苑
Villa Lotto

← 234m米(比例尺 Scale 1:7,463) →

跑馬地
HAPPY VALLEY

養和醫院
H.K.Sanatorium
& Hospital

譚公廟

正斗粥麵專家 (跑馬地)
Tasty (Happy Valley)

奕蔭街
YIK YAM ST

景光街
KING KWONG ST

毓秀街
YUK SAU ST

希雲街
HI PO LANE

駿景
Valley
View
Terr

譽滿坊
Dim Sum

景文街
TSUI MAN ST

賢平街

猶太墳場
JEWISH
CEMETERY

跑馬地
警署

藍塘別墅

冬青道 HOLLY RD

STUBBS

司 徒 拔

道 ROAD

賽馬會
體育綜合大樓

賽馬會會所
Jockey Club
Clubhouse

寶血

綠鍵坊
GREEN LANE

395

A　　　　B

北角
NORTH POINT

北角渡輪碼頭
North Point Ferry Pier
To Kowloon City
To Kwun Tong / Tseung Kwan O
To Hung Hom

←313m米(比例尺 Scale 1:10,417)→

WEST EMBANKMENT

HARBOUR PARADE

維多利亞港
VICTORIA HARBOUR

北角
NORTH POINT

僑冠中心
Quorum Centre

加藤壽司
Sushi Kato

KING'S ROAD

利苑酒家 (北角)
Lei Garden (North Point)

城市花園
City Gardens
城市
花園
City Gardens

電機中心
The Electric
Centre

FORTRESS HILL RD

北角
邮政局

摩天大廈
Sky Scraper 雲峰大廈
Summit Court

珊瑚閣
Coral Court

夏慧台 富澤園
Harbour View Ter Beverly
翠景園 富麗閣 Height
Hanking Flora Garden Hilltop
Court

EASTERN

CORRIDOR

KING WAH RD
OIL ST

海景閣
Harbour Heights

宏利保障中心
Manulife
Tower

ISLAND

東湖花園
Fortress Metro Tw
金文泰 Clementi
富澤花園
Fortress
Garden

WAN TIN PATH

朗澤閣 潤人閣
Sky Sky
Horizon Horizon
雲景閣 維景台 樹仁大學
Broadview Shue Yan
Ter University

TSUI

Orkney Shelland
Braemer
Heights

CLOUD VIEW ROAD

威景閣
Yiking Villas

東院李調用
Lee Ching Dea Mem. Coll.
北角福海 麵
Concordia
Lutheran Sch

翠景台 (雲景道)

觀景閣
Seaview
Garden
雲景台
Evelyn
Towers

TSUI
WAN

香港
日本人
學校

鰂魚涌
Quarry B.
School

漢基
國際學校
Chinese
International
School

Victoria Crkt KCC
威非路道 New John
Watson Rd

GORDON RD

WATSON RD

MERLIN ST

COMFORT TERR

COMFORT TER

JUPITER ST

MERCURY ST

WING HING ST

水星街
Belilios
Pub. Sch

留家廚房
Kin's Kitchen

皇輪 (天后)
Palki (Tin Hau)

KING'S

TSING FUNG ST

LAU LI ST

LAU SIN

NEW EASTERN

YEE KING ROAD

維多利亞公園泳池
Victoria Park
Swimming Pool

VICTORIA PARK RD

維園花園
Park Towers

北海
花園
Park Towers

TIN HAU

HING FAT ST

金龍大廈
Dragon Court

維多利亞公園
VICTORIA PARK

Metropark
銅鑼灣維景

A　　　　B

C

D

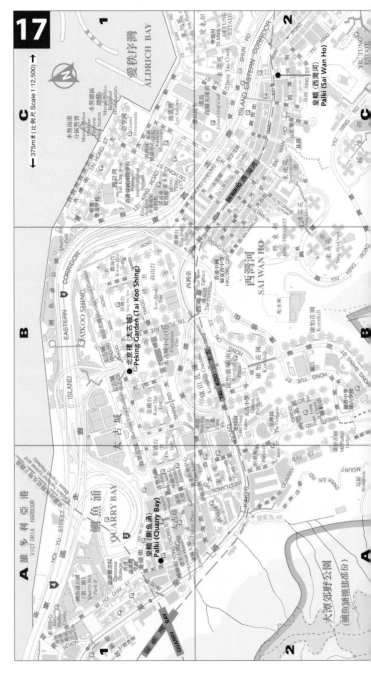

← 375m米(比例尺 Scale 1:12,500) →

N

愛秩序灣
ALDRICH BAY

水警碼頭
Marine Police
分區警署
Division Station
水警總區
Marine Police
總部大樓
Headquarters

嘉亨灣
Grand
Promenade

基利路
TAI HONG ST

太古小學
Tai Koo Primary
School

太康街

LEI KING ROAD

茜發道

筲箕灣
香港國際函授學院
Hong Kong
International
Film Fund School

ISLAND EASTERN CORRIDOR

港島

香港高爾夫球會
Island Golf Club

柴灣道

SAI WAN HO

西灣河
SAI WAN HO

皇棍 (西灣河)
Palki (Sai Wan Ho)

筲箕灣道

YIU TUNG
ESTATE

愛東邨
St.Mary's C

東濤苑
Tung Tao Court

愛蝶灣
Oi Shun

SUN SING ST.

OI HING RD.

YIU HING RD.

YIU TUNG ESTATE

C

英皇道
QUARRY BAY

EASTERN CORRIDOR

太古城
TAIKOO SHING

北京樓 (大古城)
Peking Garden (Tai Koo Shing)

ISLAND

康怡花園
Kornhill

康山花園
Kornhill
Gardens

太古
TAI KOO

康怡廣場
Kornhill
Plaza

希慎中學
HKCWC Coll

西灣河
SAI WAN HO

康怡花園
Kornhill

HING TUNG

英皇道

筲箕灣道

B

維多利亞港
VICTORIA HARBOUR

QUARRY BAY
鰂魚涌

皇棍 (鰂魚涌)
Palki (Quarry Bay)

ON CHONG ST

太古坊
Taikoo Place

英皇道
KING'S ROAD

WESTLANDS

ABBRDG

QUARRY BAY

PARK-ER RD.

鰂魚涌

CARROSSA
College

柴灣道
QUARRY BAY

大潭郊野公園
(鰂魚涌擴建部份)

A

1   **2**

南山
Nam Shan

木棉山
Muk Min Shan

Tyburn House

TAI MONG

沙下
Sha Ha

沙角尾
Sha Kok Mei

邊朗新村
Pin Long
San Tsuen

SHA KOK MEI

甲頭朗
Kap Pin Long

米芝蓮
MEI LUK ST

惠民路遊樂場

西貢鄧肇堅運動場
Sai Kung Tang Shiu Kin Sports Ground

西貢中心
李少葵

滘西洲高爾夫球場
停車場

西貢游泳池

滘西洲

滘西洲高爾夫球場
Ferries to
Kau Sai Chau

天主教墳場

西貢崇真
Sung Tsun

營場

西貢崇真

灰窰下
Fui Yiu Ha

油麻莆
Yau Ma Po

FUK MAN RD

西貢海濱公園

碼頭
(往橋咀、鹽田等)

TAN CHEUNG RD

PO TUNG

HONG TING RD

新安村
Sun On
Tsuen

灰窰里
FUI YIU LANE

康定路

西貢篤
Sai Kung Tuk

翠塘花園
Lakeside Garden

CHUI TONG ROAD

YI CHUN ST

全記海鮮菜館
Chuen Kee Seafood

西貢
SAI KUNG

碼頭
Pier

西貢戶外康樂中心
Sai Kung Outdoor
Recreation Centre

對面海
Tui Min Hoi

宮門漁邨
Hong Kin

漁民村

漁民新邨

明順村

太湖角村

HONG FU RD

水警
東分區基地
Marine Police East
Division Base

污水處理廠

蕉坑特別地區

蕉坑
Tsiu Hang

CHE KENG TUK ROAD

鯽徑篤
Che Keng Tuk

蕉坑口
Tsiu Hang Hau

← 400米 (比例尺 Scale 1:13,323) →

1

2

3

A

B

MACAU
澳門

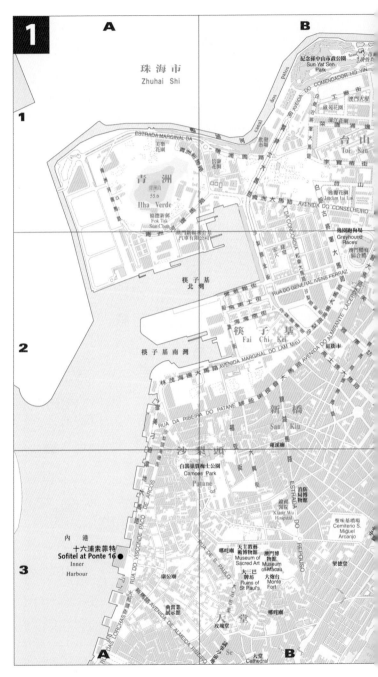

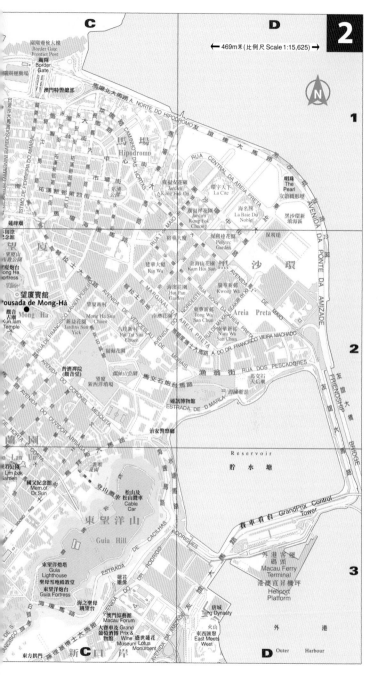

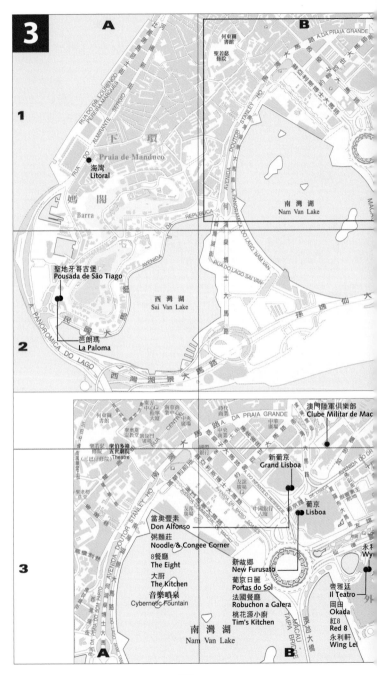

3

A   B

RUA DA LORENÇO
RUA ALMIRANTE SERGIO PEREIRA MARQUES

何東圖書館
聖若瑟修院

1

下環

RUA DO 媽閣
Praia de Manduco

海灣
Litoral

媽閣
Barra

A. DA PRAIA GRANDE

MACAU

A. PANORAMICA DO LAGO NAM VAN

南灣湖
Nam Van Lake

2

聖地牙哥古堡
Pousada de São Tiago

西灣湖
Sai Van Lake

RUA DO LAGO SAI VAN

孫逸仙大

芭朗瑪
La Paloma

A. PANORAMICA DO LAGO

西灣湖景大馬路

何東圖書館

南歐商業中心

DA PRAIA GRANDE

澳門陸軍俱樂部
Clube Militar de Mac

聖若瑟修院
(三巴仔修院)
Theatre

AVENIDA DOUTOR STANLEY HO

新葡京
Grand Lisboa

葡京
Lisboa

當奧豐素
Don Alfonso

3

粥麵莊
Noodle & Congee Corner

8餐廳
The Eight

大廚
The Kitchen

音樂噴泉
Cybernetic Fountain

新故鄉
New Furusato

葡京日麗
Portas do Sol

法國餐廳
Robuchon a Galera

桃花源小廚
Tim's Kitchen

MACAU TAIPA BRIDGE

永利
Wy

帝雅廷
Il Teatro

岡由
Okada

紅8
Red 8

永利軒
Wing Lei

南灣湖
Nam Van Lake

A   B

C   D

新口岸
Outer Habour
Reclamation Area

過仙橋碼頭
Legend
Wharf

過阿密館

文化中心
廣場

仙
大
馬
路

1

萊斯
Rocks

外 港 新 填
海 區

N A P E

美高梅金殿
MGM Grand

壹號湖畔
One Central

參考下面
See below

寶雅座
Aux Beaux Arts

金殿堂
Imperial Court

盛事
Rossio

食·八方
Square Eight

嘉
樂
庇
總
督
大
橋

PONTE GOVERNADOR
DE

2

中學

利澳
Rio

新口岸

南方
大廈

置地廣場酒店
The Landmark

星際
StarWorld

稻菊
Inagiku

文華東方
Mandarin Oriental

Outer Habour
Reclamation Area

瀟
Naam

東怡軒
Tung Yee Heen

漁
人
碼
頭
Fisherman's
Wharf

金沙
Sands

澳門
回歸賀禮
陳列館
Macau
Handover
Pavilion

文化中心
廣場

澳門文化中心
Macao Cultural Centre

澳門藝術博物館
Museum of Art

3

港 新 填
海 區

N A P E

娘湖畔
e Central

宋玉生
音樂
噴泉

←356m米(比例尺 Scale 1:11,856)→

觀音像
Statue of
Kuh Iam

D

← 627m米 (比例尺 Scale 1:20,909) →

澳氹大橋
Macau-Taipa Bridge

西灣大橋
Sai Van Bridge

氹仔東
史伯泰海軍馬路

奧羅拉
Aurora
吉良
Kira
天政
Tenmasa
帝影樓
Ying

觀音岩 澳門大
University of Mac

海洋花園本馬路

海洋
會所
Est dos Sete Tanques

氹仔雕塑
Taipa
Monument
110.8

將軍馬路

皇冠
Crown Tower

海洋花園

小澳山

菩提禪院
Pou Tai Un
Monastery

Estrada Monte

玫瑰山莊

氹仔炮臺

柯維納馬路
Est Governador Albano Oliveira

Avenida de Kwong Tung

四面佛
Four-Faces
Buddha

澳門賽馬會
Macau Jockey Club

賽馬場
Macau Jockey Club

澳門
運動場
Stadium &
Aquatic Centre

氹
仔
大
橋
Taipa
Bridge

官也街

東亞運大馬路

Avenida dos Jogos da Asia Oriental

奧林匹克
游泳館
Stadium &
Aquatic Centre

A Petisqueira
葡國美食天地

安東尼奧
Antonio

蓮
花
海
濱
大
馬
路

嘉德聖母灣大馬路 Estrada da Baia de No

Avenida de Cotai

珠 海 市
ZHU HAI CITY

路

A
MARGINAL
FLOR
DE
LOTUS

西
堤
馬
路

人工濕地

通往珠海市，橫琴
To Zhu Hai City

蓮花大橋
Lotus Bridge

蓮

ESTRADA
FLOR D

澳門氹仔臨時客運碼頭
（北安碼頭）
Taipa Temporary Ferry Terminal

友誼大橋
Friendship Bridge

北安大馬路 Estrada de Pac On

信安馬路 Avenida Son On

氹仔

159.2
大潭山

Taipa

天文台斜路

雞頸馬路

Avenida Wai Long

客運大樓
Terminal Building

澳門國際機場
Macau International Airport

嘉樂庇總督馬路 Avenida Dr. Sun Yat Sen

大潭山
壹號

氹仔住宅式
博物館
Taipa Houses-Museum

澳門
科技大學
Macau University of
Science &
Technology

喜粵
Canton
利苑酒家
Lei Garden
Morton's of Chicago
Roka

威尼斯人
Venetian

氹城

星麗門
Cotai

澳門東亞運動會
體育館(澳門蛋)
Macau East
Asian
Games
Dome

ISTMO DO ESTRADA

蓮花路

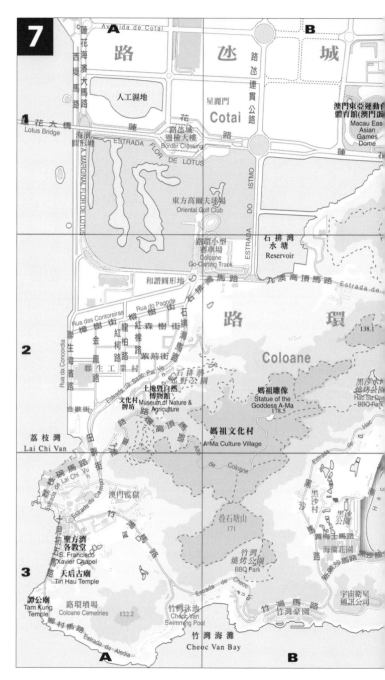

A B

路 氹 城

西堤馬路
蓮花海濱大馬路
Avenida de Cotai

人工濕地

星麗門
Cotai

澳門東亞運動會
體育館(澳門蛋)
Macau East
Asian
Games
Dome

花大橋
Lotus Bridge

海灣圓形地

ESTRADA FLOR DE LOTUS

路氹城
驗檢大樓
Border Crossing

蓮
花
路

蓮

A. MARGINAL FLOR DE LOTUS

東方高爾夫球場
Oriental Golf Club

路環小型
賽車場
Coloane
Go-Carting Track

石排灣
水塘
Reservoir

ESTRADA DO ISTMO

和諧圓形地

石排灣馬路

九澳高頂馬路 Estrada de

Rua do Pagode
Rua das Contoreiras

榕樹街
石排灣

路 環
Coloane

138.1

生海濱馬路
Rua da Concordia

樟樹街
金柯路
紅龍
紅棉街
柏

鳳凰村
聯生工業村
紫荊街

石排灣
郊野公園
Pai Van

媽祖雕像
Statue of the
Goddess A-Ma
178.5

黑沙海
燒烤公園
Hac Sa San
BBQ-Park

合歡街
Estrada de Seac Pai Van
文化村
牌坊
土地暨自然
博物館
Museum of Nature &
Agriculture

高頂馬路

媽祖文化村
A-Ma Culture Village

荔枝灣
Lai Chi Van

Estrada de Lai Chi Vu

Estrada de Cataquil

澳門監獄

竹灣馬路

Estrada de Cologne

叠石塘山
171

竹灣
燒烤公園
BBQ Park

黑沙村
黑沙

Estrada de Hac Sa

聖方濟
各教堂
I. S. Francisco
Xavier Chapel

天后古廟
Tin Hau Temple

譚公廟
Tam Kung
Temple

路環墳場
Coloane Cemeteries

122.2

竹灣泳池
Cheoc Van
Swimming Pool

Estrada de Cheoc

竹灣馬路
竹灣豪園

譚公廟
賈梅士馬園
海蘭花園

宇宙衛星
通訊公司

新黑沙馬路黑沙園

Estrada da Aledia

竹灣海灘
Cheoc Van Bay

A B

1

九澳發電廠
Power Station

三聖廟
Sam Seng
Temple

九澳堤灘海路

九澳水庫
郊野公園

九澳水庫
Ka-Ho Dam

九澳村

九澳深水碼頭

水泥廠

九澳
聖約瑟學校

九澳村路

聖路濟亞
中心

九澳
老人院

七苦
聖母小堂

九澳
燈塔

大擔角

濾水站路

112.6
九澳山

蝙蝠洞

鷹鷹洞

九澳高頂
燒烤公園

nho' de Ka-Ho

水上樂園
Water Fun Park

黑沙路

澳門哥爾夫球
鄉村俱樂部
Macau Golf and
Country Club

觀海軒
Kwun Hoi Heen

威斯汀度假酒店
The Westin Resort

2

Beach

黑沙海灣
Hae Sa Bay

海海灣灣
輝半島

3

← 690m米 (比例尺 Scale 1:23,000) →

PICTURE COPYRIGHT
圖片版權

NOTES
備註

Manufacture française des pneumatiques Michelin
Société en commandite par actions au capital de 304 000 000 EUR
Place des Carmes-Déchaux – 63000 Clermont-Ferrand (France)
R.C.S. Clermont-Fd B 855 200 507

Made in Japan

Published in 2008

Maps : (C) 2008 Cartographic data Universal Publications, Ltd / Michelin
Design : Akita Design Kan Inc. Tokyo, Japan

E-mail : michelinguide.hongkong-macau@cn.michelin.com

Pre-Press: Nord Compo, Villeneuve-d'Ascq, (France)
Printing and Binding: Toppan, Tokyo (Japan)